"Daniel Lee writes especially for his Asian Ai
leaders, and fellow theologians and colleagues. ... . ..up.. ..a..y ..u..–Asian Americans read this book, not to eavesdrop on our conversation but to attend to how
Doing Asian American Theology testifies through dissonant accents the wondrous
work of God among Asian American believers in North American contexts. The
result may be a lot of perplexity and even 'What does this mean?' but also new possibilities for a revitalized church and witness anticipating the justice and shalom of
the coming divine reign."

Amos Yong, dean of the School of Mission and Theology at Fuller Theological Seminary

"Daniel Lee provides a robust framework that is deeply rooted in the particularity of
contextual realities and the universality of truths as revealed to us in Jesus Christ.
Doing Asian American Theology adeptly covers the historical, sociocultural, psychological, migratory, generational, and theological dimensions common to all dis-
placed people without dumbing down their complexities. I strongly recommend this
book for all diaspora communities in North America and as a must-read for all
Asian American pastors, missionaries, ministry leaders, and serious thinkers."

Sam George, catalyst of diasporas for the Lausanne Movement and editor of the Asian
Diaspora Christianity series

"Daniel D. Lee skillfully draws on the rich resources of Judeo-Christian thought and
the diversity of Asian American cultural experiences to point the way forward in
doing Asian American theology. The present volume is a clarion call and road map
for constructing contextual theology in service to the Asian American Christian
community, and in turn the universal church. All theological practitioners in the
United States would benefit greatly from reflecting deeply on *Doing Asian American
Theology* in the effort to bear true and meaningful witness to the gospel of Jesus
Christ in their diverse settings in our racialized, American cultural context."

Paul Louis Metzger, professor of theology and culture at Multnomah University and
Seminary, coauthor of *Exploring Ecclesiology: An Evangelical and Ecumenical Introduction*

"With the current demographic trends in US Christianity and the social reality and
challenges related to Asian American Christianity, Daniel Lee offers this timely and
essential work. With a profound commitment to lift up the revelation of God in the
person of Jesus, this text takes on the additional challenge of framing this revelation
in the context of the human covenant with the Asian American community. Daniel
Lee is able to give honor and value to the larger redemptive narrative of Jesus while
also honoring the story of the Asian American community. The text is both a prophetic call and an intellectual enactment of an invitation to a holy calling."

Soong-Chan Rah, Robert Munger Professor of Evangelism at Fuller Theological Seminary
and author of *The Next Evangelicalism*

DOING ASIAN AMERICAN THEOLOGY

A Contextual Framework for Faith and Practice

DANIEL D. LEE

IVP Academic
An imprint of InterVarsity Press
Downers Grove, Illinois

InterVarsity Press
P.O. Box 1400 | Downers Grove, IL 60515-1426
ivpress.com | email@ivpress.com

InterVarsity Press® is the publishing division of InterVarsity Christian Fellowship/USA®. For more information, visit intervarsity.org.

Scripture quotations, unless otherwise noted, are from the New Revised Standard Version Bible, copyright © 1989 National Council of the Churches of Christ in the United States of America. Used by permission. All rights reserved worldwide.

The publisher cannot verify the accuracy or functionality of website URLs used in this book beyond the date of publication.

Cover design and image composite: Derek Thronton / Notch Design

Interior design: Jeanna Wiggins

ISBN 978-1-5140-0082-3 (print) | ISBN 978-1-5140-0083-0 (digital)

Library of Congress Cataloging-in-Publication Data
Names: Lee, Daniel D., author.
Title: Doing Asian American theology : a contextual framework for faith and practice / Daniel D. Lee.
Description: Downers Grove, IL : IVP Academic, [2022] | Includes bibliographical references and index.
Identifiers: LCCN 2022031808 (print) | LCCN 2022031809 (ebook) | ISBN 9781514000823 (print) | ISBN 9781514000830 (digital)
Subjects: LCSH: Asian Americans–Religion. | Asian American theology.
Classification: LCC BR563.A82 L438 2022 (print) | LCC BR563.A82 (ebook) | DDC 230.089/95–dc23/eng/20220725
LC record available at https://lccn.loc.gov/2022031808
LC ebook record available at https://lccn.loc.gov/2022031809

29 27 28 26 25 24 23 22 | 8 7 6 5 4 3 2 1

TO JUDY

CONTENTS

ACKNOWLEDGMENTS

IN THE PROCESS OF WRITING this book overwhelming self-doubt caught me off guard. Along with your garden-variety writer's block and my perfectionism, the seemingly impossible comparison in my mind to all the "great White theologians" that I studied, and the fear of hypercriticism within the Asian American community would have been crippling without the support of friends, co-conspirators, and family members. I am truly indebted to their invaluable support and encouragement, affirming the contribution that this book hopes to make.

The early testing of the Asian American Quadrilateral and its related concepts were honed while working together with Ken Fong at Fuller's Asian American Initiative. Remembering all the hours we spent discussing the problem of grace within Asian American churches still brings joy to my heart. Good conversations draw out ideas that you could not articulate by yourself. Every time I talked to Kevin Doi, his empathy and encouragement drew out many of the ideas that I was able to express in this book. Jason Chu has been an indispensable supporter and friend through the writing process, giving feedback and recommendations for earlier versions of various chapters. Sooho Lee generously read and gave constructive input on the early chapters. The wisdom of Jane Iwamura about writing as an Asian American religious scholar arrived just at the nick of time to save me from falling into despair. Through all the meals that Sam Bang brought me as I sought to find my administrative footing, he graciously mentored me to navigate Fuller and understand higher education. Josh Ritnimit deserves my deepest gratitude for not only being my long-time theology interlocuter, but also my teacher and guide into backpacking, which started my journey toward a more holistic view of life. I am thankful for the support of Joe Lee, my loyal friend through thick and thin, who has journeyed with me since the first days of seminary.

Many generous colleagues helped me to get a handle on the various academic fields required for this interdisciplinary work. Jennifer Rosner was one of my first teachers on the parting of the ways of Jews and Christians and the larger issues around Jewish-Christian relations. Kendall Soulen gave me insightful feedback on my idea of a particular Gentileness as related to theological contextuality. Stuart Dauermann affirmed my connection of the Jewishness of Jesus to my Asian Americanness.

In terms of trauma and psychology, the late Evelyne Reisacher showed me how modern-day attachment theory could be used for cultural attachment, introducing me to the field of interpersonal neurobiology and its potential for theology and ministry. Cynthia Eriksson's seminar on trauma and ministry led me to think about microaggressive trauma as a (de)formative force for Asian American identity.

My two good friends Russell Jeung and Justin Tse served as my guides and tutors in the field of Asian American studies. Without them I would still be trying to make some sense of this diverse and heterogenous academic field. Through their edited volume and in my personal interactions with them, Nita Tewari and Alvin Alvarez were such kind teachers and mentors into Asian American psychology. My friends at Southeast Asian Catalyst, Ken Kong, Thi Mitsamphanh, and others, as well as Der Lor and Daniel Yang, taught me the contours of the diverse Southeast Asian American communities. I am grateful to Sam George and the Connext Conference, which served as my introduction into the Indian American Christian community a decade ago. Working with Gabriel Catanus on Fuller's Filipino American Ministry Initiative has been a joy, giving me a chance to deepen my insights about the Filipino American community.

My Fuller Seminary students from TM528 Asian American Identity and Ministry, ST544 Asian American Theologies, as well as Asian American Spiritual Formation Groups from the last eight years have helped to sharpen and test ideas of this book. For the gracious sharing of their personal lives in the course discussions and assignments, I am humbled and grateful. So many friends from InterVarsity Christian Fellowship and Cru's Epic Movement gave me helpful feedback and helped to bring clarity to my ideas.

I have had my share of heartaches and difficulties here, but I am an Asian American theologian today because Fuller Seminary invested in the development of the Center for Asian American Theology and Ministry and in me personally for the last twelve years. I must give thanks for my doktorvater Howard Loewen, who has truly been my academic father. He was a pivotal leader in the initial planning stages of establishing the Asian American program at Fuller as well. The friendship and support of Amos Yong has been invaluable in recent years, especially through his diaconal leadership.

The staff and friends at my local climbing gym Hangar 18 Arcadia kept me sane and helped me beat the stress out of my mind and body. I am grateful for the supportive community and camaraderie as we struggle and wrestle with boulder problems.

My spiritual director Steve Summerell, who has been more of a pastor to me than any other in my life, serves as a witness to the Ebenezer moments of my life, reminding me of God's faithfulness through and beyond my vocational roadblocks. The ways that he encourages me to be attentive to God's voice, and to pray from where I am and not where I think I should be, has been a source of life through my writing journey.

I am grateful that the Institute for Cultural Engagement: New Wine, New Wineskins at Multnomah University and Seminary gave approval to expand and incorporate my article "Cultural Archetypes for a Theology of Culture in a Global Age," *Cultural Encounters: A Journal for the Theology of Culture* 12, no. 1 (2016): 37-52—which served as the heart of chapter four on Asian Heritage and Cultural Archetypes.

Also, Bloomsbury Publishing and Innovative Space for Asian American Christianity (ISAAC) graciously gave approval to revise and use my chapter "Spirit of Integration and Solidarity: Asian American Pneumatologies," in *T&T Clark Handbook of Pneumatology*, ed. Daniel Castelo and Kenneth M. Loyer, 291-300 (New York: T&T Clark, 2020) and my article "God's Shalom to All of Ourselves: Integrating the Asian American Double Self," *ChristianityNext Journal* 5 (2021): 53-74—which are part of chapter eight on fragmentation and integration.

The initial idea for this book came out of my conversation with David Congdon. Al Hsu, who eventually became my editor, has been so patient and understanding through all the multiple delays. To both of them and InterVarsity Press I express my deep appreciation.

My family puts everything that I do in perspective and grounds me as a person. Annabel, Priscilla, and Teresa, my three pearls, bring so much joy and delight to my life. I hope my daughters will find this book a bit easier to read than my dissertation.

This book is dedicated to Judy, my wife, my partner in crime for the gospel. Her love and partnership have made my life more full, joyous, and fun. I am so grateful that we share our convictions about what makes the gospel the *good* news.

INTRODUCTION

Theology is autobiographical, but it is not an autobiography.
My theology is not just a story of my life. It is the story of my faith
journey in the world. It is my story of how God formed me, nurtures
me, guides me, loves and allows me to age, and will end my life.

JUNG YOUNG LEE

ASIAN AMERICAN THEOLOGY *is about God revealed in Jesus Christ.*
The proper subject matter of all theology is God. What is unique in Asian
American theology is the identity of the witness that points to that revealed
God. Like John the Baptist, my desire as an Asian American theologian is
that Christ must increase and I must decrease. Given this beginning, in
what sense are Asian American witnesses qua (specifically as) Asian Americans theologically significant? How are Asian Americans significant as
Asian Americans *coram Deo* (in God's presence) and not merely *coram
mundi* (in the presence of the world), in divine encounter and not just in
sociopolitical context?

The revealed God is not a unitarian deity, pure and transcendent above
the sociopolitical fray. Rather, the revealed God is a triune God, who entered
a particular time and space and has made flesh a part of the divine life.
Moreover, this triune God sought and entered into a relationship with a
community and with all creation—a genuine covenantal partnership, not

Epigraph: Jung Young Lee, *Marginality: The Key to Multicultural Theology* (Minneapolis, MN:
Fortress Press, 1995), 7.

mere contractual subservience. The separation between the theological from sociopolitical is invalid, even as they should not be confused. Because God has revealed the divine self as a trinitarian and covenantal God, who encounters humanity in their particularities, human witnesses also must own and engage their own particularities in their own response to God. In this covenantal line of thought, the statement *Asian American theology is about God revealed in Jesus Christ* can be expanded to *Asian American theology is about God revealed in Jesus Christ in covenantal relationship with Asian Americans qua Asian Americans. Thus, Asian American theology is about Asian Americans as human covenant partners alongside of God.* While this human-divine relationship is asymmetric and contingent on divine being and will, no generic, neutral, non-covenantal theology is possible with this God. No theology can implicitly pose as objective universal science, as White-normative theologies have done for too long.[1]

These first paragraphs provide a snapshot of where I have arrived in my journey as an Asian American, ecclesial, charismatic, Reformed theologian, a journey that began over twenty years ago when I became convinced of the desperate need for deep theological reflection in the Asian American church. I am pursuing an Asian American theology that is *theological*, rooted in the very being of God, and not one that exists because of cultural, sociopolitical reasons, that is, limits or agendas of human perspectives and experiences.[2] In this book, I will present a way to understand Asian American theology: what it is, why we need it, and most importantly how to do it. Asian American theology is a way to understand our engagement and experience of God and the gospel more deeply and holistically as Asian Americans. In a sense, Asian American theology articulates how the gospel penetrates and permeates all of who we are for healing, transformation, and mission. The urgency of this task is not only for the Asian American church and Asian American Christians in diverse ministry contexts, but also for the life of the universal church that would benefit from all the gifts that Asian Americans bring.

---

[1] I will discuss how normativities, such as White racial normativity, function in theology in chapter one.

[2] I am using this tautology of a *theological* theology in the manner of how Nelson describes Jüngel's works. R. David Nelson, "Foreword to the 2014 English Edition" in Eberhard Jüngel's *Justification: The Heart of the Christian Faith* (London: T&T Clark, 2014), xlii-li.

For years, I fumbled in the dark for answers without even knowing the right questions, constantly feeling "a splinter in your mind, driving you mad," as Morpheus describes to Neo in the movie *The Matrix*.[3] That splinter is real and has a name: it is the experience of being an Asian American Christian in all of its complexity. This book seeks to provide identifying labels for the wide spectrum of Asian American experiences, and to enable the articulation of spiritual frustrations more intelligibly. Moreover, it offers theological tools to discern God's presence and work in our lives.

The organization of this book and many of its insights are the result of my work at Fuller Seminary's Center for Asian American Theology and Ministry, and the courses I teach regularly on Asian American identity, ministry, and theology. Seeing what resonates with students, what eludes them, and what questions they raise have honed my theories and sharpened my arguments. While this book is written primarily for seminarians, pastors, and other ministry practitioners, I believe it will also contribute to ongoing academic conversations on Asian American theology, especially among those with a more ecclesial and ministerial orientation. While my own story is East Asian American, particularly of Korean heritage, this book frames Asian American context much more broadly to be inclusive of East Asian, Southeast Asian, and South Asian heritages as well as multiracial Asian Americans and adoptees.[4]

THE LONG JOURNEY TO MYSELF

While the Asian American experience is incredibly diverse in multiple ways, I begin with my journey. I do so not only to clarify my own *locus theologicus*, but also because my struggle in coming to understand the place and impact of Asian American theology is a rather common one. Reflecting on my former naive beliefs about identity and race from the vantage of our present, post-Trump, post-Covid-19 era is rather embarrassing. However, the kinds of ignorance of or prejudice against Asian American theology that I held earlier are still ubiquitous among Asian

---

[3]*The Matrix*, directed by Andy Wachowski and Larry Wachowski (Burbank, CA: Warner Home Video, 1999), DVD.

[4]I am focusing on US Americans of Asian descent. While some choose to use the term *Asian North American*, I have not, given that my framing does not include Asian Canadians or Asian Mexicans.

American Christians. Hopefully, my journey will inform as well as challenge these all too prevalent notions.

Our family emigrated from South Korea to the United States in the early 1980s and settled in Northern Virginia, when it was just beginning to diversify ethnically. I was one of the handful of students of Asian heritage in my elementary school; every year, more and more Asian immigrants moved into our community. As one of the earlier Asian immigrants to the area in this wave of migration, I found myself assimilating to the dominant White culture, trying hard to fit in. It was not that I rejected my Korean heritage, but I simply believed that being American meant moving on, "evolving" from this Asian heritage to mainstream White culture. My father reasoned this transition with the proverb, "when in Rome, do as the Romans do," meaning that we should try to fit into White culture by adopting White American names and customs.

During this stressful transition, my Korean American immigrant church provided communal support as well as deep spiritual experiences. Interestingly, the spirituality that I encountered in the Korean American Christian community was both culture-blind with my Korean American identity as inconsequential, as well as ethnic-centric with Korean spiritual roots touted as superior and salutary for the decadent White American society. I remember a Korean American preacher using Daniel and his friends in Babylon as an illustration for the importance of retaining my Korean (assumedly Christian) identity and the spiritual fruit that this identity would bear in this American spiritual wasteland. Our immigration was spiritually interpreted as a mission. God had sent us Koreans to the US to bring a revival to a dying White church.

This conflation of ethnic and spiritual identities and the missionary interpretation of immigration, however, seemed forced and hard to believe, especially given contentious politics and even physical fights in many of our churches, leading to splits. It seemed like most Korean American churches that I knew around me had either gone through a split or were formed out of a split. Later in college, after stumbling upon a class in Confucianism and Taoism, my questions primarily resided in what I perceived to be Asian cultural influences corrupting our Korean American churches and Asian American ministries with high East Asian American presence, with heavy-handed moralism, legalism, and authoritarianism overshadowing grace and freedom.

When I read my first Asian American discipleship book, *Following Jesus Without Dishonoring Your Parents*, I found it both stimulating and frustrating, because I resonated so much with the themes but came away with more questions. Like me, the authors were also frustrated by Asian cultural influences and sought a more gracious and joyful gospel. While sympathetic to their proposals, I was hungry to understand how to pose theological questions and discern a faithful response given particular circumstances and experiences. As helpful as these kinds of Asian American ministry books were, the numerous unaddressed theoretical, especially methodological, issues were obviously beyond their scope.[5] So I turned to seek out this theoretical content elsewhere. As I became even more determined to get to the heart of the gospel, the Reformed tradition and its insights appeared to provide a roadmap out of this "syncretistic" spiritual quagmire that I believed I was raised in. I will later come to see that the idea of syncretism was fraught with many questions. In this Reformed tradition, I sought an all-encompassing, Christocentric, gospel-centered theology that was completely grace-infused.

Later at seminary, I drank deeply from the theological wells of the Reformation theologians to quench my spiritual thirst for God's radical grace. Thinking I had arrived at the end of my spiritual search, I tried to leave my Asian American identity behind, yet it kept pestering me with its lingering presence. When I reluctantly took a class on Asian American theology, I found the readings underwhelming and dissonant with my experience of faith. Compared to the rich fare of mainstream White American and Western theological traditions, Asian American theology frankly sounded like ghettoized sectarian offerings from ethnic enclaves. Their concerns about identity, culture, and racism sounded distant and peripheral to the radical grace that nourished my spirit in the Reformed tradition I had come to love.

---

[5]I still consider *Following Jesus Without Dishonoring Your Parents* a great resource as well as others such as *Growing Healthy Asian American Churches* and *Honoring the Generations.* Jeanette Yep et al., *Following Jesus Without Dishonoring Your Parents* (Downers Grove, IL: InterVarsity, 1998); Peter Cha, S. Steve Kang, and Helen Lee, eds., *Growing Healthy Asian American Churches: Ministry Insights from Groundbreaking Congregations* (Downers Grove, IL: InterVarsity, 2006); M. Sydney Park, Soong-Chan Rah, and Al Tizon, eds., *Honoring the Generations: Learning with Asian North American Congregations* (Valley Forge, PA: Judson, 2012).

Asian American theology, as well as other contextual theologies, appeared as *advocacy* theologies, driven by ideological and political agendas. At worst, such theologies seem to fall into a Babylonian captivity of sorts; at best, they were too limited, missing the grand narrative of God's story. Why quibble about using "pagan" Asian images of God or recovering Asian religious resources since my goal was to become more Christian and not Buddhist or Taoist?[6] Would that not be returning to the fleshpots of Egypt? Also, the racism that these mostly first-generation Asian American theologians faced appeared to me at that time as problems mainly encountered by those "fresh off the boat." I thought these issues did not concern me because I was an American and, more importantly, a Christian. These cultural and racial concerns of recent immigrants seemed irrelevant to later generations of Asian Americans. Having an Asian heritage or being Asian American did not seem to help me be a better disciple of Christ, but it was rather baggage that I hoped to leave behind.

As you can see, I did not always believe that my Asian American identity mattered for my faith. Rather, I seriously doubted the usefulness and the legitimacy of contextual theologies in general and Asian American theologies in particular. Ironically, it was not in an affirmation of my Asian American identity, but in the full pursuit of God's gospel and kingdom that I became convicted about the significance and power of Asian American theology. The heart of the matter for me was and still is knowing God's disruptive grace, being fully and deeply transformed in that divine encounter, and offering all of myself for God's kingdom. The task of Asian American theology met me exactly in my pursuit of these core concerns.

Despite my rather nonchalant view of Asian American identity and a dismissive opinion of Asian American theology, three moments during the latter years of seminary provoked me to take "contextuality" seriously.[7] These were the beginnings of my "Asian American awakening," when I realized I was not going to move smoothly from immigrant to (White) American.

---

[6]Some examples of theologies that take up Asian cultural themes are Jung Young Lee, *The Trinity in Asian Perspective* (Nashville: Abingdon Press, 1996) and Michael Amaladoss, *The Asian Jesus* (Maryknoll, NY: Orbis, 2006).
[7]I will explain in chapter one the difference between *contextuality* and *contextual theology* and why the latter nomenclature is problematic.

First, psychologically, my wedding and marriage exposed how my Korean family heritage functioned in my life. Getting married during my second year of seminary taught me that cultural heritage and generational patterns are always with us. The largely unconscious "scripts" that my wife and I brought into our marriage from our families of origin had just as much or even more influence than any pop culture representations of "typical" White American family life.[8] As a so-called assimilated person, I had mistakenly believed that my Korean parents with their old Korean ways were no longer significant for me because I did not care to continue them in my life. But, whether I valued their ways or not, I had to deal with them. If I did not acknowledge and process them, they were going to impact my life, family, spirituality, and ministry, mostly in unconscious ways. The only way to write a new script for my marriage and later parenting would be to first learn and become aware of the scripts in my life. Knowing my extended family system and allowing the gospel to bring God's shalom within it is the key to a healthy marriage and parenting, as well as every aspect of my life.[9]

Second, racially, there was no way to escape from all the pains and problems of Asian American identity and the Asian American church. At seminary, I wanted to leave behind my Korean and Asian American "pond" to become a theologian in the bigger mainstream "ocean." However, I came to realize that wherever I go I take my Asian American self with me. Of course, not all Asian Americans are called to be part of Asian American churches. However, reactively running away from the Asian American church is not necessarily a calling to some other ministry context either. Because I was enveloped in Asian American campus ministry in college, I wanted to break free from that enclave in seminary. But the mostly midwestern and southern White student body at my seminary made it quite clear that my wife and I were foreigners and strangers through just treating us as though we were invisible. In social contexts, they would literally talk to everyone around us, like we were not even there. We had no recourse but to seek an Asian American community there. Also, in discerning ordination

---

[8]Margaret Kornfeld, *Cultivating Wholeness: A Guide to Care and Counseling in Faith Communities* (New York: Continuum, 1998), 161-62.

[9]For an introduction to Murray Bowen family systems theory as it relates to ministry context, see Edwin H. Friedman, *Generation to Generation: Family Process in Church and Synagogue* (New York: Guilford, 1985).

in a more conservative and mostly White Presbyterian denomination, I was confronted with their blatant and subtle othering, although I lacked the capacity to concretely describe it at the time.

Over the years, I have seen too many Asian American pastors complain about all the suffering and abuse experienced under first generation pastors, or cultural problems of Asian American ministries, only to perpetuate the same patterns in their newly formed ministries that were supposedly nothing like their parents' churches, that is, "not your mama's church." For those Asian Americans who reactively escape to White or "multiethnic" churches, their particular pains and hurts often remain undealt with, even years later, because many of these so-called multiethnic churches fail to spiritually address the issues that lie below the surface of ourselves as Asian Americans.[10] In that sense, all ministries who reach out to Asian Americans need to understand theologically to whom they are ministering.

Third, sociologically, I began to think of my Asian American identity much more dynamically. This movement came about as I became more exposed to different kinds of Asian Americans around the country, especially different generations and regions. Thinking beyond the narrow second generation Korean American from the East Coast perspective, I no longer thought of "being Asian American" as defined by scolding mothers or grandmothers: look in the mirror and know who you truly are, make sure to learn your language, and marry your own people, and so on. Such concepts of "authentic identity" or "true self" can be oppressive and suffocating, ignoring the genuine diversity of experiences, backgrounds, and personalities. Without falling into racist stereotypes or essentialist categories, I realized I still needed a way to articulate my existence in concrete categories and definitions that acknowledged my cultural, ethnic, and racial particularities.

While these moments were instrumental, the critical element came theologically at the end of my seminary years as I was confronted with the importance of my own vocation as an Asian American theologian through my studies of the Reformed tradition, and the burning questions that I must take up as an Asian American theologian.[11]

---

[10]I will discuss the problems of these so-called multiethnic churches in chapter nine.
[11]By broadly defining Reformed, I am here including Reformed as well as Lutheran traditions.

Burning Questions

When Dietrich Bonhoeffer, contemplating a life of research apart from the political maelstrom back in Nazi Germany, wrote to his mentor Karl Barth for guidance, Barth responded, "[T]hink only of one thing: that you are a German, that your church's house is on fire, that you know enough, and know well enough how to say what you know, to be able to help, and in fact you ought to return to your post by the next ship!"[12] I remember reading this letter during my last year at seminary. I chose Princeton Seminary to study the gospel at its "purest" in the form of Reformed tradition, dedicating myself to study Martin Luther, John Calvin, Jonathan Edwards, Karl Barth, and Dietrich Bonhoeffer. Yet, at the end of my years, I was confronted with the urgency of theological concerns for the Asian American context like a burning fire shut up in my bones. Reading Barth's letter about remembering who you are and returning to your burning church took a hold of me. This was the final confirmation among many others that God was calling me back to the Asian American church that I was desperately seeking to leave behind. I knew that I was no Dietrich Bonhoeffer, but through Barth's words God reminded me of all the pain and confusion that I felt growing up in the Korean immigrant church—and that, somehow, I might be able to help alleviate not only my own confusions, but those of others as well.

Along with a call to return to my Asian American church, reading this letter had a profound impact on my understanding about the nature of theological endeavors, something I should had already known given my studies. Following Anselm of Canterbury, the theological task is often described as *fides quaerens intellectum*, "faith seeking understanding." That is to say, the theologian tries to comprehend reasonably the mysteries of faith. According to Daniel Migliore, there are two roots of our theological questions: the object of faith and the situation of faith.[13] In every question that we ask, we are dealing with both the object and the situation. In a sense, *faith seeking understanding* means seeking answers to the burning questions of our faith,

---

[12]Barth's letter to Bonhoeffer, *Dietrich Bonhoeffer Works*, vol. 13, *London, 1933-1935*, ed. Keith W. Clements, trans. Isabel Best (Minneapolis: Fortress, 2007), 41. Barth would later come to woefully regret his charge after Bonhoeffer's death. Karl Barth, *Letters 1961-1968* (Grand Rapids, MI: Eerdmans, 1981), 316. Offering counsel is not without its risks and God's calling is not without its dangers.

[13]Daniel L. Migliore, *Faith Seeking Understanding* (Grand Rapids, MI: Eerdmans, 1998), 1-14.

looking for God's work and presence amid our experiences of pain and
struggle as well as of beauty. These questions are never asked in abstraction,
from a neutral, objective place, but rather every question is situated. Bonhoeffer's theological task was to seek answers to the burning question of his
German church in a state of crisis. I realized that I needed to do the same
for myself and my church.

Of course, there are other ways to think about the task of theology. Karl
Barth describes theology as "self-examination" of a church's proclamation
and life, sort of an audit to make sure that our gospel embodiment is faithful
to God's revelation.[14] Even here, the location of our ecclesial community and
its witness are very specifically situated. Each faith community in context
must take up the missional challenges that it faces and audit the faithfulness
of its theological existence and proclamation. In this sense, Asian American
churches were already living out an expression of "Asian American theology,"
but unaware of the forces and powers at hand. While we could and should
learn from other theological sources and traditions, we cannot simply adopt
someone else's theological audit. Also, we could not expect others to do our
theological self-examination for us, nor could we do their work for them.

Realizing the truth of contextuality while reading a White male European
theologian is a bit ironic, since this same truth was argued by Black, Hispanic, Asian American, and other non-Western theologians. In various
classes, I read James Cone, Gustavo Gutiérrez, and other liberation theologians, but still missed the message. In their own way, they all accused the
theological establishment of universalizing White norms and marginalizing
non-White voices to the contextual or missiological hinterlands. In my own
journey, it is as if I resisted this idea of contextuality and ran away to the
Whitest theology that I could find only to be confronted with it there. God
had reached me even through my internalized racism, theological density,
and spiritual resistance to my calling.

However, the version of theological contextuality that I came to acquire
through my strange route had particular traits. The idea of inseparability of
object and situation of faith echoes American liberal theologian Paul Tillich's method of correlation, where the questions from the situation are

---

[14]Karl Barth, *Church Dogmatics*, eds., G. W. Bromiley and T. F. Torrance, vol. 1.1, *The Doctrine of the Word of God* (Edinburgh: T&T Clark, 1975), 4.

answered by the message of faith.[15] Tillich argues that apologetical theology that is oriented toward the context, and kerygmatic theology that is oriented toward the message, need each other. While I agree with Tillich's assessment about the importance of the situation and message in a general sense, his approach lacks the dialectical dimension that recognizes the limitations of our own questions. For Barth, even our questions arising from our situation are under God's correction and judgment. Our burning questions must be transformed by God's revelation before they can be properly answered. The necessity of this radical conversion is what distinguishes my approach, following Barth, from those of Tillich and liberation theologies.

While I sought to develop a different starting point for my vision of Asian American theology from liberation theologies, over time I came to see that the Asian American liberationist themes are indispensable. As I became better informed and moved closer to centers of institutional power, I shed my earlier post-racial naiveté. I began to take Asian American studies more seriously, learning about Asian American history with egregious injustices like the Chinese Exclusion Act and Japanese American removal and incarceration during World War II, as well as Asian American invisibility and misrepresentation in popular culture. With a growing awareness regarding the realities of systemic and structural racism in theological education, I came to see that not only cultural, but political dimensions had to be deeply incorporated into a broader understanding of the gospel and God's kingdom. Of course, the blatant White Christian nationalism around the rise of Donald Trump and the painful anti-Asian hate all around the nation and beyond made all this very clear.

Even as I gleaned much wisdom from them, I was frustrated by the reactivity of many postcolonial and liberationist works that seem to bypass ecclesial concerns.[16] My concern with some liberationist Asian American theologies was that they seemed to lack a robust theological basis to undergird their contextuality: How is Asian American identity or context connected to the God who is revealed in Christ? Theology must be rooted in God, not

---

[15]Paul Tillich, *Systematic Theology, Volume 1* (Chicago: University of Chicago Press, 1973), 8.

[16]Chan makes a similar argument about what he considers to be "elitist" liberationist Asian theologies. While I can appreciate his concern, that fact that he also dismisses the real sociopolitical issues raised by these theologies is quite problematic. Simon Chan, *Grassroots Asian Theology: Thinking the Faith from the Ground Up* (Downers Grove, IL: InterVarsity, 2014).

only our experiences; otherwise, Asian American theology would devolve into mere anthropology.[17] A *theological* foundation for Asian American theology, and not just a *sociopolitical* one, had to be firmly laid.

In a sense, my distinct methodology distinguishes between *theologia crucis* and *theologia gloriae*.[18] In Martin Luther's parlance *theologia crucis*, or theology of the cross, is a way of doing theology that begins with our own inability to reach God, seeking and gratefully receiving God's condescension in divine revelation. *Theologia gloriae*, or theology of glory, is a theology that strives after God, thinking we can, through our own resources, reach God. Applying *theologia crucis* to the relationship between context and the gospel, the connection between the theological answer and the contextual questions can only occur by faith and by the miraculous grace of God. God's answers take hold of our presuppositions and reorder them so that the gospel can be comprehended. In a sense, without a paradigm shift in our plausibility structures, which is how missiologist Lesslie Newbigin describes conversions, this connection cannot be made.[19] Of course, this is why Barth stressed Kierkegaard's *infinite qualitative distinction* between humanity and God, a separation that cannot be overcome from the human side of the gulf. This maneuver establishes the gratuitousness of God's work and presence at the core of our theology. God's grace cannot be assumed as a given, but only be entreated in faith and received gratefully.

Practically speaking, this Barthian *diastasis*, the separation between God and humanity, means that God's answers can surprise us sometimes. Contextuality is often understood as making the gospel more palatable to a particular context, an adjustment that can be suspected as "dumbing down" the gospel or capitulating to the context. To the contrary, engaging the context should mean that the gospel, with its assurances and demands, are

---

[17]Jue raises similar concerns, yet his solution merely points to a scriptural faithfulness as the solution to avoid his anthropological temptation without acknowledging the challenges of hermeneutical presuppositions that we all possess and must wrestle with. Jeffery K. Jue, "Asian American Theology: A Modern and Postmodern Dilemma," in *Conversations: Asian American Evangelical Theologies in Formation*, ed. D. J. Chuang and Timothy Tseng (Washington DC: L² Foundation, 2006), 99-119.

[18]Martin Luther, "Heidelberg Disputation," in *Luther's Works*, vol. 31, *Career of the Reformer I*, ed. Jaroslav Pelikan, Hilton C. Oswald, and Helmut T. Lehmann (Philadelphia: Fortress, 1957), 52-53.

[19]Lesslie Newbigin, *Foolishness to the Greeks: The Gospel and Western Culture* (Grand Rapids, MI: Eerdmans, 1986), 62-63.

clearly understood and not distorted in the act of reformulation, and also include a sharper identification of sin and brokenness so that true repentance can occur.

This latter point about contextuality leading to a sharper accusation of sin is crucial. Attacking the compromised cultural Christianity of his Danish Christendom, Søren Kierkegaard articulated the necessity of "the possibility of offense" for a faithful gospel presentation.[20] This possibility of offense brought the listener to a crossroad of faith, where they must decide whether they will submit themselves to God in faith or be offended and reject the gospel. Similarly, the basic concern of theological contextuality is knowing how to present the possibility of offense effectively. A vital part of the contextual work is to understand the offense well, to remove cultural or sociopolitical offenses to sharpen the presentation of the theological offense leading to conversion (1 Cor 1:23).

Framing our approach in terms of asking theological questions from the Asian American context bypasses a problematic line of thinking: How Asian should Asian American theology be? What we seek is not necessarily more Asianness in some Orientalist fashion, but rather an encounter with God with all of who we are as Asian Americans. Of course, that holistic encounter might result in a recovery and greater affirmation of our Asian heritage, but assuming that Asian American theology always has to look a certain way or display particular features should be avoided as racial stereotyping. The goal is to faithfully witness to God as Asian Americans, not necessarily to jump through hoops about cultural resource requirements, even as I believe that Asian cultural resources could be a vital part of Asian American lives. The Asian American experience and Asian American theology is greater than Asian cultural heritage. How to talk intelligently about Asian America in all its complexity is the special focus of chapter three and the general concern of this book.

Our burning questions about the gospel are about encountering a holy God who loves, who can comfort as well as afflict. Because a generic version of the gospel is too dull and misses the nuances of sin and salvation within a given context, theologies in various contexts exist to wrestle with these

---

[20]Søren Kierkegaard, *Practice in Christianity* (Princeton, NJ: Princeton University Press, 1991), 99.

questions of faithfully knowing and living the message of Jesus Christ in particular situations and lives.

SUMMARY OF THE CHAPTERS

While I am cognizant of my own Korean American male identity, here I offer meta-categories and methodological concepts that cut across the Asian American community in its diversity and heterogeneity, framing and guiding the development of various ethnic-specific Asian American theologies.[21] Also, this work reflects my own commitments to the Reformed tradition. While some jest that the Reformed tradition could be understood as an ethnic or racial group, namely, White European, and there are real problems of Whiteness in how some understand it, my experience of appreciating and working within it as a living and diverse tradition has been enriching. For those of different ecclesial traditions, I hope my thoughts can serve as a catalyst to encourage and stimulate your own journey of doing theology for yourselves and your communities. For those desiring to learn the genesis of my ideas, much of the crucial moves of this book were developed in my previous work on Karl Barth and Asian American theology.[22]

The rest of this book is as follows. Chapters one and two develop the concept of theological contextuality. Chapter one begins with a presentation of theological contextuality as related to the very nature of all theologies. Because all theology is contextual—meaning answers to our burning questions that arise out of our lives—a "neutral" approach to theology is misguided. Along with faith seeking understanding through our burning questions, the nature of theology is about knowing the contextuality of all theology, being aware of the various unnamed normativities that oppress and distort our theological existence, and discerning the relationship between particularity and universality. Without understanding these three dimensions of theology—contextuality, normativities, and particularity/universality—the basis of Asian American theology would be incomprehensible.

---

[21]My social location, of course, also includes my identity as a cisgender male, middle-class, Gen Xer, who grew up in northern Virginia but now resides in greater Los Angeles.

[22]Daniel D. Lee, *Karl Barth, Contextuality, and Asian American Theology* (Minneapolis: Fortress, 2017).

Chapter two points to the election of and God's covenantal relationship with Israel as the biblical basis of contextuality. Supersessionist theology that made Israel irrelevant has the consequence of losing theological contextuality as well. Theological contextuality arises out of divine self-revelation of a covenantal God who enters history, making creation part of the divine being. Because Jesus is eternally Jewish, our present particularities matter as well. Our living God is a God who encounters us in time and space in our particularities. If we are to deal with the God of the Bible, we must contend with the idea of theological contextuality.

Applying this idea of theological contextuality to the Asian American context, the next five chapters present the Asian American Quadrilateral (AAQ), the methodological apparatus or grammar for doing Asian American theology. Every Asian American already deals with these contextual aspects of life; the important question is the level of awareness, articulation, and sophistication of theological reflection that we possess.

In chapter three, I begin by describing how Asian American identity and contexts feel like swimming around in murky water that is complex, diverse, and largely unconscious, yet impacts us deeply. In these waters lurk histories, influences, proclivities, and tendencies that we cannot name. Therefore, the first step to theological methodology is to "name the demon," in a manner of speaking. As a heuristic interpretive tool, I propose the AAQ, a fourfold framework that describes the Asian American experience as the intersection of Asian heritage, migration experience, American culture, and racialization. Within the matrix of these four themes, we struggle with matters of faith, family, church, leadership, scholarship, gender, and all other concerns. All Asian Americans negotiate these four themes very differently; these categories provide a common language to discern the similarities and distinctions between groups.

Chapter four covers what Asian heritage is and how to deal with it theologically. By Asian heritage, I mean the Asian cultural, religious, and philosophical heritage that is shared with contemporary Asians, many of whom, like Asian Americans, must also negotiate between this heritage and Western/global influences. This theme describes these traditions with their long development and many interpretations and embodiments, which function implicitly as well as explicitly within the Asian American context.

They include Confucianism, Taoism, Buddhism, Shinto, Shamanism, Hinduism, folk religions as well as Asian Christianities. These heritages act, however, as lived cultural realities, not as abstract ideas or academic concepts. The theology of culture I propose works with this heritage in the form of *cultural archetypes*, for example, a family-centric Confucian worldview, as opposed to essentialist stereotypes like "Asians are communal." Moreover, a *dialectical* view of these cultural archetypes allows a much more nimble and dynamic critique and construction for theology.

In chapter five, I deal with the theme of migration as immigration, refugee experience, and its related phenomena such as transnationalism, the acculturation or assimilation process, intergenerational conflict, and identity formation. While immigrants and refugees from Asia share many commonalities with those from elsewhere, their experiences are filtered through their Asian heritage, and, as we shall see, are impacted by their racialization. In this sense, we must keep in mind that all of these four elements of the AAQ influence and color the others, thus creating a distinctive context for Asian Americans. Also, the narrative and trauma of this transitional experience often leaves residual effects on the generations that follow the first one. I will analyze the possible theological significance of migration for Asian American immigrants and refugees as well as the meaning of America as a promised land and an empire. The particular weight of Asian American experiences of marginality will serve as an analogy to the alien status of Christians in the world.

Chapter six lays out American culture that encompasses not only the multicultural contemporary American culture, in which Asian Americans actively participate, but also the Western intellectual tradition, missionary/colonial history, and particularly Asian American representation in broader society and popular culture. The American pluralistic post-Christendom context in general, and the evangelical movement in particular, serve as the situation in which many Asian American Christians find themselves. As a result, Asian American Christianity is heavily influenced by the Enlightenment's rationalistic influence, as well as by the Puritanism and revivalism of evangelicalism. Of course, the church's contemporary struggles with postmodernity and a post-Christendom environment apply to Asian Americans as well. Drawing from and critiquing both missional theology that engages the North American culture as a mission field and postcolonial theology that challenges the Western hegemony, I explain why the matrix of Asian American experience provides unique insights for broader significance.

Chapter seven describes the Asian American experience of racialization. This fourth and final theme of the AAQ articulates the process of racial identity formation, navigating the Black/White binary, and the particular forms of discrimination that Asian Americans face as people of color. While all minorities face microaggressions and structural racism in various expressions and degrees, Asian American marginality might be best summed up in its "perpetual foreigner" status, the inability to fully affirm the Americanness of their identity. In this discussion, I explain the merits and limits of understanding Black Americans as the racial ancestors of Asian Americans.

The last two chapters look at the personal and the communal aspects of Asian American theology. In chapter eight, I offer what a process of integration and reconciliation might look like. Using trauma theory and interpersonal neurobiology, I propose that the journey of discipleship is also a process of creating a coherent narrative of our lives, where disparate, repressed, or dissociative aspects of our lives are made conscious and integrated to our senses of selves. This integration is a vital part of a holistic discipleship where all of ourselves are brought into God's purview to be reconciled and transformed. Furthermore, this process is crucial to our relationships and leadership as well. I propose the Holy Spirit as the agent of intrapersonal reconciliation, gathering and holding together our disparate selves, expressing our unarticulated pains and hurts, and uniting all that to Christ.

In chapter nine, taking to task the failing ideals of multiethnic ecclesiology and its toxic impact on Asian Americans, I argue that a "critical mixed economy embodied ecclesiology" better addresses the church in the eschatological in-between. Following the Chalcedonian pattern, our ecclesiology must not only be rooted in the God who gathers his people, but also the real humans who make up the community, with their bodies, cultures, contexts, and so on. This embodied ecclesiology must not only take the neighborhood into account, but the whole societal context. As a particular example of this embodied ecclesiology, I propose that Asian American churches in their various ministry models live in the tension of calling and temptation, which requires continual spiritual vigilance and theological conversion.

In the concluding invitation, I invite Asian Americans to do theology for themselves and their communities. There is a desperate need for Asian American communities of various ethnic heritages to articulate and struggle with their own concerns toward Asian American theologies of every kind in service of Asian American Christian communities of every kind. Asian American theology is the common task and calling of Asian American Christians in their complex diversity. We must all join in.

CONTEXTUALITY AND PARTICULARITY

*Christian faith is not available as an abstraction. The Word is
made flesh in human lives. Theology is historical to its core.*

FUMITAKA MATSUOKA

AT AN ASIAN AMERICAN CONFERENCE, after presenting a survey
of current scholarship on Asian American theology, the speaker asked the
attendees, mostly Asian American pastors, *Is this helpful? Do we need this?*
While the speaker phrased the question as one of usefulness, underlying it
was the question of the legitimacy and place of Asian American theology.
He was not asking a rhetorical question, but truly wondering whether we
need an Asian American theology. His question, a common one, exposes
the deep and widespread misunderstanding about the nature of the theological task in general, and the task of Asian American theology in particular.

This chapter is a non-apology for the existence of Asian American theologies.
I offer no justification or defense for the existence and the importance of Asian
American theologies, no answer to the question of whether Asian American
theologies should exist or if they deserve attention, because the basic premise
of that question is fundamentally flawed. I will, however, lay out the nature of
theology, as it relates to questions about contextuality, normativity, and the
dynamic tension between particularity and universality. In understanding
the nature of theology, we will be able to understand how the task of Asian
American theology fits into the broader global and multiethnic landscape.

Epigraph: Fumitaka Matsuoka, *Out of Silence: Emerging Themes in Asian American Churches*
(Cleveland, OH: Pilgrim Press, 1995), 4.

THE COVENANTAL BASIS OF CONTEXTUALITY

The notion of theology being an objective science is faulty because God is a living person and not a dead artifact. This reality that every theology is contextual is not new. Stephen Bevans, for example, points to a number of external sociopolitical and internal theological factors for theology being contextual.[1] While the concept of contextualization first arose out of missiology where the need for translation of the gospel was pressing, the growing global consciousness made it clear that no one was culture free. That realization served as a catalyst for missiologists to rethink the nature of theology.

Unfortunately, the label *contextual* remains in many theological circles and minds as a descriptor separating out non-Western, Majority World theologies or non-White theologies in the US. Theologies bearing this label might be relegated to the hinterlands of missiology or be seen as pertinent only in discussions about global or liberation theology. A common misunderstanding about contextual theology or contextualization is that people often mean a universal kernel of truth or gospel that is simply clothed in various cultures. The problem with this conceptualization of theology is that the White European tradition is often assumed to be this universal core theology, as though it is *a*contextual or neutral.

Since all theology is contextual, although some are implicitly while others are explicitly so, we could just drop the contextual label altogether. Instead of *contextual* as a label, I propose that we use the concept of contextuality as a category that applies to all theologies, describing the manner in which every theology is situated and engages their context.

This contextuality could be understood as a human limitation that we must work to move beyond. In that case, we might argue either that we are tragically bound by human limitations of cognition and perception or socio-politically determined to be ideologically disposed. We might also frame contextuality in terms of human need, or practical necessity to make the theology and the Bible relevant to different situations around the world. Instead of cultural and sociopolitical reasoning, I am interested in the theological understanding of contextuality as rooted in the very identity of God.

---

[1]Stephen B. Bevans, *Models of Contextual Theology* (Maryknoll, NY: Orbis, 1992), 5-10.

There are two popular versions of theological contextuality, namely incarnation and Pentecost.[2]

In terms of the incarnation, the Word becoming flesh is too universalistic to serve as theological grounds for contextuality. There is no significance to the differentiation of various flesh, as in particular human embodiments, or even flesh in a general sense, including, for example, animals as well.[3] Also, this is an analogical argument, not a proper theological one because properly speaking there is only one incarnation. If analogically we argue that the "incarnational" dynamic occurs in every culture or context, it is the same eternal Word in every contextual incarnation. This eternal Word in differing flesh is the support for theological contextuality as *translation*; in this case, Asian American bodies, communities, and cultures are merely husks that have no impact on the kernel that is the Word. There is a static superficiality to contextuality in that God is not impacted at all. God says the same thing but in a different language in a sense. Does God say or do something different when interacting within a certain context?

Pentecost offers another perspective on theological contextuality. Here the outpouring of the Spirit "upon all flesh" (Acts 2:17) could be interpreted in terms of universality; however, the speaking of many tongues leads to a "divinely ordered diversity and pluralism."[4] Through linguistic diversity, cultural and religious diversities could be taken up as theologically significant as well.[5] Willie Jennings contends that Pentecost should be interpreted as speaking the language of another instead of one's own, thereby expressing new kinship and intimacy across identities.[6] A possible concern here is that this version of contextuality accentuates foreignness, emphasizing the exoticism of Asian language and culture. While perhaps appropriate for the global context, stressing language and culture tends to Orientalize Asian Americans. What about the particular experiences of Asian Americans that

---

[2]Bevans, *Models of Contextual Theology*, 7-8.

[3]David L. Clough, *On Animals, Volume 1: Systematic Theology* (New York: T&T Clark, 2012), 81-103.

[4]Amos Yong, *The Future of Evangelical Theology: Soundings from the Asian American Diaspora* (Downers Grove, IL: InterVarsity, 2014), 136.

[5]Yong, *Future of Evangelical Theology*, 139.

[6]Willie Jennings, *The Christian Imagination: Theology and the Origins of Race* (New Haven, CT: Yale University Press, 2010), 266.

are not cultural or linguistic, but rather political or sociological, that is, marginality or invisibility?

While accepting the benefits and insights of the incarnation and Pentecost, I propose God's revelation as a covenantal God as the ground of theological contextuality. In proposing God's being as covenantal, I am stating that God sees and interacts with every people and every person in their particularity, for their reconciliation and vocation. Our relationship with this living God is an I-Thou encounter.[7] Jewish philosopher Martin Buber knew the danger of objectifying God, making the eternal Thou into an It. We can so easily reduce our living God into ideas or concepts, whether they be a worldview, law, morality, or even love or grace. More education or knowledge does not necessarily protect us from this danger of theological abstraction. Dietrich Bonhoeffer warns that the first theological question was asked by the serpent, inquiring about God in the third person as an object of our study.[8] It is always tempting to think of God as an idea that we can grasp, rather than a free person that I must attend to. Rather than a universal idea or an abstract concept, our God is "the God of Abraham, God of Isaac, God of Jacob, not of the philosophers and savants" as Blaise Pascal would confess.[9] Another way of expressing this I-Thou relationality is to confess that our God is a covenantal God. This covenantal God is alive and not dead, actively working and interacting with us and the world. Affirming God's covenantal aliveness means at least three things.

First, the living God encounters us in our particular existence. Our God encounters us as a person. This personal encounter occurs concretely in time and space, within a particular context; it does not happen abstractly. As Pascal notes above, in Scripture God does not reveal himself as a universalizing philosophical idea, but rather as a God of a particular people and definite relationships. God reveals himself personally, stopping people dead in their tracks and sending them forth to a radically different life afterward.

As we encounter the living God, we are called to follow Christ in our particular contexts, in our particular times, in our particular bodies. While all of us are called to follow Christ, where and how the path of discipleship

---

[7]Martin Buber, *I and Thou* (New York: Touchstone, 1970).

[8]Dietrich Bonhoeffer, *Dietrich Bonhoeffer Works*, vol. 3, *Creation and Fall: A Theological Exposition of Genesis 1-3*, ed. John W. de Gruchy, trans. Douglas Stephen Bax (Minneapolis: Fortress, 1997), 107.

[9]Blaise Pascal, *Pensées* (New York: Penguin, 1966), 285.

takes us is different for all of us and that's because God encounters us concretely. We read Scripture not only to follow in the wake of God's past actions or words. We are also opening ourselves to hearing the living God speak—not just to anyone, but to us in our particularity.[10] As we pray and listen to God, God responds not with generic one-size-fits-all responses, but with specific answers to our particular supplications.

Second, the living God invites our whole selves to be reconciled. Confessing that "God is all, and we are naught" might sound pious, but it is not biblical. Emil Brunner points out how we can distort biblical faith by emphasizing God at the expense of humanity.[11] He poses this covenantal reality of our faith in terms of objectivity and subjectivity, both who God is in and of himself and our experience of God, respectively. Especially when the church feels threatened by various trials and temptations, it can resort to a reactionary exclusivism, embracing objectivity while rejecting notions of subjectivity.[12] There definitely are times when the church needs to recover the otherness of God and critique anthropocentric distortions of faith. However, this kind of correction does not reflect the full picture of our faith and more importantly does not express the covenantal nature of our God, who in divine freedom creates room for our human freedom.

Just as we can reduce God to an It, it is also possible to not bring our whole selves to this relationship, failing to be an authentic I. Walter Brueggemann talks about this kind of distortion in terms of us becoming mere yes-men or yes-women to God's commands, failing to have a "genuine covenant interaction" with God.[13] With the struggles of White assimilation and being presented with a White version of Christianity that ignores parts of our identity, it is so easy for Asian Americans to be become a truncated self, a self that represses parts of ourselves that we deem unpresentable. In a

---

[10]Karl Barth's rejection of casuistry is getting at the very same thing. God is alive and we cannot treat him as though he is dead and has left us a book in his stead. See Daniel D. Lee, "Reading Scripture in our Context: Double Particularity in Karl Barth's Actualistic View of Scripture," in *The Voice of God in the Text of Scripture: Explorations in Constructive Dogmatics*, ed. Oliver D. Crisp and Fred Sanders (Grand Rapids, MI: Zondervan, 2016).

[11]Even with their infamous rift over natural theology, Karl Barth affirmed this same point later in his career. See Karl Barth, "Humanity of God," in *The Humanity of God* (Richmond, VA: John Knox, 1960), 37-65.

[12]Emil Brunner, *Truth as Encounter* (Philadelphia: Westminster Press, 1964), 82.

[13]Walter Brueggemann, *The Psalms and the Life of Faith* (Minneapolis: Fortress Press, 1995), 102-104.

sense, we can die to ourselves in a misguided way, thinking that our Asian American aspects are the problem.

The failure to bring our whole selves into God's presence means that there are parts of ourselves that are not reconciled to God, missing from God's shalom. In a sense, Christ's reconciliation is not just cosmic, social, and interpersonal, but also *intra*personal: it involves all of ourselves, even parts that we do not value or are unaware of. Through the gospel, God transforms us deep below the surface of our lives, healing our hurts and affirming our seemingly unpresentable aspects.

Third, the living God sends us out with particular callings. Encountering us in our place and station in life and taking ahold of our whole selves, God sends us out to join his mission in the world. God had particular callings for Moses, Daniel, and Esther, as he has for us. We are not just getting a generic call to follow a universal spiritual code. Such a general God, a mechanistic universality that is objective and the same for all, arises from reducing the gospel to a set of objective beliefs or static spiritual concepts. Now, this idea of particular callings can be twisted into an egotistical self-affirmation about our uniqueness and God's way of bringing that to fruition. But even as we recognize the danger of such narcissistic thinking, a covenantal understanding of God's calling cannot be simplified into a set of common laws or plans that everyone follows.[14]

A different way of thinking about this I-Thou dynamic of our living God and our particularity can be drawn from John Calvin. Calvin begins his *Institutes* (I.i.1) with the interrelated nature of the knowledge of God and knowledge of ourselves.[15] He is not sure which one precedes or follows the other; this theme of double knowledge is one of the fundamental themes that runs through his theology.[16] Here, Calvin displays his deeply covenantal imagination that affirms the place of humanity with God, even as the stress clearly falls on God's work and glory.

---

[14]Kierkegaard's "teleological suspension of the ethical" in regarding Abraham's call is getting at this very idea of particular callings. Søren Kierkegaard, *Kierkegaard's Writings*, vol. 6, *Fear and Trembling/Repetition*, ed. an trans. Edna H. Hong and Howard V. Hong (Princeton, NJ: Princeton University Press, 1983), 54-67.

[15]John Calvin, *Institutes of Christian Religion* (Louisville, KY: Westminster John Knox, 1960), 35.

[16]Richard A. Muller, *The Unaccommodated Calvin: Studies in the Foundation of a Theological Tradition* (New York: Oxford University Press, 2000), 8.

While for Calvin self-knowledge meant knowing ourselves to be fallen and redeemed in Christ, we might analogically extend his train of thought to include sociopolitical and cultural location. In continuing Calvin's framework in a more hermeneutical vein, our knowledge of God is filtered and impacted by the knowledge of ourselves and vice versa. That includes cultural, ethnic, racial, and sociopolitical particularities. We must be honest with ourselves about the insights and limits of our encounter with God. The knowledge of ourselves guides us into being an authentic "I" and to evaluating critically our particular understanding of God. The knowledge of God revealed in Christ leads us to a living "Thou," who reveals who we are and who we are called to be, which includes both how we can distort our knowledge of God as well as how we are specifically in need of God's grace.

Incarnation, Pentecost, and covenantal relationality are all important for theological contextuality. However, they can all become theoretical abstractions untethered from the biblical witness unless we recover God's election of Israel. It matters that Word became flesh in a Jewish body, that different languages were spoken by Spirit-filled diasporic Jews, and that the divine self-revelation of God occurred in the covenantal election of Israel as God's people. Because this election of Israel is the basis and the core of theological contextuality, the next chapter will address why all theology must be post-supersessionist. In recovering the Jewishness of Jesus, we affirm the significance of our own particular Gentileness. While covenant serves as a formal foundation of contextuality, its material basis is this particular Gentileness that exists as a foil to the election of Israel.

HIDDEN NORMATIVITIES

The importance of having a clear notion of theological contextuality is not just about multicultural and global hospitality, making room for non-Western theologies. Lacking a deep awareness of our own situatedness exposes us to contextual captivities and distortions of the gospel. Lesslie Newbigin, and missional theologians thinking after him, have made this point clear. When Newbigin returned to the UK after his long missionary work in India, he found that Western Christianity was hopelessly captive to modernism and pluralism and yet was unaware of this bondage.[17] In a sense, the

---

[17]Lesslie Newbigin, *Foolishness to the Greeks: The Gospel and Western Culture* (Grand Rapids, MI: Eerdmans, 1986).

so-called West has been sending missionaries to the Majority World without realizing that they come bearing their own context as well. Many Western countries thought, because of their long historical engagement with Christianity, that they and their context had been thoroughly converted. However, Darrell Guder points out that without a continual conversion we will find ourselves with a gospel reduction, because gospel-culture interaction requires continual vigilance.[18] This conversion is not a once-and-for-all kind of affair, but rather an again-and-again reality. Only by continually being aware of where we are situated and how that impacts our theology can we avoid cultural captivities of the gospel.

If contextuality is an inescapable human phenomenon that is also vital for our faithfulness, why do we keep thinking that some theologies are not contextual, that some are above the cultural sociopolitical fray? The culprit for this blindness is the "exnomination" of White Eurocentric normativity. Exnomination is a concept developed by Roland Barthes that describes how a pervasive aspect of culture can be accepted as normative, as "a given," by remaining unnamed.[19] It is a way of describing how one particular perspective becomes a universal norm by staying invisible.

The contextuality of many White male theologians remains invisible because, through the process of exnomination, we do not see their works as perspectival. This is analogous to how *American* is often assumed to mean *White* American, whereas every other race feels that they must label or hyphenate themselves as Asian Americans, Black Americans, Hispanic Americans, and so on. Because this normativity is unnamed, we cannot see its distinctiveness. At Fuller, I have met many well-meaning White students from the Midwest who express their excitement about being exposed to so many different cultures because they feel that they themselves are cultureless or neutral, sort of like a blank whiteboard or vanilla ice cream. This illusion of universal neutrality is what exnomination does to White normativity.

---

[18]Darrell L. Guder, *The Continuing Conversion of the Church* (Grand Rapids, MI: Eerdmans, 2000), 98.

[19]Roland Barthes, "Mythology Today," in *Mythologies* (New York: Hill and Wang, 2012), 250-52. Spencer applies Barthes's concept of exnomination to the dynamics of racial realities and politics of representation. Stephen Spencer, *Race and Ethnicity: Culture, Identity and Representation*, 2nd ed. (New York: Routledge, 2014), xxiv, 294.

Being blind to our own contextuality makes us vulnerable to contextual captivities. Like Newbigin, Stanley Hauerwas and William Willimon have noted in *Resident Aliens* how American culture can be confused for Christianity.[20] In our contextual sloth, the American church has confused ideas of individual freedom, political privilege, and intellectual assent for the gospel. In a similar manner, Soong-Chan Rah has described a White captivity of evangelicalism with unnamed racism, individualism, and consumerism hijacking our faith.[21] The issue is not that American Christianity is in danger of becoming captive to cultural forces, but rather that, because of the exnomination of White normativity, invisible and unrecognized cultural forces have already taken over. Cultural captivity of the gospel is a universal and continual danger for everyone, no matter where you may be in the world. This danger can arise out of misunderstanding your theological context, making the context into an idol and judge of the gospel, or by being oblivious to your context, thinking that you work in a contextless manner when in fact your context is invisibly limiting, guiding, distorting, and coopting your faith.

Along with exnomination, Barthes describes how modern myths function through the deprivation of history.[22] Within the conservative evangelical tradition, I was nurtured with a very clear historical sensibility of one continuous, storied Western tradition. From this perspective, what I am calling "White Eurocentric theology" was perceived as the historically-rooted theology that can be traced all the way back to the apostles. From this perspective, non-White, non-Western faith communities can and should make appropriate cultural accommodations and applications based on this universal tradition, but they are not allowed to develop their own ethnic or racial theologies deviating or revising it.

While this view of tradition sounds appealing, the truth is that there is no such single continuous monolithic Christian tradition. Andrew Walls argues that the transmission of Christianity is more "serial" through various contexts and different times than "progressive" as one continual tradition

---

[20]Stanley Hauerwas and William Willimon, *Resident Aliens: Life in the Christian Colony* (Nashville: Abingdon, 1989), 30-36.

[21]Soong-Chan Rah, *The Next Evangelicalism: Freeing the Church from Western Cultural Captivity* (Downers Grove, IL: InterVarsity, 2009), 18-23.

[22]Barthes, *Mythologies*, 264.

spreading from a single center (for example, the "Western" context).[23] This idea limits how much the church fathers should be considered as "older and more experienced elders," since this older wisdom might not apply across the board in other contexts. While helpful to relativize and contextualize all of church history, we should note that this idea of serial transmission, when positing Israel as only one context among many, is problematic as we will see in the next chapter.

Now given that, in order to make sure that our talk of contextuality does not devolve into some sort of postmodern subjective relativism, we must now clarify the relationship between particularity and universality, and the place of a global tradition.

PARTICULARITY AND UNIVERSALITY

The dynamics of contextuality can be understood in this double statement: *Universality must be mediated by particularity; particularity must be in service of universality.*[24] Similarly, Andrew Walls proposes two concepts that highlight how the gospel lives in tension with the host culture.[25] The *indigenous principle* states the need for contextualization, for the gospel to feel at home in a particular context. The *pilgrim principle*, on the contrary, points to the constant reforming dimension that counters the indigenous principle and connects each embodiment of the gospel to the universal faith community.

The first statement, *universality must be mediated by particularity*, means that God chooses to communicate God's universal message through the mediation of a particular manifestation, first and foremost, through Israel and the Jewish Christ. There is no pure, acultural, unadulterated gospel. All Christianity is mediated through a culture, and all theology is contextual theology.

The second statement, *particularity must be in service of universality*, means that no contextual theology can have a privileged position over others. No contextual theology can have a specific claim on God. All contextual expressions of the gospel must in the end serve the one, holy, catholic, and apostolic

[23]Andrew F. Walls, *The Cross-Cultural Process in Christian History: Studies in the Transmission and Appropriation of Faith* (Maryknoll, NY: Orbis, 2002), 145.
[24]Daniel D. Lee, *Double Particularity: Karl Barth, Contextuality, and Asian American Theology* (Minneapolis: Fortress, 2017), 82.
[25]Andrew F. Walls, *The Missionary Movement in Christian History: Studies in the Transmission of Faith* (Maryknoll, NY: Orbis, 1996), 7-9.

church. Theological contextuality must not lead to a tribal theology that is self-serving to the ethnocentric exclusion of others, such as the German Christianity of the Third Reich. Newbigin relates particular cultures with the universal community and its universal mission and points out that this dialectical process leads to a deeper understanding of the gospel itself:

> The Christian community, the universal Church, embracing more and more fully all the cultural traditions of humankind, is called to be that community in which a tradition of rational discourse is developed which leads to a true understanding of reality, because it takes as its starting point and as its permanent criterion of truth the self-revelation of God in Jesus Christ.[26]

To understand how this works, cartography can serve as an analogy of how the global theological tradition develops as all the particular theological expressions work together in service of the one gospel, one church, and one God. Imagine a vast world where each community explores and maps out the geography of their own lands. After years of familiarity and study, each community will have mapped out their own lands to every road and side street, while lands distant from them will be represented with vague sketches. Now, if the map that a particular community developed was used for all, the people who live in other lands will have only meager outlines for understanding their own lands. Jonathan Bonk introduces the term "ecclesiastical cartography" in describing how church sees the world. He bemoans how some parts of this map remain *terra incognita*, with no names or labels.[27] Beyond thinking of this cartography in a geographic sense as Bonk does, I mean for us to imagine the landscape of theological and contextual concerns, questions, and concepts.

It is important to clarify that I am not here talking about superficial and easily packaged "cultural gifts" such as family orientation, communalism, or hospitality. Rather, I am imagining those Asian American theological contributions that come about as we ask theological questions about our contextual struggles. I once heard an Asian American speaker, who is very active in multicultural ministry circles, bemoan the fact that while African American churches have their spirituals and gospel choir, and Hispanic

---

[26]Lesslie Newbigin, *The Gospel in a Pluralist Society* (Grand Rapids, MI: Eerdmans, 1989), 87-88.

[27]Jonathan J. Bonk, "Ecclesiastical Cartography and the Invisible Continent," *International Bulletin of Missionary Research* 28, no. 4 (October 2004): 153-58.

ministries have their celebratory worship in Spanish, Asian Americans do not really have "distinct gifts" to share with others. But rather than fretting about what we are or are not bringing to the table, our primary concern should be identifying and taking up our pressing theological questions because in attending to that task we find our contribution to the world. The particular Asian American gift to the global church arises out of our spiritual struggle with God, seeking and responding to God in our specific place of discipleship and mission. For example, the distinct gift of the Asian American church is not just cultural collectivism but the theological reflections and spiritual practices about brokenness, sin, transformation, and redemption around cultural collectivism in a racialized world.

Using this rough analogy of cartography, we can imagine how each of the communities might raise questions and develop theology as they experience God in their own situation. Specific questions will be asked in one context, whereas those in another context might pursue different inquiries. For example, within the European context, with its long history of Christendom, the question of church and state has been a pivotal question leading to various proposals for what faithfulness might mean, whether it be the Lutheran two kingdoms approach, the Anabaptist free church, or a Dutch Reformed Christian political party as Abraham Kuyper proposes. This question is storied, with each approach developed with historic depth.

However, what if the pressing question is not only church and state, but church and family as well, as it is for many Asian Americans? Of course, the issue of church and state is relevant for Asian Americans living in the United States. However, the relationship between church and family, which is not commonly recognized as a theological problem but rather simply a spirituality or ministry problem, plagues the lives of many Asian Americans. In a sense, this is a different area of the theological map that is not well-developed, it is *terra incognita*.

Within the Western Protestant tradition, with its Enlightenment-influenced individualism, family is not a significant theological locus. Thus, it is not only possible, but quite probable, to graduate from seminary without ever dealing with family as a theological category. And yet, it is a burning question for many Asian Americans. The resources that developed Western theological traditions are inadequate not only because they come from a different cultural background, but also because they do not pursue this issue with the requisite level of depth and nuance. They are just not pursuing these kinds of questions. Of course, the fact that family has been so ignored as a theological locus does not mean that this development was not needed for the broader White American situation either. In asking their burning questions about the relationship between church and family, Asian Americans here would expand theological insights toward uncharted frontiers that not only would benefit their community but serve the global theological tradition as well.

That is just one example, but the larger point is that, only as we work together can the global theological map be developed to sufficient detail and distinctions. And just like any real map of our world, we need to continually work on this map as our world continues to change all the time.

In continuing this cartography analogy, a factoid I learned recently in my hobby of backpacking might help illustrate how having one interpretation of Scripture as our theological norm still does not lead to uniformity of perspectives. Most of us grow up thinking that the compass always points north. However, that's only half true. What the compass points to is called the "magnetic north," and it differs from "true north." The difference in degrees between magnetic and true north is called the "declination." These magnetic declinations vary significantly from place to place and even change over time.[28] When in the backcountry, in order to navigate correctly you must first learn the current declination at your location, then account for this deviation before referring to your map. Otherwise, you can end up miles away from where you intend to go.

When I first encountered this idea of magnetic north, it did not register in my head because I couldn't understand how the compass could be "wrong" or, more accurately, relative over time and space. Moving beyond the shock, I was baffled that I had not known about this, and that so many people still have no idea that the compass does not point us to true north. Analogously, I offer that while God's revelation is the "true north" that Scripture points us to, our readings of Scripture are more like the "magnetic north" of biblical interpretation, which vary based on time and space. In a sense, how we read Scripture and even what we see as pressing or relevant varies over time and

---

[28]To see what these magnetic declinations look like over time and location, refer to www.ncei.noaa.gov/maps/historical_declination/. Accessed on August 9, 2017.

space. Moreover, unlike having the benefit of GPS technology and satellite maps for traversing geography, we must depend on historical and ecumenical wisdom for our theological bearings, and even more importantly on God's spirit to discern the changing contextual declinations.

Through this rather crude analogy, I am pointing to our epistemological limitations and how theology is not God, but rather a witness to God. To bring all these ideas together, missiologist Paul Hiebert's concept of epistemological shifts provides an interpretative paradigm to comprehend this dynamic between particularity and universality.[29]

Hiebert describes the epistemology of modernity to be positivism, which holds that our knowledge "corresponds one-to-one with reality."[30] With the supreme optimism of the Enlightenment, scientific knowledge, for example, was understood to be purely objective. The impact of this epistemology on theology was that theology and the gospel were equated with one another. Taking this understanding of their theology, Western missionaries sought to share an "acultural and ahistorical" gospel to other nations.[31]

With the demise of modernity, human optimism gave way to the skepticism of postmodernity, or pessimism in the form of an instrumental epistemology. Within this view, our knowledge is so tainted with our presuppositions and our interests that imposing it on others is always a form of oppression. From this perspective, theology is just a subjective expression of the gospel in one's own context and worldview with no claim to any sort of objectivity. Therefore, it is more accurate to "speak of theologies, not Theology, for there are as many theologies as there are human points of view."[32]

However, Hiebert suggests that we have matured to a critical realistic view of theology, holding that "reason and empiricism are not sufficient to discern the truth, but they are useful guides we can draw upon. . . . It recognizes that as humans we see through a glass darkly, but that we do see."[33] This humble view of human knowledge shows that "none can claim sole authority

[29]Paul G. Hiebert, "Anthropology, Missions, and Epistemological Shifts," in *Paradigm Shifts in Christian Witness: Insights from Anthropology, Communication, Spiritual Power*, ed. Charles E. Van Engen, Darrell Whiteman, and J. Dudley Woodberry (Maryknoll, NY: Orbis, 2008), 13-22.
[30]Hiebert, "Anthropology," 13.
[31]Hiebert, "Anthropology," 14.
[32]Hiebert, "Anthropology," 17.
[33]Hiebert, "Anthropology," 19.

to judge the others."[34] All human theology is culturally and historically biased, yet it still points to the gospel that saves us. Theology is not the gospel itself, but it still bears useful witness to the gospel.

This critical realistic perspective on theology is "based on community hermeneutic" because no one person can see the whole picture in detail, but rather requires others to compare and sharpen their view.[35] The *critical* element reminds us that other theologians are sinners just like us; the *realist* element states that, even as sinners, their insights can still help us as we struggle with Scripture in our context to discern God's work and presence.

In my long theological journey, the above reflections are what have led me to not try to justify Asian American theology, but to see it within the backdrop of what theology is in general. When I was writing my dissertation on Karl Barth, I kept wanting to go beyond the edges of where Barth could take me. I had been attracted to Barth because of his radical Christocentricity and grace-centeredness. I just needed to find a way to apply Barth's wisdom to the Asian American context, I thought. However, despite my urgent questions, I found that Barth either refused to go down the line of questioning I found necessary or provided superficial responses lacking the nuance I sought. As a good student at the foot of a modern-day church father, I remained subservient, thinking that the fault laid with me.[36] Gradually, however, I overcame this sense of mute prostration before theological greatness, and began to realize that Barth himself, even as he took up certain questions, avoided pursuing others. As I studied the dynamics of his own contextuality, his fight to move beyond the ghost of Friedrich Schleiermacher, exposing the idolatry of German racist Christianity, or jousting with the existentialism of Rudolf Bultmann, I discovered that Barth was taking up the burning questions of his situation while ignoring others. Even with the sheer volume of his *Church Dogmatics*, Barth's theological project was not exhaustive in a universal sense, nor was that his intent. Many of his

---

[34]Hiebert, "Anthropology," 20.

[35]Hiebert, "Anthropology."

[36]Torrance describes Karl Barth as "the great Church Father of Evangelical Christendom, the one genuine Doctor of the universal Church the modern era has known. . . . Only Athanasius, Augustine, Aquinas and Calvin have performed comparable service." T. F. Torrance, editor's preface to *Church Dogmatics*, vol. 4, part 4, *The Doctrine of Reconciliation*, by Karl Barth (Edinburgh: T&T Clark, 1969), vi.

Barthian admirers, including myself at one point, fail to see it, but I now see that Barth knew, or at least came to understand, the limits of his own contextuality. That is why Barth encouraged others not to merely copy or repeat his thoughts in their own context, to not be Barthians, but to do theology for themselves.[37]

Looking through the venerated theologians of the broader tradition, I found that every single one struggled with the burning questions of their time and place. Seeing this, I conclude that I, just like Barth, Bonhoeffer, Calvin, Luther, and Augustine, as well as James Cone, Gustavo Gutiérrez, Kwak Pui-lan, and others, need to take up the burning questions of my situation. I am an Asian American, and my church's house is on fire. When many Asian Americans read works of their favorite prominent White male theologians or pastors, they are also reading a particular and limited perspective. As Asian Americans, we share certain aspects of their context, and hence can benefit from reading these works. But what we must also realize is that there are other questions that these writers do not know about or do not take up, questions that are particular to us as Asian Americans.

For me, realizing this hidden normativity of White theology, especially in the Reformed tradition, was a long journey. I understood intellectually that theologies existed in context. However, with a firm conviction about the universality of the gospel, and the primacy of spiritual identity over human distinctions, I believed that being a follower of Christ meant that our cultural, ethnic, and racial identities are theologically irrelevant. To focus on these creaturely particularities seemed like distractions at best, and idolatries at worst, in comparison to the all-consuming calling to seek and love God who breaks down all walls of division and hostilities. However, I have come to understand that the idea of contextual theologies came with the assumption that "normative" theology and tradition do not address particular situations and perspectives. While true in some sense, this way of labeling left untouched the hidden supposedly universal and objective assumptions of the tradition and of theologies free of any descriptors. And through the process of exnomination these descriptor-less theologies asserted their normative ideologies along with their theological ideas.

---

[37] Karl Barth, "No Boring Theology! A Letter from Karl Barth," *South East Asia Journal of Theology* 11 (1969): 3-5.

There are more theologians now who would accept the reality of such a thing as the social location of the theologian, but a flippant acceptance matters little if it is not methodologically substantive. Moving forward we have two options. On the one hand, we label nothing because labeling is being used to marginalize. Thus, all are just theologies with the assumption that all are perspectival and all are only contributions. While theoretically possible, this option wouldn't work given that the seemingly universal, objective theologies would continue business as usual. Alternatively, we label everything and expose all the hidden assumptions. Locate yourself as a theologian and your theological work explicitly. This labeling is your theological and ethical responsibility. In this sense, Asian American theology is just theology, aware of its particular context, the place in which we ask theological questions.

We should stop using the word *contextual* for only certain theologies and not others. That selective usage itself is problematic and confusing. Rather, we need to discuss the contextuality of every single theology. In all this, we must especially make explicit a theology's relationship with historical and structural normativities. This is one of the main reasons we are talking about all this in the first place, to understand the relationship between knowledge and power.

Given its importance, our efforts should be directed toward developing the concept of theological contextuality. That is exactly what the next chapter does in identifying the importance of Israel for contextuality and supersessionism as the chief problem that we must address. While not a commonly made connection, this link between contextuality and the election of Israel, I argue, is *the* proper foundation of this concept.

2

ELECTION AND GENTILENESS

The kind of liberation we are calling for is not a liberation from ethnicity, but liberation through ethnicity.

ROY SANO

I JEST THAT MY RESURRECTED BODY will not look like Brad Pitt. It will not be White, nor will it be some generic human body. My glorified body will be Asian American. As a few students in this Asian American identity and ministry class chuckle, they collectively pause to ponder what that means. Somehow many had assumed that our eschatological glorified bodies would be free from and beyond the strictures of cultural, racial, and ethnic particularities. Given the implicit White normativity mentioned in chapter one, glorified neutral humanity defaulted to Whiteness in their minds.

In the history of doctrine, the famous saying of Gregory Nazianzen, "the unassumed is the unhealed," serves as a guide to framing soteriological reflections. In his historical context opposing Apollinarianism, Gregory sought to protect the full humanity of Christ so that human body, soul, and mind are all redeemed through the person and works of the incarnate one. The Word indeed became flesh, assuming all aspects of humanity so that all are saved. However, what does this assumption of full humanity mean for Asian American identity as a cultural, sociopolitical, and ethnoracial matrix?

Epigraph: Roy I. Sano, "Ministry for a Liberating Ethnicity: The Biblical and Theological Foundation for Ethnic Ministries," in *The Theologies of Asian American and Pacific Peoples: A Reader*, complied by Roy I. Sano (Oakland, CA: Asian Center for Theology & Strategies, Pacific School of Religion, 1976), 291.

What happens to these identifiers in our union with Christ? Are they left behind as worldly dross or do they continue even unto the eschaton?

Because Jesus Christ as the new Adam reveals to us what it means to be authentically human, these theological anthropological questions are basically christological. How is Jesus Christ human and what has he assumed for our redemption? This chapter exposes the problem of the abstract humanity of Christ and its implication for a whitewashed redemption, proposing instead a recovery of a Jewish Jesus, particularly as that reality impacts our human identities. In order for all of ourselves to be healed in Christ, all must be assumed by Christ, including our cultural, sociopolitical, and ethnoracial identities.

So often soteriological concerns drive our theological pursuits, which is understandable given the urgency of seeking the presence of God in our suffering and brokenness. This soteriological concern should not be anthropocentric but cosmic in scope. In that broad vista, we remember that to know Christ is to know his benefits, as proposed by second-generation Lutheran Reformer Philipp Melanchthon. Revelation and reconciliation are two sides of the same coin of encountering the living God. To know God is to know the God who saves. While we began with posing the redemption of our Asian American bodies, our soteriological question leads us to the very nature of God and of the theological task in general.

In chapter one, I proposed that contextuality is rooted in the very identity of God, not just the sociopolitical varieties of our lives. That God is revealed as a covenantal God comes to a concrete focus in the divine election to be the God of Israel and, through Israel, the world. This election is not merely an instrumental fashion where Israel serves as a means to an end, to be jettisoned after divine usage, but rather in an everlasting manner so that the nations are included by being grafted to this chosen people. Election of Israel and revelation of God are intertwined. Divine self-revelation comes to us as the God of this people. Contextuality for Asian American theology in light of Israel means discerning what kind of Gentile theology is Asian American theology. Just as the particularity of Israel remains, even in its hybridity and commixture throughout history, being a particular Gentile is the basis of Asian American theology.

The argument of the chapter is as follows: First, I explain the problem of anti-Judaism and anti-Semitism throughout church history and how that has led to the double problem of ethnocentricity and abstract anthropology. Second, I critique various proposals for the meaning of Jesus' Jewishness, offering a thicker "carnal" Jewishness à la Michael Wyschogrod. Third, I present the theological implications of this carnal Jewishness of Jesus for Asian American theology as a particular Gentile theology.

ERASED JEWISHNESS AND THE DANGERS
OF ABSTRACT HUMANITY

"Truly God and truly human" is how the Chalcedonian Creed of 451 grasps the person of Jesus Christ. Beset by distortions that either sundered the mystery of the incarnation or denied its reality, this two natures solution, divine and human, guided the church amid its contemporary challenges. However, while it affirmed the humanity of Jesus as a general ontological category, this humanity lacked any material content. The Jesus of this and other ecumenical creeds is only abstractly human but not concretely so. While the historic events of the virgin birth by Mary, crucifixion under Pontius Pilate, and resurrection are acknowledged, Jesus' Jewishness is nowhere mentioned. His concrete humanity as a Jewish Messiah is not of theological import. This omission is not simply accidental but betrays a deeply rooted anti-Judaism and anti-Semitism that took root from the early church and on.[1]

The biblical witness takes pains to establish Jesus' blood lineage, his genealogical identity. Jesus is "Son of David" (Mt 9:27; 15:22; 20:30-31) and Abraham's seed (Rom 4:13; Gal 3:16). "Salvation is from the Jews" and more specifically from this Jew, the one Jesus Christ (Jn 4:22). According to the New Testament, the "Jewish origins, the Jewish nature, and the Jewish life of Jesus" is at the heart of its witness to the Savior of the world.[2] The incarnate God in Jesus Christ is the God of Abraham, Isaac, and Jacob, the God of Israel, the elected people. The gospel is that this ethnic God is the God almighty, Creator of heaven and earth.

The first Christians were Jewish followers of Jesus, one among broad and diverse expressions of Judaism. This small community did not believe

---

[1] I am indebted to the guidance and insights of my colleague, Messianic Jewish theologian, Jennifer Rosner regarding the Jewish-Christian schism.
[2] Markus Barth, *Jesus the Jew* (Atlanta: John Knox Press, 1978), 27.

that they were part of a religious tradition distinct from Judaism. The God of Israel had become incarnate as the long-awaited Messiah. The New Testament attests to how Jewish Christ followers struggled to follow the Spirit in including Gentiles into their community. The separation of Christ followers, encompassing Jews and Gentiles, from the rest of Judaism occurred through a gradual process that has been called the "parting of the ways," or more accurately "partings" because this schism occurred over many centuries.[3]

At its early stage, the leadership of the growing Christ-following community was situated in Jerusalem with a firm connection to its Jewish identity. Thus, the fundamental Jewishness of the Christian faith was assured. However, with the fall of the Second Temple in 70 AD and later the exile of all Jews, including Christ-following Jews from Jerusalem after the Bar Kochba Rebellion in 135 AD, the Gentile Christ followers lost their tangible connection to their Jewish roots through Jerusalem. Along with the loss of Jerusalem, these Jewish revolts escalated the tensions within the Jewish-Gentile Christ-believing community. As a movement within the greater Jewish community, Christ followers shared Judaism's legal protection as well as respectability given Jewish "ancient and venerable pedigree."[4] As anti-Jewish sentiments arose throughout the Roman Empire in response to the rebellions, this "[a]ssociation with the Jewish world was now a liability rather than an asset."[5] Anti-Jewish sentiment also came from Jewish missionary zeal and their proselytizing of converts from many faiths.[6] Gentile Christ-believing leaders fearing the loss of their flock to Judaism castigated this Jewish mission along with Judaism itself. The decentralized rabbinic Judaism that came after the fall of the Second Temple and the predominately Gentile Christ followers continued to develop in a mutually exclusive manner, so that the Jewish elements within Christianity were erased and

---

[3]See, for example, James D. G. Dunn, *The Partings of the Ways: Between Christianity and Judaism and their Significance for the Character of Christianity* (Philadelphia: Trinity Press International, 1991).

[4]Mark S. Kinzer, *Postmissionary Messianic Judaism: Redefining Christian Engagement with the Jewish People* (Grand Rapids, MI: Brazos Press, 2005), 184.

[5]Kinzer, *Postmissionary Messianic Judaism*, 184.

[6]Lee Martin McDonald, "Anti-Judaism in the Early Church Fathers," in *Anti-Semitism and Early Christianity: Issues of Polemic and Faith*, ed. Craig A. Evans and Donald A. Hagner (Minneapolis: Fortress, 1993), 221.

Christ-accepting elements within Judaism were also rejected. In this mutual rejection Christianity and Judaism defined each other as distinct religions.[7]

While this complex history of the parting of ways continues to be researched and debated, looking to the history of doctrine, the Council of Nicea, convened by Emperor Constantine, stands out as one of the earliest definitive moments. As the first ecumenical council of the church, the Council and its resulting Creed began the process of defining orthodoxy. Also, as a display of the sociopolitical power of Gentile Christianity, this Council marks the establishment of Christendom, the merging of Christianity with the Roman Empire.

Along with affirming the full deity of Jesus Christ against the Arian proposal, this Council also resolved the Quartodeciman Controversy, which debated the legitimacy of aligning the date of Easter celebration with the Jewish Passover. During the Council, Constantine expressed blatant anti-Judaism and argued for the decoupling of Easter and Passover, saying that Christians should have nothing in common with the hated Jews:

> It was declared to be particularly unworthy for this, the holiest of all festivals, to follow the custom [the calculation] of the Jews, who had soiled their hands with the most fearful of crimes, and whose minds were blinded. . . . We ought not, therefore, to have anything in common with the Jews, for the Saviour has shown us another way; our worship follows a more legitimate and more convenient course (the order of the days of the week); and consequently, in unanimously adopting this mode, we desire, dearest brethren, to separate ourselves from the detestable company of the Jews. . . . It would still be your duty not to tarnish your soul by communications with such wicked people [the Jews].[8]

Nicea sees a church with "no place for Judaism and no place for Jews," saying "no to the Jewish people and its ancestral way of life."[9] Whereas the New Testament witnesses to a struggle for Gentile inclusion, now the Jewish believers are rejected unless they denounced all aspect of their particular identity and traditions. Along with this explicit anti-Judaism, Nicea was also

---

[7]See Daniel Boyarin, *Border Lines: The Partition of Judaeo-Christianity* (Philadelphia: University of Pennsylvania Press, 2004), 130.

[8]*Nicene and Post-Nicene Fathers of the Christian Church*, 2nd ser., vol. 14, *The Seven Ecumenical Councils*, ed. Philip Schaff and Henry Wace (Grand Rapids, MI: Eerdmans, 1983), 54. Quoted by Kinzer, *Postmissionary Messianic Judaism*, 201.

[9]Kinzer, *Postmissionary Messianic Judaism*, 209.

destructive in its implicit denial of Israel or the God of Israel in relation to the definition of orthodoxy, especially in terms of Christology. The Chalcedonian Creed's "fully human and fully divine" suffers from this same lineage of Jewish omission, of rendering Israel theologically irrelevant. The biblical witness to Jesus as the Son of David or Abraham's seed might be allowed, but the theological import of this Jewish truth for the heart of the gospel is now denied. The supersessionism that states that church replaced Israel, that faith in Christ makes Jewish election void, rejects the biblical witness that "God has not rejected his people whom he foreknew" and the "gifts and the calling of God are irrevocable" (Rom 11:2, 29).

For the sake of theological contextuality, affirming the Jewishness of Jesus protects us from the double error of ethnocentricity and of abstract anthropology. On the one hand, the truth of Israel's election means that the place of the chosen people is occupied. Peoples throughout history have repeatedly taken up the mantle of being the divinely elect people, defined ethnically, racially, or nationally. Shinto attributes this chosen status to the Japanese people, for example. Or Sun Myung Moon of the Unification Church believed that Korea is a chosen nation and himself a new Messiah figure. This ethnocentricity as related to election existed and persists among Christians as well. As Willie Jennings states, "[w]ithout Israel as the point of elected stability, the idea of an elected people [becomes] an idea without its authentic compass and thereby subject to strange new human discernment."[10] This chosenness often coincided with a vocation and a task, as well as self-perceived rights and privileges. The Doctrine of Discovery, formed by *Inter caetera* and related papal bulls, gave Portugal and Spain the permission to enslave and subjugate the pagan world; the doctrine of manifest destiny justified US settler expansion and colonization of the Americas. These religious ideologies took up divine election for their own worldly purposes, exchanging "white European election for Jewish election."[11]

Even in the sense of a spiritual election for the purpose of divine mission, superseding Israel as the chosen people is not without theological dangers and aberrations. For example, with the explosive growth during

---

[10]Willie James Jennings, *The Christian Imagination: Theology and the Origins of Race* (New Haven, CT: Yale University Press, 2010), 34.

[11]Jennings, *Christian Imagination*, 36.

the 1960s to 1980s, Korean Christians believed that they were "now the chosen people of God . . . with a special providence of God" for missions.[12] But this belief fails to accept that Israel was elected "not because [it was] more numerous than any other people" but because it was the smallest (Deut 7:7). Its election meant a covenantal struggle with the living God, not supremacy over all the other peoples of the earth or numeral superlatives in missions. Understanding what it means to be God's people without a reference to ancient Israel allows an understanding of God's favor and election that is defined by a contemporary cultural sense of greatness, rather than in the "patterns of thought from their embodiment in Israel." By having this "small" chosen people at the center, all ethnicities, races, and nations are decentered. Israel's election "disrupts the connection of all peoples to their gods."[13]

This resulting ethnocentricity in lieu of Israel is closely tied to the idea of abstract humanity, as two sides of the same coin. Traditional orthodox Christology affirmed that Christ was fully human but not necessarily Jewish, human form without the particularity of Jewishness. This abstract and generic humanity of Jesus functions like a blank screen for us to project whatever versions of concretion we desire. To put it differently, this abstraction leaves a vacuum that is filled with whatever is normative within a context.

In the formation of modern thought, Immanuel Kant's project of a rational Christianity means rarifying the universal from dregs of particularity. In "Religion Within the Boundaries of Mere Reason," Kant rejects all superstition, what he calls "counterfeit service to God," as all that does not serve human moral development, framed by his idea of categorical imperative and universal law.[14] J. Kameron Carter points out that for Kant human perfection meant transcending the ethnic and racial particularity toward universality.[15] Consequently, Kant proposes White Europeans as the base universal

---

[12]Frieder Ludwig, Klaus Koschorke, and Mariano Delgado, eds. "South Korea: Explosive Church Growth," in *A History of Christianity in Asia, Africa, and Latin America, 1450-1990: A Documentary Sourcebook* (Grand Rapids, MI: Eerdmans, 2007), 126.

[13]Jennings, *Christian Imagination*, 254.

[14]See Immanuel Kant, "Religion within the Boundaries of Mere Reason," in *Religion and Rational Theology*, ed. and trans. Allen W. Wood (New York: Cambridge University Press, 1996), 190-94.

[15]J. Kameron Carter, *Race: A Theological Account* (New York: Oxford University Press, 2008), 89.

humanity, "one closest to that of the phyletic species" outside the racial categories, from which all other races developed.[16] For Kant, human qua human
means possessing the technical, pragmatic, and moral disposition to ma-
nipulate the world, use other humans, and educate the self.[17] Kant points to
White Europeans as not only the foundation, but also the maturity and perfection of all humanity.

Even without Kant's explicit connections to Whiteness, the idea of a generic humanity can arrive at White normativity. In his *Essence of Christianity*, Ludwig Feuerbach theorized that theology is truly anthropology. In
the very needs and desires of humanity God becomes the corresponding
solution and we ultimately "project [humanity's] own image as God."[18] While
not subscribing to his vision of theology, we can appreciate Feuerbach's exposure of how we can project ourselves in our perception of God. This projection can be quite explicit and intentional, or implicit and passive. The
passivity of how this anthropological projection can occur is especially significant. Given the exnomination of normative social images and values, an
active or explicit act of making Christ into our own image is not necessary.
Like the mechanism of implicit bias, projecting ourselves in the humanity
of Christ can bypass our volition. The result is that the empty canvas of
universal or generic humanity is filled with whatever is normative in the
context, which in our case is Whiteness.

The abstraction of Christ's humanity has direct soteriological implications for all Christians. If Christ can be human generically, so can we. Our
particularities are of no spiritual import either. We can be human apart from
any particularities. Uniting with this understanding of a truly human Christ,
our human particularities are not engaged in salvation. We have shown
repeatedly that without engaging all aspects of our lives for God's reconciliation, parts of ourselves remain under our own wayward control.

Obscuring the Jewishness of Jesus leaves us with a myth of a Savior at the
mercy of endless self-serving interpretations. But if we affirm the Jewishness

---

[16]Immanuel Kant, "Of the Different Races of Human Beings," in *Anthropology, History, and Education*, ed. Günter Zöller and Robert B. Louden (New York: Cambridge University Press, 2007),
95.

[17]Immanuel Kant, "Anthropology from a Pragmatic Point of View," in *Anthropology, History, and
Education*, 417.

[18]Ludwig Feuerbach, *The Essence of* Christianity (New York: Harper Torch, 1957), 63.

of Jesus, then we must clearly understand the meaning of this Jewishness to overcome this myth and its interpretive vulnerabilities.

THE JEWISHNESS OF JESUS

In recovering the Jewishness of Jesus, we establish his concrete humanity, a humanity not merely as an ontological category, but the embodiment of his particularities. However, the content of this Jewishness for theological anthropology could be interpreted differently. The following examples show the possible range of interpretation and meaning.

First, for missiologists Andrew Walls and Lamin Sanneh, Israel and Jewishness represent a moment in salvation history, a particular beginning that serves as a model as we move toward a culturally pluralistic future. Andrew Walls organizes church history in six ages starting with the Jewish age moving on to Hellenistic-Roman, Barbarian, and others.[19] Walls's thesis that "Incarnation is translation" leads him to affirm that in Christ God was translated into humanity, where true humanity must be particular, "in a particular locality and in a particular ethnic group, at a particular place and time."[20] Incarnation becomes a general missiological principle of particularity but not a unique event regarding Israel, meaning that there are other "incarnations" when the gospel becomes flesh in new cultures and contexts. Similarly, Sanneh, drawing attention to the nature of the gospel message for crosscultural translatability, conceptualizes the Jewish-Gentile encounter as a missiological breakthrough where "Jews and Gentiles became interchangeable."[21]

What is missing in both is the theological import of Israel and the Jewish Christ as a mediator of revelation and reconciliation that Torrance highlights. Willie Jennings points out "a subtle form of supersessionism" that exists in both of these missiologists; after Israel serves its purpose as a source, there is no longer any particular usage for it.[22] The problem here is the functional erasure of Israel and the Jewishness of Christ, as one ethnic group

---

[19]Andrew F. Walls, *The Missionary Movement in Christian History: Studies in the Transmission of Faith* (Maryknoll, NY: Orbis, 1996), 16.

[20]Walls, *Missionary Movement*, 27.

[21]Lamin Sanneh, *Translating the Message: The Missionary Impact on Culture* (Maryknoll, NY: Orbis, 1989), 6.

[22]Jennings, *Christian Imagination*, 159.

among many. The need for a particularized encounter with God is rightly affirmed and anthropology concretized. However, dismissing the election of Israel and the Jewish character of the gospel leaves open the possibility of anti-Semitism and ethnocentricity.

Thomas Torrance adds an important distinction between Israel as the people of God as opposed to a nation. He proposes that Israel is "not just a nation, an *ethnos*, but a people of God, a *laos*."[23] The historical kingdoms of Israel embodied Israel as the people of God so that even if the kingdoms fell the people still existed. This should not mean some spiritualized Israel, but it is a warning against an ideological co-option of Israel's election for political expediency, even by the current state of Israel.

Second, where Walls and Sanneh reduce Israel to a moment in salvation history, Mennonite Theologian John Howard Yoder stresses the political significance of Jewishness. Yoder wisely grasps the heart of the matter by questioning the historical necessity of the Christian-Jewish schism and pointing out that this parting has led to Christianity and Judaism defining themselves through increasing exclusivity.[24] Yoder argues that Jewishness is defined functionally, as the people of God seeking faithfulness while living in *galut* or diaspora. In recovering the lost Jewishness of the gospel Yoder finds "the rootage of [Jesus'] message in the particular heritage of Abraham, Moses, and Jeremiah," especially Jeremiah's vision of living in exile as an alternate community in empire.[25] Jesus' message of a kingdom of justice and peace as opposed to a worldly kingdom of power is what actually makes it specifically Jewish. The peace, which resides at the heart of the gospel, envisions "mission without provincialism, cosmopolitan vision without empire."[26] However, when Christianity lost its Jewishness and become Roman with its Constantinianism, the pacifism was done away with as well. Yoder recovers how the Jewishness of Jesus entails concrete ethical and political ramifications for the whole people of God. The danger here is that the abstract idea of *galut* could simply replace the concrete

---

[23]Thomas F. Torrance, *The Mediation of Christ* (Colorado Springs, CO: Helmers & Howard, 1992), 14.
[24]See Yoder, "It Did Not Have to Be," in *The Jewish-Christian Schism Revisited*, ed. Michael G. Cartwright and Peter Ochs (Grand Rapids, MI: Eerdmans, 2003), 43-66.
[25]Yoder, "It Did Not Have to Be," 75.
[26]Yoder "It Did Not Have to Be," 75.

Jewish people, a peace principle similar to the indigenizing principle of Walls and Sanneh.

Third, along with missiological, political abstractions, we also find racial instrumentalizations of Jewishness. For example, James Cone's Black Jesus is one such an interpretation of Jewishness in racial terms.[27] Cone's Christology is based on a dialectical affirmation of "Jesus Christ in terms of his past, present, and future."[28] The Jewish Jesus of the past means the Jesus of the present is Black, because Jesus was a liberator of the oppressed and at the present the oppressed are Black. Jesus is at one with "the least of these" and the least in America is Black people, therefore Jesus is Black.[29] Cone describes Blackness as "a christological title" or as a way to confess Christ in a particular context.[30] If we accept the Black/White binary for perceiving oppression, the existential or analogical idea of Jewish Jesus being Black is not only appropriate, but prophetic in its urgency. Of course, as discussed in chapter seven, the Black/White binary has its continual relevance as well as its problematic limitations. While Cone offers theoretical nuances of what this symbolic Blackness means, popularly Jesus being Black results in erasing Jewishness so that Black Americans take the place of Israel as the elect. While this is a potent antiracist response to a White Jesus, Black Jesus suffers from an instrumentalization of Israel.

J. Kameron Carter shares Cone's pressing concerns regarding race and racism, but also recognizes the danger of losing Jewishness in Cone's Blackness. Recognizing Whiteness as an idol to thwart, Carter interprets Christ's Jewish flesh as covenantal flesh "into which the Gentiles are received," making Jesus "mulatto," multiracial, and "*intra*racial."[31] Within this mulatto body of Christ the different bodies come together as one without losing their own particularities.[32] By interpreting Jewish flesh as covenantal flesh, Carter underscores the hybridic history of Jew in diaspora through the

---

[27]James H. Cone, *A Black Theology of Liberation*, Twentieth Anniversary Edition (Maryknoll, NY: Orbis, 1990), 119.

[28]Cone, *Black Theology of Liberation*, 120.

[29]See Anderson's incisive critique of Cone's symbolic Blackness as being totalizing and therefore idolatrous. Victor Anderson, *Beyond Ontological Blackness: An Essay on African American Religious and Cultural Criticism* (New York: Continuum, 1999) 86-92.

[30]Cone, *Black Theology of Liberation*, 122.

[31]Carter, *Race*, 30.

[32]Carter, *Race*, 364.

course of its history with God, that boundaries of Jewishness have been and are porous. Also, in terms of Augustinian *Totus Christus*, with Jesus as the head and the church as his body, the flesh of the Savior is indeed "mulatto" or "*intra*racial." However, Jewish flesh is in danger of becoming a concept of inclusive unity, an expression of the instrumentalization of Jewishness with real Jews made into abstract ideas.

The Asian American Christologies of Jung Young Lee, Sang Hyun Lee, and Kwok Pui-lan all share Cone's analogical interpretation of Jesus. Jung Young Lee sees in Jesus "the marginal person *par excellence*," given his "class, economic, political, social, and ethnic orientation."[33] This assessment follows Lee's identification of marginality as the "common cord" that gathers various racial minorities and that can help us toward an appropriate theology for our multicultural context.[34] Similarly, Sang Lee identifies liminality in the Galilean origins of Jesus, Galilee meaning a place of political, cultural and religious fringe land.[35] Kwok Pui-lan speaks of Jesus/Christ as a "hybrid concept" as opposed to "white and colonial constructs of Christ" with its sense of historical rootage.[36] Ironically, Pui-lan asserts this point even as she acknowledges the problem of denying the Jewishness of Jesus. Her reasoning is that this Jewishness simply means that we need to guard against anti-Judaism.[37] There is no theological significance to the Jewishness of Jesus. The concepts of marginality, liminality, and hybridity are all helpful tools. Yet again, they result in obscuring or, more accurately, using the Jewishness of Jesus as an abstract idea.

Along with his clear affirmation of Israel's election and its mediation of salvation for all, Willie Jennings takes up this question of Israel as an ethnic group. Overall, the ways in which Jennings articulates the radical importance of Israel and the parting of the ways for the nature of the gospel message is commendable. Jennings seeks to establish "the organic connection between Israel, Jesus, and Gentile existence."[38] Jesus

---

[33]Jung Yong Lee, *Marginality: The Key to Multicultural Theology* (Minneapolis: Fortress, 1995), 79.

[34]Lee, *Marginality*, 27.

[35]Sang Hyun Lee, *From a Liminal Place: An Asian American Theology* (Minneapolis: Fortress, 2010), 43-47.

[36]Kwok Pui-lan, *Postcolonial Imagination and Feminist Theology* (Louisville, KY: Westminster John Knox, 2005), 182.

[37]Pui-lan, *Postcolonial Imagination*, 173.

[38]Carter, *Race*, 259.

"re-creates" Israel so that it is not defined by kinship but faith and commitment in him. Furthermore, Christ becomes an entrance for all Gentiles to be in Israel, that through him a new kind of communion and cultural intimacy can exist. In all this, Jennings specifically rejects the idea of Israel as an ethnic group with its definitive relationship to the land in that identity.[39] In this sense, Israel's identity cannot be land or ethnic kinship, but rather defined by its covenant with God.[40] In pitting kinship in opposition to covenant, Jennings addresses the heart of the matter. In Christ, is Jewish ethnic identity done away with? Is Jesus Christ of the present and the future any less Jewish?

As opposed to the missiological, political, and racial conceptualization of Jewishness, Jewish theologian Michael Wyschogrod offers a "carnal" one that affirms the real existence of Jewish people. For Wyschogrod "the acid test of the church's theological posture toward Israel's election is the church's conduct toward Jews in its own midst."[41] Faith in Christ does not erase the Jewish identity as the chosen people. Wyschogrodian Jewishness is about the particularities of the physical body and the family biologically connected to that body. Wyschogrod contends that "Israel's election is . . . a carnal election that is transmitted through the body."[42] In this election, kinship is "sanctified," not destroyed but confirmed "by placing it under [divine] service."[43] Wyschogrod reminds us that Judaism "rejects [the] bifurcation between spirit and matter."[44] And in that sense, it is about a sanctified peoplehood and a national or ethnic identity. This thick Jewishness is about being a carnally elected people.

In all the creeds and confessions of the church throughout history, the Presbyterian Confession of 1967 stands out in its affirmation of Jesus' Jewishness. Its authors state that in "Jesus of Nazareth true humanity was realized once for all" that he was "a Palestinian Jew" who "lived among his own

---

[39]Jennings, *Christian Imagination*, 254.
[40]Jennings, *Christian Imagination*, 256.
[41]R. Kendall Soulen, *The God of Israel and Christian Theology* (Minneapolis: Fortress, 1996), 11, referring to Michael Wyschogrod, "Israel, the Church, and the Elect," in *Brothers in Hope*, ed. John M. Oesterreicher (New York: Herder and Herder, 1970), 83.
[42]Michael Wyschogrod, *The Body of Faith: God in the People Israel* (Lanham, MD: Aronson, 1996), 176.
[43]Wyschogrod, *Body of Faith*, 67.
[44]Wyschogrod, *Body of Faith*, 177.

people and shared their needs, temptations, joys, and sorrows."[45] Jesus' divinity was *in* this Jewish body with its familial, cultural, ethnic, and racial particularities. This flesh was not just a vehicle or a husk for a divinity that transcended these human distinctions with their limitations. The meaning of Jesus' humanity is found in these particularities and not in some theological concepts, because being human means boundaries, distinctions, and limitations. Whatever Jewishness means—be it particularity, peace, liberation, inclusivity, or even divine action—it cannot be less than this carnality. The Jesus of the past is Jewish, but so is the Jesus of the present and the future. Any other Jesus than the Jewish one, who mediates the election of Israel for all to share in, is not the Jesus attested in Scripture, is not the incarnate God of Abraham, Isaac, and Jacob.

ENCOUNTERING GOD AS PARTICULAR GENTILES

Affirming and protecting the Jewishness of Jesus and God's election of Israel means that as Asian Americans we encounter God as particular Gentiles. This encounter has profound implications for the task of theology.

First, Christians are chosen in Christ *through* Israel. Salvation comes through Israel in the person of Jesus Christ. There is one elect and one chosen people, Israel. For all Gentiles, we are elect or chosen indirectly or through the mediation of Christ who is the embodiment of Israel. Technically speaking, being God's chosen people in Christ (Eph 1:11) means being grafted to Israel, the chosen people (Rom 11:17). The fact that this longer theological formula is not unpacked at every mention of Gentile election in Christ should not obscure its truth. Jesus does not reside in some transcendent place above or neutral space between Jews and Gentiles. But, rather than bypassing Israel and putting our hopes directly in the Jewish Christ, Gentiles are invited to join Israel, the chosen people of God, to partake in their election through the person and work of the Mediator.

Given that Israel is the one and only chosen people, no ethnic, racial, and national group can claim to be the elect, no American manifest destiny, no Korean chosen people as missionaries to the world, and so on.

---

[45]Office of the General Assembly, Presbyterian Church (USA), *The Book of Confessions* (Louisville, KY: Office of the General Assembly, Presbyterian Church [USA], 2004), 288.

No other incarnation of the Holy Spirit or Jesus Christ appears in the person of Sun Myung Moon. The idea of Asian Americans being the new Jews, although meant in terms of racial politics and upward mobility, is fraught with unsavory theological problems as well as other problematic model minority distortions.[46] The burden of being the elect people of God falls on Israel alone.

Second, the particular Jewishness of Jesus' humanity serves as a model and a mirror for our own concrete humanity. A "non-Jewish Jesus" is "blasphemous."[47] The schism between Jews and the Gentile church that emerges from a non-Jewish Jesus obscures the gospel and leads to a theological anthropology that is abstract and contextless, as well as a corresponding soteriology that has no real place for our human identities. The Jewishness of Jesus recognizes and confronts our Gentileness in whatever particularity. Just as Jewishness should not be distilled to an abstract theological concept, Gentileness must be affirmed concretely with its familial, cultural, ethnic, and racial particularities.

As we unite with Christ, we retain and bring our own limited particularities so that sacramentally, we abide in Christ *in* and *through* these particularities, instead of transcending them. Being in Christ does not erase all our human cultural, sociopolitical identities. Rather, confessing a Jewish Jesus affirms a concrete Gentileness for the non-Jews. Since by faith, we are uniting with a Jewish Savior, even after the resurrection, with a concrete humanity, we correspondingly must acknowledge ourselves to be Gentile and concretely human. The idea that Jewish believers of Christ are a contradiction in terms, a *tertium quid*, is unbiblical. The biblical witness does not account for such an understanding. In the book of Acts, it is Gentile believers of Christ who are the problem, not the Jewish ones, calling for a special council to determine the place and practice of these Gentile abnormalities (Acts 15:1-35).

---

[46]Jason L. Riley, "The New Jews of Harvard Admissions: Asian-Americans are Rebelling over Evidence that They are Held to a Much Higher Standard, but Elite Colleges Deny Using Quotas," *Wall Street Journal,* May 19, 2015, www.wsj.com/articles/the-new-jews-of-harvard-admissions-1432077157; Jerome Karabel, "No, Affirmative Action Has not Made Asian-Americans the 'New Jews,'" *HuffPost,* October 11, 2018, www.huffpost.com/entry/opinion-harvard-affirmative-action-lawsuit_n_5bbe62b8e4b0c8fa1367c1c1.

[47]Robert T. Osborn, "The Christian Blasphemy: A Non-Jewish Jesus," in *Jews and Christian: Exploring the Past, Present, and Future,* ed. James H. Charlesworth (New York: Crossroad, 1990).

Denise Duell reminds us that universalist claims can be liberating or oppressive "depending on who is making them, in what contexts, and to what ends."[48] Too often we naively assume that the erasure of difference in Christ means equality and freedom. Beleaguered by contemporary racism and tribalism we can be tempted to escape to the abstract universality that a post-ethnic Jesus offers. However, not only is this "universal" Jesus a denial of revelation and anti-Semitic, it can also become "a kind of imperialism that insists that we are all one and that demands an obliteration of difference."[49]

Third, Jewishness and Gentileness are concrete but not essentialistic. We must be careful not to equate the human particularity that we are discussing with essentialism, which in this context refers to an existence of a core, unchanging, defining essence. Jewishness possesses no eternal essence in terms of blood, culture, language, and so on. Even the biblical witness shows that racial, ethnic, or cultural purity of lineage does not exist. A case in point is the genealogy of Jesus that includes Tamar, Rahab, Ruth, and Bathsheba (Mt 1:3, 5, 6). Even without an essence, there is a carnal particularity; there is such a people with a particular family lineage, a cultural-ethnic-racial-linguistic matrix, albeit fluid and hybrid. Our particularities, including Jewish particularity, are never pure and could never be essentialized into one or two features. Nevertheless, in their hybridity they still exist in particular historic contexts, at the intersection of culture, customs, language, bodies, and so on.

Revelation 7:9 should be read in this dynamic and hybrid manner. The "great multitude that no one could count, from every nation, from all tribes and peoples and languages" must be read figuratively. It is not as though essential human features are eternal. They are not. Nations rise and fall; people groups defined by their languages are born and die. The United States did not exist a couple hundred years ago, but out of many nations, a people who call themselves Americans now exist. While they have ethnic heritages—many of them with multiple ethnic heritages—these do not define their contextual matrix. This eschatological vision of human diversity can

---

[48]Denise Kimber Buell, *Why This New Race: Ethnic Reasoning in Early Christianity* (New York: Columbia University Press, 2005), 151.

[49]Regina Schwartz, *The Curse of Cain: The Violent Legacy of Monotheism* (Chicago: University of Chicago Press, 1997), 88, quoted in Buell, *Why This New Race,* 151.

only be read as an image of human diversity-in-particularity, ever dynamic and fluid and yet concrete for those who are living it. In this sense, the distinction between race and ethnicity is moot. It is not the case that ethnicity is biblical and eternal, whereas race is secular and temporal. They are both human cultural creations of social meaning and identity. While particular expressions of ethnicity and race are forever part of who we are, the categories themselves are fluid and porous, changing over time, whether centuries for ethnicity or decades for race. The point is that even with their differences, we must contend with both—culture/ethnicity and race—for the sake of our faith and discipleship.

Fourth, the elect status of Israel means that this special covenantal people bear a particular witness to God. There is a Gentile witness to God as well, but the witness of Israel takes precedence. Focusing our attention on Jesus, Thomas Torrance argues that when we "detach patterns of thought from their embodiment in Israel . . . , and then schematise them to our own culture, a western culture, a Black culture, an oriental [sic] culture" and "seek to interpret Jesus in that culture . . . we inevitably lose him."[50] Quite simply, abstracting Jesus from Israel makes him a naked symbol that in turn can be taken up for any ideological purpose. In that vein, Asian American Christology cannot mean simply replacing the Old Testament with Buddhist or Hindu scriptures, nor can it witness to a Jesus extracted from Israel as a Buddha or a Krishna.

Given the priority and precedence of the witness of Israel, there is yet a place for an extrabiblical witness. In that sense, we must go further than Torrance. I point out in chapter four that the reconciliation of our whole selves leads us to put the biblical witness in dialogue with the categories of Asian religious and philosophical heritage. As Indian Jesuit theologian Michael Amaladoss puts in, this dialogue often occurs within ourselves.[51] In this dialogue the biblical and Jewish witness must take precedence so that theological engagement works in service of a deeper revelation of Christ, a Jewish Christ revealing the God of Israel. Any faithful theological endeavor strives to order ourselves to revelation, not align revelation to our culture,

---

[50]Thomas F. Torrance, *The Mediation of Christ: Evangelical Theology and Scientific Culture*, 2nd ed. (Edinburgh: T&T Clark, 1992), 19.

[51]Michael Amaladoss, *The Asian Jesus* (Maryknoll, NY: Orbis, 2006), 6-7.

although this task is not at all an easy nor a straightforward one. The scandal of particularity in the election of Israel and in Jesus meditating that election for the whole world is part and parcel of the gospel.

In his provocative *The Divine Name(s) and the Holy Trinity*, Kendall Soulen proposes a way to bring together various naming patterns of the triune God that is post-supersessionist, affirming the biblical witness while still being open to the dynamic and continuing move of God.[52] Soulen identifies three naming patterns of the Trinity: A *theological* pattern of the mysterious and unspoken Tetragrammaton and other oblique references to God, a *christological* pattern of the three persons as the Father, the Son, and the Holy Spirit, and the *pneumatological* pattern of contextually generative ternaries such as "Love, Lover, Beloved" or "God, Word, Breathe." This last open-ended pattern affirms the multiple images of God that we find not only in Scripture, like mother, lover, friend, wind, and so many others, but also as various cultural heritages and contexts.

Soulen states that these three general patterns are *distinct*, each having its one integrity; *equally important*, each adding to the full vision of God; and *interrelated*, each deeply relating to the others. We might think of these patterns in concentric circles with the *theological* proper name, the Tetragrammaton, at the center, the *christological* pattern of Father, Son, and Holy Spirit, surrounding that, and the *pneumatological* and ever open-ended names from cultures, experiences, and contexts as the outer ring.

Following Soulen's proposal, we may affirm a place for divine naming patterns and divine images that arise as the presence and work of the triune God manifests in various contexts. And yet, the particular precedence of God's witness through Israel and its patterns of thought must be retained and affirmed.

Fifth, when recovering the election of Israel, politics and justice take on a new significance for the church, not just culture and language.[53] Just like acknowledging the particularities of humanity in and among our local ecclesial bodies, racial and political justice cannot remain a peripheral and optional issue regarding our confessional orthodoxy. Just as our bodies

---

[52]R. Kendall Soulen, *The Divine Name(s) and the Holy Trinity*, vol. 1, *Distinguishing the Voice* (Louisville, KY: Westminster John Knox, 2011), 22.

[53]Osborn, "The Christian Blasphemy," 227.

matter, the sociological, political, and physical world matter too. The christological insights discussed above are allowed as long as it does not erase or
supersede the actual Jewish people. Of course, Yoder and others argued for
this ethical and political dimension of recovering Israel and Jewishness.
For example, recognizing the election of Israel in Jesus' Jewish flesh means
rejecting any expression of ethnocentricity and spiritual nationalism as anti-
Semitic supersessionism. There is only one chosen people, and the church
is grafted in among this elected body through Christ. God acknowledges
cultural, political, and social contexts and identities. As Cone avers, the
gospel is for the oppressed and Jesus is "Black" if meant as a metaphorical
or homiletical shorthand.[54] The Gospel of Luke testifies, "Blessed are the
poor"; God is not neutral to the sociopolitical and economic plight of the
oppressed. This truth simply cannot be spiritually neutralized. This aspect
of embodied concreteness stands side by side with the Matthean "Blessed
are the poor in spirit." We must not affirm one at the expense of the other.

Contextuality is rooted in the very identity of God, who elected Israel by
entering into a covenantal I-Thou relationship. Because God is at core a
covenantal God, we deal with this particular God in our human particularities, where not only who God is but who we are matters as well. In the
next chapter I offer a way that we can concretely describe and engage the
particularity of Asian Americans.

---

[54]See Victor Anderson, *Beyond Ontological Blackness: An Essay on African American Religious and Cultural Criticism* (New York: Continuum, 1995), on ontological Blackness as an expression of problematic essentialism, "idolatry" in Anderson's words.

3

ASIAN AMERICA AND THE ASIAN AMERICAN QUADRILATERAL

Rather than considering "Asian American identity" as a fixed, established "given," perhaps we can consider instead "Asian American cultural practices" that produce identity.

LISA LOWE

A VETERAN ASIAN AMERICAN campus ministry staff once shared a story with me about the difficulty of getting a handle on the Asian American label. When an Asian American campus ministry decided to have "the challenges of dealing with parents" as their retreat theme, one of the students raised a question. She said, "I have a great relationship with my parents, and they are not the stereotypical Asian tiger parents. I guess I'm not very Asian American." She continued by questioning if she really belonged in this ministry.

Just what does it mean to be Asian American? The term *Asian American* was developed in the formation of the Asian American Political Alliance (AAPA) by Yuji Ichioka and Emma Gee in 1968.[1] This panethnic, racial identifier sought to replace *Oriental*, a label loaded with colonial and racist baggage. Given its history, *Asian American* could be understood as a

---

Epigraph: Lisa Lowe, *Immigrant Acts: On Asian American Cultural Politics* (Durham, NC: Duke University Press, 1996), 64.

[1]Karen Ishizuka, *Serve the People: Making Asian America in the Long Sixties* (Brooklyn: Verso Books, 2016), 62.

political and racial term meant for strategic alliance, a way to assert our empowered agency and self-determination. However, a number of issues complicate this broad panethnic umbrella category. For one, it can feel like a concession to external impositions because of the dynamics of racialization in our society.[2] Many Asian Americans, both in their family life and in their faith communities, still live primarily out of ethnic-specific identities rather than racial and political ones. Moreover, the process of becoming aware of one's racial identity as an Asian American, that is, being both a racial minority and a person of color, requires an awakening or conversion of sorts.

Much Asian American theological literature often falls victim to a general East Asian monopolizing, where Korean or Chinese Americans dominate the discussion.[3] Of course, the term *Asian American*, properly speaking, must at least include those individuals and communities of East Asian, Southeast Asian, and South Asian heritages, as well as those of multiracial heritage, and adoptees.[4] Filipino American activist-psychologist Kevin Nadal rightly argues for a Brown Asian American Movement to resist the continuing erasure of non-East Asian American communities under the panethnic Asian American umbrella.[5] The East Asian American (or in Christian circles we might even identify a Korean American) dominance or supremacy is a pernicious sin that should be repented of and actively addressed by East Asian Americans.

---

[2]See Espiritu for various dimensions of the Asian American panethnic label and identity. Yen Le Espiritu, *Asian American Panethnicity: Bridging Institutions and Identities* (Philadelphia: Temple University Press, 1992).

[3]Jung Young Lee, *Marginality: The Key to Multicultural Theology* (Minneapolis: Fortress, 1995) and Sang Hyun Lee, *From a Liminal Place: An Asian American Theology* (Minneapolis: Fortress, 2010). David Ng, ed., *People on the Way: Asian North Americans Discovering Christ, Culture, and Community* (Valley Forge, PA: Judson, 1996).

[4]While much of what I propose would apply to West Asian Americans as well, they are not racially and politically included in the category of Asian America. There is always a possibility of this changing, as in the case of South Asian Americans, who were included as part of Asian America through their activism starting with the 1980 US Census. Regarding Pacific Islanders, their distinction from Asian Americans is significant even though the nomenclature of AAPI (Asian Americans and Pacific Islanders), APA (Asian Pacific American), and others is common. My delimitation of context regarding Asian Americans reflects the concern over the problematic nominal inclusion of Pacific Islander without substantive incorporation. That kind of inclusion would again be an example of ethnic monopolizing that I seek to avoid.

[5]Kevin L. Nadal, "The Brown Asian American Movement: Advocating for South Asian, Southeast Asian, and Filipino American Communities," *Asian American Policy Review* 29: 1-11.

This broad diversity of Asian Americans does not share a common language, racial phenotype, colonial legacy, cultural heritage, or migration history. While the concept of marginality in some shape or form is often used in Asian American theology to circumvent this diversity issue toward a common theme, such a strategy results in ignoring disparate experiences and dulling the particularities so crucial for any theology that takes context seriously. If we focus on cultural heritage, even though there might be similarities among those of different ethnicities, there is no one culture common to all Asian Americans. If we narrow the term to refer only to East Asians, this cultural categorization might begin to seem appropriate, as these heritage cultures generally share the influences of Confucianism, Taoism, and Buddhism. But even then, what about the differences between communities, generations, and families?

The issue of defining Asian America is crucial for understanding the gospel for Asian American lives and, of course, for doing Asian American theology. The task of defining Asian American identity is not preparation for theology, but it is itself the theological work that is so urgently needed. Since there is no one definitive and essential Asian Americanness, we need a way of talking about Asian American identity and context in a fluid, dynamic, and multilayered way, a way that is concrete to everyday life and yet broadly encompassing of our diversity.

All Asian Americans have personal experiences of being Asian American, which might come from growing up in Asian American families or attending Asian American churches. However, those experiences are not critical knowledge that is gained through study with historical and analytical concepts beyond our experiential horizon. In this chapter I offer a hermeneutical rubric, an interpretative framework to identify and organize the meaning of Asian Americanness. Named the *Asian American Quadrilateral* (AAQ), it is a heuristic tool for mapping diverse Asian American identities and experiences as residing at the intersection of four closely related themes: Asian heritage, migration experience, American culture, and racialization. I will discuss why and how I came to develop the AAQ, as well as its main features and strengths. We cannot meaningfully ask the theological question of what the gospel means in a particular context if we cannot even grasp the scope and boundaries of that context.

FISH IN MURKY WATERS

I began the introduction speaking about the feeling of having a splinter in your mind, of the inability to identify the phantoms that haunt our lives, not even knowing clearly the nature of our questions. Alluding to Max Weber, anthropologist Clifford Geertz argues that "man is an animal suspended in webs of significance that he himself has spun" and that culture is these webs.[6] The idea of culture as webs is compelling on a species or community level, but fails to capture how we as individuals experience culture. We do not spin these webs by ourselves, but rather are born into such webs, a complex cultural matrix that easily becomes part of our innate consciousness. In this sense, I imagine us as fish living in murky waters. However, the awareness of this culture is quite challenging. As a Chinese proverb says, "If you want a definition of water, don't ask a fish."[7] Our whole existence is located in this aquatic world: born, eating, swimming, mating, and dying, all the while breathing in and out the waters around us. Because these waters are all-encompassing, they are an invisible medium whose properties and existence we take for granted. We might only notice the murkiness of these waters upon a move to different waters. And, even then, the murkiness of our home waters would still only be relative since we never swim in "neutral" waters. In a sense, all waters are murky, but simply in different ways. As a fish in its home waters experiences murkiness in an immersive way, unable to distinguish or identify the differing elements of its experience, so we encounter the "maddening splinters" of our minds.

Without being able to name this murkiness, we are merely its oblivious victims, influenced, controlled, and even manipulated, unaware of its effects. It is interesting to note that Jesus in his exorcisms first names the demons before he casts them out. Biblically speaking, knowing the name of something is connected to authority and power. For example, God names and renames God's covenant people, determining God's relationship with them and directing their mission. Humanity is called to name the animals and be their steward. Names allow us to get a handle on an otherwise elusive thing

---

[6]Clifford Geertz, *The Interpretation of Cultures* (New York: Basic, 1977), 5, referring to Max Weber, *On the Methodology of the Social Sciences* (Glencoe, IL: Free Press, 1949), 84, 149.
[7]Quoted by Lesslie Newbigin, *Foolishness to the Greeks: The Gospel and Western Culture* (Grand Rapids, MI: Eerdmans, 1986), 21.

in our minds. They can reveal the true nature of a thing or determine its path and usage. Also, names can establish a relationship that was previously unimagined, moving toward familiarity and warmth or rejection and antipathy. While the various elements in these waters cannot be sharply separated from each other, we can try to distinguish and label distinct elements of this amorphous and amalgamated whole. We cannot theologically engage the undifferentiated whole, but we can analyze and discern what the gospel means for various identifiable elements. From there, we come closer to navigating the complex contextual matrix in which we reside.

In an interview, Maya Lin, a renowned artist and architect who submitted the winning design for the Vietnam Veterans Memorial as an undergraduate, confessed that she didn't realize that her design reflected Taoist influences and was taken aback when a report pointed it out.[8] Upon later reflection, however, she realized that Taoist and other inclinations were part of her childhood environment, growing up in a Chinese American family with an artist father and a poet mother. This cultural influence occurred even though Lin grew up quite assimilated, thinking she was just American without realizing or valuing her Chinese heritage. She did not have the linguistic and cultural ability to recognize what was in her life already, and when she finally acquired it, her sense of self shifted. Later, Lin designed the Museum of Chinese in America, her first Chinese-related project, because she came to value this aspect of her identity and also wanted to share it with her two daughters.[9]

Surprisingly, acquiring a sufficient vocabulary for contextual elements does not simply describe our experience, but rather helps create our reality. We not only use language descriptively, but formatively or generatively as well. The linguistic dimension can function in a pre-experiential a priori fashion, giving meaning to our experiences and shaping the way we experience the world or construct our personal narrative.[10] In a sense, raw

---

[8]Maya Lin, "A Personal Journey with Maya Lin, Artist and Architect," *Becoming American: The Chinese Experience*, interviewed by Bill Moyers, produced by Thomas Lennon (Princeton, NJ: Films Media Group, 2003), www.films.com/id/5519.

[9]Paul Berger, "Ancient Echoes in a Modern Space," *The New York Times*, November 5, 2006, accessed October 31, 2017, www.nytimes.com/2006/11/05/nyregion/thecity/05maya.html.

[10]George A. Lindbeck, *The Nature of Doctrine: Religion and Theology in a Postliberal Age* (Louisville, KY: Westminster John Knox, 1984), 23.

experiences and interpreted meaning are two different things. Two people can experience the same event and yet derive different meanings from it depending on the conceptual vocabulary that they possess. Referring to the connection between our conceptual maps and experiences, Clifford Geertz proposes a semiotic concept of culture, believing there are layers of meaning that we need to interpret to achieve a "thick description" of experience.[11] Rather than thick, deep might be a better descriptor for what I am seeking to do in this volume. Without the knowledge of symbols and signs, or the names of elements, we only have a shallow understanding that misses the deeper significance of how experiences and cultural elements function in our lives. A "deep description" means that we interrogate our experience for subterranean (i.e., subconscious) myths, themes, and structures that undergird the apparent.

My experience of teaching illustrates how language forms and shapes our experience. A couple of years ago, when I began teaching my course on Asian American identity and ministry, I ask the students to share in small groups their experiences of racism. As we debriefed together, one student said, "I've never experienced racism. I mean, when I was growing up people called me 'ch—k' and stuff, but everyone goes through that." In his mind, his life had been just like everyone else's, even as a racial minority. As we continued the class and he learned about microaggressions, everyday slights and insults that can be more damaging than overt racism, he began to rethink not only his encounters with racism, but his whole life and sense of identity.[12] I realized, through interacting with this student and others like him, that I was not simply giving them a descriptive vocabulary, but also a generative one, in which they shaped their memories, experiences, identities, and lives.

Acquiring contextual language is akin to the process of "critical consciousness," as Paulo Freire would say, in which a person becomes aware of the structural undercurrents of their lives.[13] Freire proposes a liberative pedagogy bringing about conscientization in those who are unaware of their true situation. I find this idea of *awareness* more helpful than *identity* as we

---

[11]Geertz, *Interpretation of Cultures*, 6.

[12]See Derald Wing Sue, *Microaggressions in Everyday Life: Race, Gender, and Sexual Orientation* (Hoboken, NJ: Wiley, 2010).

[13]Paulo Freire, *Pedagogy of the Oppressed*, 30th anniversary ed. (New York: Bloomsbury Academic, 2000).

discuss our Asian Americanness. We will address concerns about identity and the process of integration later in chapter eight, but so often fixation over identity ends up moving us toward a rhetoric of "the true, essential self" that leans closer to notions of purity or ethnic authenticity. That stereotypical and reductive sense of self is what we are trying to avoid with the AAQ contextual awareness framework.

The growing number of multiethnic and multiracial Asian Americans further complicates our notions of identity. If our identity discourse becomes that of "authenticity" and "truth," then we marginalize these increasing number of Asian Americans as "half-," "quarter-," etc. They can easily feel defensive amid judgment about whether or not they can really claim inclusion in the Asian American community. While there is an important conversation to be had about the phenotypical features that may lead to multiethnic and multiracial Asian Americans experiencing life differently, enjoying distinct privileges or suffering particular oppression, we cannot draw our concepts of Asian American identity so narrowly as to preclude them from belonging.

Offering a different take, David Hollinger offers the idea of *affiliation* instead of *identity*. He proposes that, given the growing number of mixed-race peoples, "affiliation" might be a better way to think of ourselves in our diversity, where given your particular ethnic and cultural makeup you would affiliate with the subgroup.[14] Hollinger points out the subjectivity of self-identification, acknowledging that historic circumstances or physical attributes do not always fully reflect our own sense of being and belonging. However, even if we affirm this sense of affiliation to a degree, there are yet structural limitations because of societal and structural forces. So, while there is a range of affiliation possibilities, we must begin with an awareness that includes those forces.

Depending on how we frame Asian American identity, we can either feel deeply understood and affirmed in this discussion or pigeonholed and suffocated by stereotypes. The choice cannot simply be a choice between "being our true and authentic selves" or "selling out to Whiteness." While many Asian Americans do suffer various expressions of self-hatred and

---

[14]Freire, *Pedagogy of the Oppressed*, 7.

hyperassimilation to Whiteness, the language of an "authentic Asian
American self" free from the entanglements of societal pressure is an es-
sentalistic fantasy. Asian Americans experience the double bind of representation, allowed only to exist as a socially-invisible nonentity, or a stereotypical reduction that fails to represent us. Whether watching an Asian
American TV show or reading an Asian American theological text, Asian
Americans can suffer *rep sweats*, the anxiety over misrepresentation or
simply a narrow representation. Sometimes, these rep sweats contribute to
Asian Americans being overly critical of other Asian Americans and even
themselves, demanding a perfect standard of public representation that is
effectively impossible to live up to. We will address further the finer aspects
of representation in chapter six.

For many Asian Americans, the multiple facets and layers of their
identity become so burdensome to sort out that they find their liberation
in accepting a spiritual identity as their true selves, saying that I am not
Asian American, but a child of God. However, we saw in the previous
chapter that our spiritual identity does not transcend and leave behind our
bodily existence, because we confess the resurrection of our bodies as part
of the good news.

When I propose that we frame our discourse on Asian Americanness
with *awareness*, I mean that we should not focus on whether one owns or
disowns their identity. I have met many Asian Americans who either feel
ambivalent about their Asian cultural heritage or are even antagonistic
toward it, believing that it is oppressive or abusive. Using the binary language of owning or disowning Asian identity, these people could be considered to be denying who they really are. Contextual awareness provides a
more specific vocabulary to critique their heritage more precisely, so that
they can metaphorically perform their cultural analysis with a scalpel instead of a sledgehammer.

My friend and colleague Ken Fong talks about how he grew up labeling
unattractive Chinese features, things, and even people as "Chinese-y." This
vague racist term encompasses being stingy, lacking in style, smelling of
tiger balm and dried mushrooms, and other aspects of Chinese culture
around him that he perceived to be un-American and undesirable. I grew
up using the term *Korean* similarly. I would say "that pastor is so Korean,"

meaning that the minister was hierarchical, authoritarian, and oppressive. I definitely did not want to be too Korean. The obvious problem with this way of speaking is that it turns ethnic heritage into an epithet. While we can and should critique and reject those parts of our cultural heritage that we find unhealthy or abusive, rejecting parts of ourselves in a wholesale manner with such blunt and broad phrases like "that's so Filipino" or "she's acting so Indian" is not productive or constructive. This way of talking about ourselves is akin to babbling or baby talk. Without more sophisticated and precise words, we can only describe our experience in such simplistic and clumsy terms.

The increased awareness of precise language works with scalpel-like focus to target exact cultural elements without collateral damage to surrounding aspects. For example, oppressively authoritarian currents within Korean cultural heritage might be identified as coming from a legalist interpretation of Confucian filial piety. By legalist, I am referring to the Legalist school of thought of Chinese political philosophy that is reflected in Sun Tzu's *The Art of War*.[15] Although not often acknowledged, there are egalitarian themes within Korean Buddhism and even Taoism. Even within Confucianism, an internal tension and balance between authoritarianism and humanness could serve to soften the oft-cited dynamics of hierarchy and power. But those Asian Americans (or others) who lack the awareness of these specific aspects of Asian culture cannot employ them for a precise and nuanced critique, and instead resort to expressing their discomfort with overly broad phrases like "that's so Korean."

Along with the ability to critique more precisely, an increased awareness of the factors of Asian American identity will reveal deeper forces that can predetermine even what we consider simply to be our own personal preferences. Some Asian Americans feel no connection or even appreciation for their Asian heritage. They honestly believe that this is "just how I am," based on their own individuality. Conscientization points out the colonizing and racist forces that press us toward rejecting our own Asianness. Now, being aware of these forces does not mean you will end up loving everything Asian, but it should make you wonder whether your

---

[15]John Minford, introduction to *The Art of War*, by Sun Tzu, trans. and ed. John Minford (New York: Penguin, 2002), xxii.

preferences are really your own, or if they arise from surrounding forces on the cultural battlefield.

Our perception of our Asianness is fluid and dynamic. Younger generations of Asian Americans may have less baggage associated with Asian culture. Those who grow up with the current rise of Asian pop culture, including Korean dramas (K-Dramas), Korean pop music (K-Pop), and Japanese animation (anime), for example, may not consider Asian culture as inferior, but rather as a source of self-affirmation. Also, if they reside in a generally progressive or racially diverse metropolitan area of the country and live with the support of a sizable ethnic community, they might not feel racially marginalized. Again, even here a deeper awareness might show that these transnationalistic tendencies only exist at the pop culture level and that their post-racial sensibilities ignore the historic and structural dimensions present nationally. In a sense, this affirmation of Asianness through pop culture can easily be an expression of escapism at the expense of their American political and sociological situation, relegating their "sacred calling" to be faithful where we are located.[16] Even here, critical awareness is required for spiritual and theological growth and maturity.

CRITICAL INTERPRETATIVE FEATURES AND THE ASIAN AMERICAN QUADRILATERAL

Within this overall framing of awareness, several critical features must be incorporated into our working interpretative language. These features are important because an inherent problem belies the term *Asian American*: it refers to a group without a common cultural heritage, history, migration narrative, and even skin color. Not only does the group itself contain multiple ethnic heritages and multiple generations, but the overall context itself is in flux amid changing global forces and cultural shifts, requiring continual hybrid negotiations. Below are four important considerations that summarize the significant features that our contextual language must account for.

First, we must affirm the *hybrid* nature of Asian American context and existence, avoiding essentialistic definitions. Essentialism, in this situation,

---

[16]Lee, *From A Liminal Place*, 105.

means the presumption that there are some essential characteristics that all Asian Americans must share. Often these so-called essential characteristics are racial stereotypes that serve to perpetually otherize Asian Americans. This essentialism is expressed in Orientalism, a way of perceiving and portraying the East as stuck in time, exotic, grotesque, feminine, and other generalizations usually presented as oppositional to Western culture and values.[17] As with many stereotypes, these generalizations might carry some modicum of descriptive truth, but the universalizing of motifs without precise details ends up becoming oppressively reductive.

Early generations of Asian American theologians sought a common essentializing experience, looking, for example, to marginality, liminality, or community. This might be an example of "strategic essentialism," where a common experience becomes a strategic core on which to build a political alliance.[18] Obviously, there are benefits and limitations to such a strategy. In a sense, this project on Asian American theology could itself be considered an expression of strategic essentialism. However, my goal is to try to complexify our understanding of Asian American commonality so that hybridity is incorporated within. There might be situations where Asian Americans can helpfully share about "the gift of being collectivist" or "the challenges of being an immigrant," but far too often that unsophisticated way of talking reinforces stereotypes and marginalizes other Asian Americans who do not share such experiences, the way model-minority tropes do. In chapter seven, along with other expressions of anti-Asian racism, we will go further into exactly how the model-minority myth works and why it is so problematic.

Second, the language must offer heuristic power for a *concrete* analysis of what this hybridity means. This is the other side of the coin in a sense. In rejecting essentialism and affirming hybridity, we could lose ways to describe the particular contextual themes and currents within the lives of Asian Americans. Hybridity can function like an amorphous catchall: since we are all a mash-up of divergent traditions and heritages, is there a

---

[17]Namsoon Kang, "Who/What is Asian? A Postcolonial Theological Reading of Orientalism and Neo-Orientalism," in *Postcolonial Theologies,* ed. Keller et al. (St. Louis, MO: Chalice, 2004), 100-117. Said's work has been formative in defining the problem of Orientalism. See Edwards Said, *Orientalism* (New York: Pantheon, 1978).

[18]Gayatri Chakravorty Spivak, *The Post-Colonial Critic: Interviews, Strategies, Dialogues* (New York: Routledge, 1990), 15.

point to deciphering the various strains of what they are, and is that even possible? Hybridity is a formal descriptor and does not offer much in the way of material content. It merely rejects as inadequate the idea of a static Orientalist essence.

However, for our purposes, contextual concreteness is required at multiple levels. On the level of racial and political categories, understanding the historical trajectory and structures that Asian Americans faced and continue to encounter must be delineated. Also, the interpretative tools must be sufficient for various ethnic-specific experiences and communities. Even among Southeast Asian communities, there are wide differences between Hmong Americans as opposed to Cambodian Americans, for example, even though both share the tragic legacy of being refugees. While various coalitions and partnership might exist between these two ethnic American communities, the groups and families themselves are very keen on the ethnic boundaries. It is important to note that these ethnic boundaries are not negative in and of themselves. Of course, these limits can be and are used to otherize, but they also help foster community and cultural values and help us understand our past and heritage. While we must be cautious with ethnic boundaries, they are a basic part of many Asian American lives, and they should not be disregarded. In light of this, we need to keep in mind the adequacy of our interpretative tools to help us organize reality at the ground level.

Third, our conceptual map for Asian American existence must account for *intersectionality*. Intersectionality, developed by Kimberlé Crenshaw, arose out of feminist theory to account for how African American women's experiences differ from those of African Americans in general and women in general. Being an African American woman bears emergent properties as a result of the interaction of race *with the addition of* gender as well, beyond each of these categories alone.[19] This idea points to how social categories such as race, class, and gender are interconnected, creating overlapping and distinctive forms of oppression that differ from those of the separate categories alone. While there are many other social identities such as sexual orientation, disability, and age that can comprise the multiple axes of intersectionality, most often race, class, and gender are the commonly

---

[19]Patrick R. Grzanka, ed., *Intersectionality: A Foundations and Frontiers Reader* (Boulder, CO: Westview, 2014).

used ones. For Asian Americans, what is needed is a breakdown of what *race* means in these common intersectional categories.

Finally, our language and categories should facilitate connections to other academic disciplines that can enrich the task of Asian American theology. As stated in the previous chapter, there is a dearth of Asian American theological works, and if we narrow them down to evangelical ones there are even less. In my office, all my Asian American theological works barely fill a single shelf on my bookcase. However, there exist other theological fields like missiology, theology of religions, missional theology, or postcolonial theology that would greatly enrich our present task. The riches of Asian American studies, Asian American psychology, and Asian American literature are indispensable resources that must be deeply studied and engaged in the theological process for Asian Americans. Compared to the still developing areas of Asian American theology and ministry resources, Asian American studies and psychology have been around for fifty years, reflecting maturity and depth of academic rigor and theoretical reflection.

Given these interpretive needs, what we need is a rubric that organizes and establishes connections to all the relevant categories, even if they are not all always in play. The Asian American Quadrilateral (AAQ) defines the Asian American context as the intersection of four contextual themes: Asian heritage, migration experience, American culture, and racialization. Each theme of the AAQ cannot be understood in isolation from the other three. Rather, they mutually inform and impact each other, further interacting with gender, class, sexual orientation, religion, age, and others.

Why *these* four themes, or why *only* four? Theoretically, there is no limit to how many others we can include; however, from the practical perspective of developing a heuristic tool with issues of simplicity, aesthetics, and hermeneutic power in mind, I have found that these four best serve our purposes. This tool has been tested and refined for its interpretative range and capacity for nearly a decade now. Of course, like all theoretical proposals, the AAQ is provisional and limited.

The AAQ is my offering to the Asian American community for us to use, modify, change, revise, or even reject in favor of a better concept. If it stimulates discussion and further theorizing, it has served its purpose for the Asian American theology that is on the way. Even if the AAQ serves our current purposes quite sufficiently, revision or overhaul may eventually be required because the context changes so drastically. Even as we learn from the past, our best theology cannot replace our attentiveness to God's future works and presence. All theology is *theologia viae* and *theologia viatorum*, theology of the way and of those on the way.

As we will see, these four themes serve as mental bins or boxes for us to organize information as we encounter them from various academic disciplines and works. They form a sort of knowledge structure with a hierarchy of framing, so that we continually keep the forest in view while gaining deeper knowledge of the trees and even specific leaves, cones, and needles. Too easily we can try to interpret a certain phenomenon in Asian American context with one narrow tool, such cultural heritage, at the exclusion of others such as migration or racialization, which might be more significant than the former, or even impact and interact with it.

For example, is structural racism the chief cause of the lack of Asian American managers and executives in Silicon Valley, or is it some other theme within the AAQ schema? Is the lack of successful Asian American creatives an issue mainly stemming from cultural heritage? What else might be happening to either contribute or aggravate these issues? The kind of interdisciplinary approach that the AAQ guides us toward is common to many theologians who are contextually aware. However, with its fourfold framing, we can even interrogate various sociological, racial, and theological works, questioning possible blind spots and reductive arguments that result from ignoring any of the four themes.

The first theme of the Quadrilateral is *Asian heritage*, including cultural, religious, and philosophical inheritances. Asian America shares this factor with contemporary Asians, many of whom must also constantly negotiate between this heritage and Western/global influences. This theme describes these traditions with their long development and manifold, often conflicting, interpretations and embodiments, which function implicitly as well as explicitly within the Asian American context. Traditions include Confucianism, Taoism, Buddhism, Shinto, Shamanism, Hinduism, and folk religions, among others, but they are lived cultural realities and not merely abstract ideologies.[20]

---

[20]For examples of these Asian religions as lived cultural realities, see Randall L. Nadeau, *Asian Religions: A Cultural Perspective* (Malden, MA: John Wiley and Sons, 2014).

This theme is the deepest layer of the Asian American context. Here, *deep* implies that it is both distant or elusive, while also almost primal or pervasive. Many Asians fail to describe or articulate the implicit, veiled, but often transgenerational epigenetic cultural influences infused in their language, food, arts, and everyday mannerisms. Is a certain social custom derived out of Buddhist roots or Shamanist practices? There might be a vague sense of these origins, but for many Asians this is just part of life as they had always known, "simply how Thais are" or "just the Japanese way." Also, none of these influences are now pristine and maybe even have become secularized for everyone involved.

At least for many Asians, the information about these historical heritages is readily available if they were to seek them in their institutions, although through various expressions of colonization, these cultural roots might have been rejected, abandoned, or buried. For many Asian Americans, however, they are twice removed, not only by time but moreover by space. While there are respectable Asian studies programs in many elite universities, making connections to the subtle vestiges of this cultural heritage in their everyday life can be a tenuous and laborious undertaking. Is parental behavior or a particular tradition something unique to one's own family or an expression of a storied ethnic cultural heritage? Discerning certain social and cultural features shared by many Mar Thoma Christians, due to its long engagement in a predominately Hindu environment, is qualitatively better than labeling something as strange, difficult, and vaguely "Indian." In any case, even if connections to original religious or philosophical roots are lost to those who are enacting these practices and embodying these sentiments, recovering these roots provides a language to conceptually take ahold of our experiences.

By identifying Asian heritage as vital for Asian American theology, we can connect the Asian American Christian experience to the disciplines of missiological research, interreligious dialogue, and Asian theologies, all of which together form a considerable resource. For example, our theological work benefits by locating a parent-child relationship not just in immigrant intergenerational conflict, or even Korean culture or cursory tropes of Confucianism, but more technically in the development of filial piety from Confucius to Mencius and the evolution of authority and hierarchy from classic

Confucianism, through state Confucianism, to later Neo-Confucianism, as well as the nascent Christian-Confucian engagement of Matteo Ricci, James Legge, Julie Ching, and Xinzong Yao.[21] Of course, learning what might we do with Confucianism from Asian American theologians such as Peter Phan or Jung Young Lee is a given.[22]

The *migration experience* is the second theme. In an earlier version of the AAQ I had called this theme the *im*migration experience, betraying my East Asian bias. Since refugee experience was not a part of my own personal history, I failed to draw this theme wide enough to include this narrative, which is crucial as well as tragic in the lives and history of many Southeast Asian Americans, into my theorizing of Asian American experience. Moreover, for Filipino Americans, because of the near fifty years of American colonization after over three hundred years of Spanish rule, their "immigration" experience is politically fraught.

Thus, this theme encompasses immigration, refugee experiences, and related phenomena such as transnationalism, the acculturation or assimilation process, intergenerational conflict, and identity formation. As with the first theme of Asian heritage we share with Asians, Asian Americans share broad contours of migration with other globally diasporic Asians, although the particular history and politics of the US make it distinctive. Those who migrate from Asia share many commonalities with immigrants to the US from elsewhere, but their experiences are filtered through their Asian heritage and, as we shall see, are impacted by American cultural perceptions as well as their racialization. In this sense, we must note that all four elements influence and color the others, thus creating a distinctive context for Asian Americans.

Among others, out of this theme comes the concerns of personal, transgenerational, as well as communal trauma, all of which directly impact spiritual formation, communal life, and leadership development in Asian

---

[21]Matteo Ricci, *The True Meaning of the Lord of Heaven (T'ien-chu Shih-i)*, trans. Douglas Lancashire and Peter Hu Kuo-chen (St. Louis: The Institute of Jesuit Sources, 1985); James Legge, *Confucianism in Relation to Christianity: A Paper Read Before the Missionary Conference in Shanghai, on May 11th 1877* (London: Trubner & Co., 1877); Julie Ching, *Confucianism and Christianity: A Comparative Study* (New York: Kodansha International, 1977); Xinzong Yao, *Confucianism and Christianity: A Comparative Study of Jen and Agape* (Brighton, UK: Sussex Academic Press, 1997).

[22]See Jung Young Lee, *The Trinity in Asian Perspective* (Nashville: Abingdon, 1996) and "Part Two: Inculturation" in Peter Phan, *Christianity with an Asian Face* (Maryknoll, NY: Orbis, 2003), 75-248.

American communities. People suffer significant traumas when they leave behind their own language, food, family, friends, and identity, and must adapt to a new and different world. Many first-generation migrants must also confront the new experience of life as a racial minority, although some of them might have been an ethnic minority in their country of origin as well, such as Hmong Americans. For those of later migration generations, the narratives of early transitional experience might be lost but still leave behind a lingering residue embedded now in family values and outlook.[23]

Of course, for recent arrivals, reflection on these matters might be of lower priority than the more pressing issues of immediate survival and just making ends meet. Or, for those arriving with the recent influx of wealthy immigrants from China, affluence might mask the psychological and political stress and trauma of their transition. Since our educational system and mainstream society marginalizes Asian American migration narratives, unless one is looking for them, one could just adopt a White European assimilation pattern for Asian Americans. Even with the vast differences between earlier Asian immigrants, post-1965 arrivals, and contemporary experiences, we can detect similar echoes and refrains that make sense of our own lives now.

This theme connects us to concepts of identity formation, assimilation theories, historical overview, and theologies of migration and globalization, all germane to the work of Asian American theologies. The history of Asian American people by Ronald Takaki or the recent notable volume by Erika Lee provide bird's eye views of this kaleidoscopic Asian American community, highlighting the ways Asian Americans as newcomers did and did not share the experience of our European immigrant neighbors.[24] Theories of segmented assimilation and acculturation versus enculturation, polycentric identity, or code-switching all fall under this theme.

The third theme, *American culture*, encompasses not only the multicultural contemporary American culture, in which Asian Americans actively participate, but also the Western intellectual tradition and missionary/colonial histories in Asia. The American pluralistic post-Christendom context in general,

---

[23]David L. Eng and Shinhee Han, "A Dialogue on Racial Melancholia," *Psychoanalytic Dialogues* 10, no. 4 (2000): 667-700.

[24]Ronald Takaki, *Strangers from a Different Shore: A History of Asian Americans* (Boston: Back Bay, 1998); Erika Lee, *The Making of Asian America: A History* (New York: Simon & Schuster, 2015).

and the evangelical movement in particular, serve as the environment in which many Asian American Christians find themselves. As a result, Asian American Christianity is heavily influenced by the Enlightenment's rationalistic influence, as well as by Puritanism and an evangelical revivalism. Of course, as part of American society, the church's contemporary struggles with postmodernity and the post-Christendom landscape apply to Asian Americans as well.[25]

Moreover, issues of Asian American representation and cultural perceptions of Asian Americans are covered under this theme. Controversies over whitewashing of Asian characters in movies like *Ghost in the Shell* with Scarlett Johansson and *Aloha* with Emma Stone, and the yellowface makeup of actors in *Cloud Atlas* are also subject to theological reflection because these kinds of cultural artifacts form and deform the sense of self for Asian Americans. On the other hand, we do not want to ignore the strides achieved in TV shows like *Fresh Off the Boat*, *Kim's Convenience*, and *Never Have I Ever*, as well as films like *Crazy Rich Asians*, *Shang-Chi and the Legend of the Ten Rings*, and *Turning Red*. While many Asian Americans see the obvious import and impact of these kinds of representation, theological connections and relevancy are yet lacking and must be developed.

Under this third theme, the field of missional theology with its agenda of engaging the North American culture as a mission field is a valuable and relevant dialogue partner for Asian American theology.[26] In that vein, understanding American evangelicalism as a product of mainstream White American culture is an important aspect of this dialogue. Of course, postcolonial theology is already serving a critical role as an entry point and resource for Asian American theologies by supplying concepts of hybridity, Orientalism, essentialism, as well as structural and power dynamics. Cultural studies and media theory as related to representation also serve to help enrich our conceptual map.

Finally, the fourth theme of *racialization* articulates the process of racial identity formation, navigating the Black/White binary, and the particular forms of discrimination that Asian Americans face as people of color.

---

[25]See Elaine Howard Ecklund, *Korean American Evangelicals: New Models for Civic Life* (New York: Oxford University Press, 2008) and Rebecca Kim, *God's New Whiz Kids: Korean American Evangelicals on Campus* (New York: New York University Press, 2006).

[26]Darrell Guder, ed., *Missional Church: A Vision for the Sending of the Church in North America* (Grand Rapids, MI: Eerdmans, 1998).

While all minorities face microaggressions and structural racism in various expressions and degrees, Asian American marginality might be best summed up in its "perpetual foreigner" status, the inability to fully affirm the Americanness of our identity.

Recent works by J. Kameron Carter and Willie Jennings on the theological genealogy of race have contributed much to our understanding of race, and we can also draw from James Cone and the broader Black theological tradition.[27] However, lest we assume that Asian Americans do not have our own resources about race, we can also draw from works like Frank Wu's *Yellow* and Yen Le Espiritu's *Asian American Panethnicity*, as well as Russell Jeung's *Faithful Generations*, the latter of which specifically covers faith and race in Asian American churches.[28]

Many Asian Americans find their ethnic identity more salient for their everyday life, especially in their familial and communal relationships. The Asian American label is more of a public racial identity, with historically activist and political roots. Acknowledging this activist and political dimension leads us to reflect and develop the inherently political reality of the gospel as the message of the kingdom, of God's reign overall. In that sense, Asian American theology is for a public witness of gospel justice, not only for Asian Americans, but all who are marginalized and oppressed.

This is the general overview of each of the four themes, explaining their meaning and outlining how they connect us to concepts, ideas, and broader resources that can serve as raw material for our Asian American theological constructions.

RECIPE, COORDINATES, AND PRESCRIPTION OF OUR PARTICULARITY

As stated above, these four themes or perspectives are interrelated and overlapping. They are also constantly changing in the tumult of

---

[27]J. Kameron Carter, *Race: A Theological Account* (New York: Oxford University Press, 2008); Willie J. Jennings, *The Christian Imagination: Theology and the Origins of Race* (New Haven, CT: Yale University Press, 2010). Among his many books, one of James Cone's most significant works is *A Black Theology of Liberation* (Maryknoll, NY: Orbis, 1970).

[28]Frank H. Wu, *Yellow: Race in America Beyond Black and White* (New York: Basic Books, 2002); Yen Le Espiritu, *Asian American Panethnicity: Bridging Institutions and Identities* (Philadelphia: Temple University Press, 1993); Russell Jeung, *Faithful Generations: Race and New Asian American Churches* (Piscataway, NJ: Rutgers University Press, 2004).

globalization. Moreover, the existential vector of these communities and individuals is also dynamic and multidirectional. Just how the four themes of the AAQ are experienced, and what Asian American identity and experience means for a particular person or a community, will depend on various factors such as *ethnic heritage, migration circumstances, generation, gender, sexuality, skin pigmentation, class, family dynamics,* and *geographical location.* For each person or community, there are contextual variations such as awareness, prominence, trajectory, continuation, appreciation, reactivity, struggles, and pains as these aspects are all related to the AAQ.

For example, a fourth-generation Chinese American man with ancestors who came as "paper sons or daughters," who grew up in Southern California, the so-called capital of Asian America, would have a very different experience and understanding of his racioethnic identity than a second-generation Vietnamese American woman with a heritage of refugee experience living in North Carolina, or a Malayali American man living in Texas whose darker complexion racializes as Black in his geographic community.[29]

While different Asian Americans might have widely varying *personal* experiences, all of us need to continually grow in our more *critical* knowledge of historical events, laws, structures, systems, and impacts regarding the broader Asian American community. Given the societal and historical forces at play, it is simply not enough to presume that *being* an Asian American automatically gives one an *understanding of* being Asian American. Without education, we can easily fall into the trap of projecting our uninformed perspectives and narrow personal experiences onto the wider Asian American community. Lacking this critical awareness, our sense of being, with our preferences, proclivities, desires, and other characteristics, could turn out to merely be expressions of structural programming and cultural formation. While it is impossible to fully extricate ourselves from our environmental influences, we can and must grow in our critical awareness of them if we are not going to be passive victims of these

---

[29]Paper sons or paper daughters refers to undocumented Chinese immigrants who purchased false documentation claiming relations to Chinese Americans who were US citizens. The Chinese Exclusion Act of 1882 created the need for such a scheme, and the 1906 San Francisco earthquake, which destroyed public birth documents, created the opportunity for its feasibility.

forces. Regardless of our individual experiences and sense of identity, we must all grow in our contextual awareness of these societal forces, and the AAQ can serve as our guide.

For our varying subjective experiences, the AAQ could be understood and used in three different ways, as *existence*, *situation*, or *lenses*. We might understand these various utilities through the analogies of *recipe*, *coordinates*, and *prescription*.

First, *existence* here means *identity* as ascribed and achieved, as well as negotiated and constructed. Thinking along these lines, we might talk about a particular *recipe* that describes how Asian American individuals or communities are formed, using various elements of the AAQ as *ingredients*. Since we are thinking of identity construction, the recipe here means how I am formed, particularly in connection to how others experience me.

Second, *situation* refers to where you find yourself, the kind of people, influences, and issues that surround you. Instead of ingredients and a recipe, we can use the metaphor of *mapping* and *coordinates*. Given your contextual terrain and community, what kind of concerns and problems do you encounter? This framing focuses more on your environment and location than your internal sense of being.

Third, *lenses* and the idea of unique personal *prescriptions* highlights that even though we might be looking at the same text or event, we could be interpreting them quite differently, focusing on different aspects. How do you see the world from your family or community background?

All three of these analogies highlight the various ways in which our contextual language helps to describe and construct our realities. It is possible at some times for these three to function in a complimentary fashion, and at other times to cause dissonance. Because the Asian American experience is so complex, these kinds of categories help explain the reasons for confusion or disconnection even among Asian Americans of a very similar background, even within the same family.

Ultimately, the point of all these vocabularies, delineations, and categories is the facilitation of theological engagement. What eludes our language cannot be understood, analyzed, or critiqued. We must name things for us to begin our theological task, to think deeply about what, why, and how our world, experience, and specifically our spiritual praxis is the way that it is, and for us to imagine a world, experience, and praxis that move closer to the kingdom of God.

This chapter provided a high-level overview of the AAQ, which will be broken down and explored in further depth in the next four chapters. We now turn to address the first theme, Asian heritage.

ASIAN HERITAGE AND CULTURAL ARCHETYPES

They are my heritage. They belong to my ancestors.
I am in dialogue with them within myself.

MICHAEL AMALADOSS

"WOULDN'T THAT BE GOING BACKWARDS?" That was the reply of a Hmong American Christian leader when I stated the importance of recovering our cultural and religious heritage and constructively engaging them in a theological manner. For him, "pagan" influences such as shamanism represented our pre-Christian past: the old humanity that we must leave behind as we embrace the new humanity in Christ. There is definitely an element of truth to that notion, in terms of our allegiance and commitment to Christ. However, this "looking ahead and moving forward" can often simply mean White assimilation as well, that is, growing up to be White, as I stated in chapter one. We can mistakenly think that we can free ourselves from all cultural influences and embrace a pristine biblical faith, without realizing that the faith in majority White churches is deeply influenced and sometimes even compromised by European cultural heritage and mainstream American culture. So, there is no escape from the necessary theological task of engaging our cultural context and

Epigraph: Michael Amaladoss, *The Asian Jesus* (Maryknoll, NY: Orbis, 2006), 6.
My article, "Cultural Archetypes for a Theology of Culture in a Global Age," *Cultural Encounters: A Journal for the Theology of Culture* 12, no. 1 (2016): 37-52, provides the core arguments for this chapter.

influences from wherever they may originate. We will focus on aspects of American cultural context and influences later in chapter six.

This chapter has a double task. First, I will provide some conceptual handles on naming and engaging the Asian heritages in ourselves and our communities. After describing the *geographic, temporal,* and *theoretical* distance in Asian American experiences of Asian heritages, I will list out some of the important heritages for the various ethnic contexts. Second, I will present a strategy for theologically engaging these heritages and other aspects of the Asian American Quadrilateral through what I call "cultural archetypes" and its related analytic tools. Unlike stereotypes, which can be pejorative or romanticized, this archetypical approach affords us a more precise and nuanced way of describing and evaluating our experiences as well as imagining possible constructive responses. Put differently, the idea of cultural archetypes could provide specificity in cultural perception and analysis while avoiding essentializing stereotypes.

A LIVED VERSION OF ASIAN HERITAGE

I often describe this Asian heritage dimension of the AAQ as the deepest aspect of our lives, both deep in the sense of primal, impacting everything in subtle ways, and deep in the sense of distant, buried, and hidden. This distance that we feel regarding our cultural heritage is true in both Asia and America. For Asians in Asia, there can be a kind of invisibility of the Asian heritage because they are simply a given and always everywhere yet seemingly distant by the passage of time as heritage, not the dynamic global and modern Asian contemporary culture, especially in urban areas.

Asian Americans are removed in multiple ways. Asian heritages can feel irrelevant, especially to later generations, and at the same time linger with their inescapable physical racial features. We might think about three key distances that we need to recognize, namely *geographic, temporal,* and *theoretical. Geographic distance* simply notes that Asian Americans are removed from the historical sites and institutions of Asian religious and intellectual heritage, such as holy sites, temples, academic institutions, and cultural centers. Because these resources are not around, it can deceive one to believe in the irrelevance of Asian heritages. Even if one desires to learn about their Asian heritage, their search can prove challenging.

Temporal distance refers to a distinction between Asian *heritage* of historical tradition against a modern global contemporary reality of Asian *culture*. These traditions and heritages are not what Asia is now, but only an aspect of them. More significantly, temporal distance refers to the phenomenon of a cultural "time capsule."[1] For later generations of Asian Americans, a particular version of Asian heritage brought over with the first generation was often preserved in sort of a time capsule and became representative of what Asianness means. We immigrated from Korea as a family in the 1980s. Later, my parents visited Korea and on returning they said that my siblings and I were more Korean than the Koreans in Korea. They meant that we displayed more traditional Korean values because our sense of Koreanness came from the 1980s, whereas Koreanness in Korea as a living reality continued to develop and transform in global interaction and exchange. This cultural "time capsule" along with an Orientalist mindset deriving from US intellectual formation can mislead Asian Americans when they refer to their own Asianness in stereotypical and racist ways.

A *theoretical distance*, a theory-praxis gap of sorts, also pertains to the teachings and ideas of a tradition and what people actually practice and believe. This gap is the critical element that we must attend to, especially for Asian American Christians who care about these matters for the purposes of Christian theology and ministry. I will explain why a cultural engagement approach is more appropriate than an interreligious one.

A direct way to theologically engage Asian heritage is through a frame of interreligious dialogue. This framing reminds us that the religious, intellectual, and cultural aspects of Asian heritage cannot be distinguished in a Western sacred/secular divide, even for seemingly secular Confucianism. Its strength is making explicit the religious and spiritual tenets, beliefs, practices, and mysteries of Asian heritages. Along similar lines, the notion of multiple religious belongings or multiple religious participation explains how Christians can continue to belong to or practice certain religious practices rooted in other religious cultures.[2] Again, the insight of this

---

[1]See Ricky Yean, "The Immigrant Time Capsule," https://rickyyean.com/2018/05/23/the-immigrant -time-capsule/, accessed August 28, 2021.

[2]John J. Thatamanil, "Eucharist Upstairs, Yoga Downstairs: On Multiple Religious Participation," in *Many Yet One? Multiple Religious Belonging*, ed. Peniel J. R. Rajkumar and Joseph P. Dayam (Geneva: World Council of Churches, 2016).

approach is that this kind of religious and spiritual multiplicity might actually be happening consciously or unconsciously. When we are not aware of these various religious influences, we do not really know how our Christian lives might also be Buddhist, Shintoist, or Hindu.

For most Asian American Christians, this interreligious or spiritual multiplicity is not how these Asian heritages manifest in their lives, or at least not how they desire to make sense of them. At least in historical orthodox Christianity, confessing Christ as Lord means that Christ followers should not seek multiple allegiances alongside him, but rather should hold captive every aspect of Asian heritage in obedience to Christ (2 Cor 10:5). Given this pursuit of Christ's rule, there can still be theological or spiritual insights gleaned from these Asian heritages. Later in the chapter, I will lay out how this can work theologically. We cannot ignore the dangers of syncretism and cultural distortions for our faith, but we should also acknowledge how White-normative theology has been so quick to raise this warning all the while remaining persistently blind to its own Western or "American" cultural engagements. A deep racist and Orientalist bias must be overcome if we are to begin taking up these heritages theologically.

In everyday life, Asian heritage, even the religious ones, look so defused and subtle that they are experienced more like culture all around them. In his *Asian Religions: A Cultural Perspective*, Randall Nadeau presents Asian religions in terms of cultural values, which I have found helpful for teaching Asian American Christians. He explains how religion is not just belief or practice, but also "the cultural spring and foundation of the needs, motivations, thoughts, and behaviors that make up the totality of human experience."[3] Nadeau's work can serve as a bridge or a cultural translator of religious tenets and practices into everyday life.

Along this line of thought, Kosuke Koyama in *Water Buffalo Theology* distinguishes between Buddhists and Buddhism.[4] In his missionary context in Thailand, Koyama stresses the importance of actual human to human encounter that cannot be reduced to analyzing doctrines or religious philosophy. People are embodied, relational beings, rather than ideals:

[3]Randall L. Nadeau, *Asian Religions: A Cultural Perspective* (Malden, MA: Wiley-Blackwell, 2015), 10.

[4]Kosuke Koyama, *Waterbuffalo Theology*, rev. ed. (Maryknoll, NY: Orbis, 1999), 93-95.

> Buddhism does not feel hunger even if it does not eat for many centuries. . . .
> Buddhism does not suffer from flood and drought. A Buddhist, on the con-
> trary is different. He, or she complains, laughs, grieves, sweats, suffers, thirsts,
> and hungers. A Buddhist is a person.[5]

Even in a Buddhist context like Thailand, there is a distinction between the academic study of Buddhism and the lives of Buddhists, who often might be more cultural or nominal Buddhists. Now, these Buddhists in Thailand might consciously identify themselves as Buddhists, and in this there is a significant difference we must acknowledge from the Asian American Christians we are talking about. However, it is important to highlight how this kind of cultural heritage exists in diffused and heterogeneous ways in real life.

For example, we are seeking to engage not an academic Confucianism that is in textbooks, but the diffused version of it in lived-out experiences. To access this lived version, however, we need the vocabulary that comes from academic studies of Confucianism as well as its historical development. Analogously, we cannot seek to understand contemporary American evangelicalism just by reading the Sermon on the Mount, because what we are living out presently is a historically developed and culturally embedded expression of what's in the Bible. Much of what we see around us in evangelicalism is a product of Christendom, or a state-appropriated view of faith. Textbook Confucianism as an idealized philosophy sounds much more benevolent than the often-fraught lived reality that many East Asians and those of East Asian heritage found or find themselves in.

Akin to Koyama's distinction between Buddhism and Buddhist, other theologians have sought to deal with the lived-out nature of this heritage by using different languages and concepts. C. S. Song used the language of stories.[6] Song understood that stories reflect religious, philosophical, and cultural values and mores much more closely to how they manifest themselves in everyday life settings than religious literature per se. He desired to use indigenous theological sources, drawing on symbols and images from the stories of the people. Michael Amaladoss echoes the same sentiment in

---

[5]Koyama, *Waterbuffalo Theology*, 94.
[6]Choang-Seng Song, *Third-Eye Theology: Theology in Formation in Asian Settings*, rev. ed. (Maryknoll, NY: Orbis, 1979), 8-16.

The Asian Jesus.[7] Amaladoss calls these Asian symbols and images *pre-theological*, in that they are part of the soil in which the gospel seed grows whether we are aware of them or not.[8] They are his heritage and belong to his ancestors, and he is in dialogue with them and himself when he uses them for theological reflection.[9]

Given their deep nature, Asian heritages have sometimes been understood as "cultural DNA," figuratively inherited and fundamentally part of our basic makeup. The idea of a cultural DNA came out of a conversation that Bill Moyers had with the world-renowned Confucian scholar Tu Weiming, discussing how people can implicitly live by Confucian values and ideas and also transmit them to their children.[10] Taking up this idea, others like David Ng and Paul Tokunaga used the idea of "Confucian" or "Asian" DNA to describe this heritage aspect of their Asian American identity.[11]

In referencing how cultural values and patterns can be passed between generations in implicit ways, this genetic metaphor resonates strongly. Familial transference through scripts, systems, or epigenetics gives some grounds for this language of cultural DNA. However, using this genetic language is not without its burdens. During World War II, racist sentiments channeling the "inscrutable Oriental" propagated the idea that Japanese Americans could never be truly American: "A viper is nonetheless a viper wherever the egg is hatched—so a Japanese American, born of Japanese parents—grows up to be a Japanese, not an American."[12] These racist views erroneously confused cultural values with political identity or allegiance, as well as oppressively assuming a White-normative understanding of American identity. In a way, the term *cultural DNA* can be misunderstood to imply cultural determinism and essentialism, limiting personal agency as well as the possibilities of cultural change and mixture. As argued in the previous chapter, Asian American

---

[7]Michael Amaladoss, *The Asian Jesus* (Maryknoll, NY: Orbis, 2006).

[8]Amaladoss, *Asian Jesus*, 5.

[9]Amaladoss, *Asian Jesus*, 6.

[10]Tu Weiming, "A Confucian Life in America: Tu Weiming," *Bill Moyers' World of Ideas*, interviewed by Bill Moyers, produced by Gail Pellett (New York: Public Affairs Television, 1990). The transcript of the interview can be found at www-tc.pbs.org/moyers/journal/archives/docs/mingwoi.pdf.

[11]David Ng, *Asian Pacific American Youth Ministry* (Valley Forge, PA: Judson Press, 1999), 88; Paul Tokunaga, *Invitation to Lead: Guidance for Emerging Asian American Leaders* (Downers Grove, IL: InterVarsity Press, 2003), 35.

[12]W. H. Anderson, "The Question of Japanese-Americans," *Los Angeles Times*, February 2, 1942.

identity and experiences are hybrid and dynamic, as well as incredibly diverse depending on family situation and geographical location within the US. For these reasons, in terms of guiding our theological engagement, this biological metaphor is too static and limited.

In thinking of the lived version of these heritages, we must recognize that Asian heritage is often steeped in patriarchy and sexism. When confronting colonial heritage and White racism, it is tempting to run to cultural heritage with an over-sympathetic eye, glorifying it wholesale. This cultural glorification can be done in the name of decolonialization and decentering Whiteness and White theology. However, while cathartic, such a simplistic move fails to be constructive and rooted in lived experiences. Doing so comes at the cost of those groups, often including women, who are themselves marginalized and oppressed within those traditions. Kwok Pui-lan warns that "[c]hallenging the colonial legacy, [many Asian male] theologians sometimes were too eager to embrace the cultural traditions of Asia, without taking sufficient notice of their elitist and sexist component."[13] Gender as well as class can influence interaction with and the willingness to receive or even consider Asian cultural heritage as worthy of recovery and discussion. We need to be wary of our own social location and privilege when handling them. Also, learning to discuss Asian heritage better does not mean that our assessment needs to be positive. As mentioned in the last chapter, sometimes the outcome of deeper awareness is learning to critique better. That is a basic part of this Asian American theological work as well.

These elements should not be seen and handled as some eternal essence of ethnic culture. Rather, the goal should be to study them to acquire a broader and layered contextual lexicon to become conversant in their presence and influence in subtle and not so subtle ways in the lives of people. The more complex and multifarious our understanding of an ethnic heritage, the more sophisticated and contoured contextual interpretative insights will be. Of course, these cultural heritages will be just one factor that intersects with the other aspects of the Asian American Quadrilateral.

Now that we have done important ground clearing, we turn to what we actually mean by Asian heritage. In this book Asian heritage refers to

---

[13]Kwok Pui-lan, *Introducing Asian Feminist Theology* (Cleveland, OH: Pilgrim Press, 2000), 30.

cultural influences that were brought from Asia when the migrant generation came to the US. The particular Asian heritage they brought from Asia is weightier than contemporary Asian culture because of the time capsule phenomenon noted above. While a more in-depth study of Asian heritage is beyond the scope of this book, here I list out some of the key elements in the six largest ethnic groups, which make up about 85 percent of Asian Americans as of 2019.[14]

Chinese heritage. Confucianism, Taoism, and Buddhism are considered the three main Chinese traditions and they have a long history of interacting with each other, mutually influencing, critiquing, and developing in a symbiotic and complementary way to cover all aspects of life.[15] It is important to study them together and not just in isolation. Folk religion with their domestic deities and spiritual practices could also be very impactful in certain families. With internal corruption and external attacks from Western and Japanese imperialism in the nineteenth century, the May Fourth Movement of 1919 served as an important self-critique of these philosophical and social heritages.[16] Marxism, particularly Maoism that later took over with its Cultural Revolution disrupted these Chinese traditions, decentralizing and scattering their institutions.[17] Their experience of Maoism also formed the reactionary political stance of the older Chinese communities in the diaspora. Even without any concrete knowledge, familial ritual and virtues can mediate Chinese cultural and religious influences in subtle ways through the generations.[18]

Indian heritage. Even with the incredible ethnic, linguistic, and religious diversity of India, Hinduism remains profoundly foundational to Indian culture. Of course, what is labeled and packaged as Hinduism is a complex phenomenon. Even for historic Indian Orthodox Christians of Kerala,

---

[14]For an overview of the latest Asian American demographics, see Abby Budiman and Neil G. Ruiz, "Key Facts About Asian Americans, a Diverse and Growing Population," Pew Research Center, April 29, 2021, https://pewrsr.ch/3e3t4nF.

[15]See Xinzhong Yao and Yanzia Zhao, *Chinese Religion: A Contextual Approach* (New York: Continuum, 2010).

[16]See, for example, Vera Schwarcz, *The Chinese Enlightenment: Intellectuals and the Legacy of the May Fourth Movement of 1919* (Berkeley: University of California Press, 1986).

[17]See Charlotte Brooks, *Between Mao and McCarthy: Chinese American Politics in the Cold War Years* (Chicago: University of Chicago Press, 2015).

[18]See Helen Jin Kim, Russell Jeung, and Seanan S. Fong, *Family Sacrifices: The Worldviews and Ethics of Chinese Americans* (New York: Oxford University Press, 2019).

Catholics of Goa, or the various Pentecostal churches, their faith and church context are framed within Hindu religious, spiritual, and philosophical tradition, in explicit or implicit dialogue with it, or in reaction against it. The great ethnic and linguistic diversity, mostly ignored by American society, plays a prominent role in what Indianness actually means. The particular features of Indian American Hinduism amid the broader American multicultural context is important, especially how the ethnic and religious identities become conflated.[19] While Hinduism can be studied as a religion, it can also be approached in terms of mythology and the ways that they seep into everyday imaginations.[20] For Mar Thoma Christians, this ancient ecclesial tradition must be considered part of their Asian heritage, not only spiritually but culturally and socially as well.[21] We must also take into consideration British colonialism, with its legacy in so many facets of sociopolitical and bureaucratic life, and Indian independence and the horrors of the Partition, which lingers as transgenerational trauma.[22] These cultural and religious heritages interact with the racial politics of how Indian Americans became South Asian Americans within Asian America and the complications therein.[23]

Filipino heritage. The archipelago, with its over seven thousand islands, has set the context in which Filipino cultures and languages have developed. The Philippine myths and indigenous spiritual beliefs are an important part of the Filipino cultural imagination. Over three hundred years of Spanish colonialism and its Catholicism have been formative in so many aspects of what it means to be Filipino and Filipino American. Because of its broad impact, with the majority of Filipinos being Catholic, Filipino Catholicism should be studied and engaged even by Filipino American Protestants.[24]

---

[19]See Prema A. Kurien, *A Place at the Multicultural Table: The Development of an American Hinduism* (New Brunswick, NJ: Rutgers University Press, 2007).

[20]See Devdutt Pattanaik, *Indian Mythology: Tales, Symbols, and Rituals from the Heart of the Subcontinent* (Rochester, VT: Inner Tradition, 2003) and his *Myth = Mithya: Decoding Hindu Mythology* (New York: Penguin, 2008).

[21]See Prema A. Kurien, *Ethnic Church Meets Megachurch: Indian American Christianity in Motion* (New York: NYU Press, 2017).

[22]See Shashi Tharoor, *Inglorious Empire: What the British Did to India* (London: Scribe, 2016), and Sanjeev Jain and Alok Sarin, eds., *The Psychological Impact of the Partition of India* (New Delhi: Sage India, 2018).

[23]Lavina Dhingra Shankar and Rajini Srikanth, eds., *A Part, Yet Apart: South Asians in Asian America* (Philadelphia: Temple University Press, 1998).

[24]See Stephen M. Cherry, *Faith, Family, and Filipino American Community Life* (New Brunswick, NJ: Rutgers University Press, 2014). Gonzalez provides a more Protestant take on Filipino

For example, the Iberian Catholic legacy and the way that it was indigenized with Filipino beliefs and practices, such as Santo Niño de Cebú or *Parol* during Christmas is culturally significant to all those of Filipino heritage. Fifty years of official American colonialism and the neocolonialism that continues have created a colonial mentality that impacts many psychologically as well as spiritually.[25] Thus, this colonial history distinguishes the relations between the US and the Philippines from other Asian countries, and critiques simplistic narratives of Filipino American immigration that ignore this imperial politics as reductive. Early Filipinos were coming to the metropole of the American empire, not moving to a different country.

Vietnamese heritage. Through various periods of Chinese colonialism and influence especially in the northern area, Confucianism, Taoism, and Buddhism have deeply engaged Vietnamese folk religions and mythology.[26] Particularly, Thiền Buddhism has a long and deep influence within Vietnamese culture as a whole. Sixty years of French colonialism brought Roman Catholicism as well as a deep impact on the Vietnamese writing system, language, education, and economy. The communist rise and the war with the US have been formative for both nations, with particular challenges around the ethics of remembrance.[27]

Korean heritage. Like the Chinese context, the three religions (Confucianism, Taoism, and Buddhism) are all present, however, the Yi dynasty with its seven centuries of rule suppressed Buddhism and established Confucianism as the social and intellectual foundation.[28] Unlike China or Japan, Korea did not have an internally driven movement to critique this Confucian core until the more recent globalizing influences. Shamanism also plays a big role in the everyday concerns and needs of the people in the language of blessings and protection, even underneath Christian practices

---

American ecclesial life. Joaquin Jay Gonzalez III, *Filipino American Faith in Action: Immigration, Religion, and Civic Engagement* (New York: New York University Press, 2009).

[25]See E. J. R. David, *Brown Skin, White Minds: Filipino-American Postcolonial Psychology* (Charlotte, NC: Information Age, 2013).

[26]Peter C. Phan, *Vietnamese-American Catholics* (Mahwah, NJ: Paulist, 2005).

[27]See Viet Thanh Nguyen, *Nothing Ever Dies: Vietnam and the Memory of War* (Cambridge, MA: Harvard University Press, 2016).

[28]See Martina Deuchler, *The Confucian Transformation of Korea: A Study of Society and Ideology* (Cambridge, MA: Council on East Asian Studies, Harvard University, 1992).

and beliefs.[29] The history of Korean Christianity incorporates all these influences deeply into its concept of discipleship, *tonsong* prayer or early morning prayer, pastoral ideals, and many other ways.[30] Also, the particular role that Korean Christianity played in opposing Japanese imperialism should be understood for its indigenizing dynamic. The Korean War, its trauma on the older generation, and its residual impact should be considered as well.[31] The central role of the Korean American church for the majority of the immigrant and later generations should be acknowledged.[32]

Japanese heritage. Shinto has the pride of place in defining Japanese spiritual heritage.[33] Buddhism and Confucianism are late imports that developed in the context of a Shinto mindset. Along those lines the wabi sabi aesthetic of Zen Buddhism as well as the Bushido warrior code also inform this heritage. As a critique of these heritages in the face of and in reaction to Western and modern threats, the Meiji Restoration marks one of the turning points of modern Japanese culture; it also began Japan's own imperialism over Asia.[34] Finally, how post-World War II Japan was reformed with American occupation and political delimitations became constitutive of modern Japan.[35] After their incarceration during World War II, Japanese Americans endured political oppression and social pressures toward assimilation, which had a powerful impact on them and their connection to their cultural heritage as opposed to their Japanese *American* identity.[36]

---

[29]See Jung Young Lee, *Korean Preaching: An Interpretation* (Nashville: Abingdon, 1997), and *Korean Shamanistic Rituals* (New York: Mouton, 1981).

[30]See Sung-Deuk Oak, *The Making of Korean Christianity: Protestant Encounters with Korean Religions, 1876-1915* (Waco, TX: Baylor University Press, 2015) and David Chung, *Syncretism: The Religious Context of Christian Beginnings in Korea* (Albany, NY: State University of New York Press, 2001).

[31]For example, see Bruce Fulton and Ju-Chan Fulton, trans., *The Red Room: Stories of Trauma in Contemporary Korea* (Honolulu: University of Hawai'i Press, 2009).

[32]Ho-Young Kwon, Kwang Chung Kim, and R. Stephen Warner, eds., *Korean Americans and Their Religions: Pilgrims and Missionaries from a Different Shore* (University Park, PA: Penn State University Press, 2001).

[33]Motohisa Yamakage, *The Essence of Shinto Japan's Spiritual Heart* (Tokyo: Kodansha International, 2010).

[34]See Mark Ravina, *To Stand with the Nations of the World: Japan's Meiji Restoration in World History* (New York: Oxford University Press, 2020).

[35]See John W. Dower, *Embracing Defeat: Japan in the Wake of World War II* (New York: W. W. Norton and Company, 1999).

[36]See David K. Yoo, *Growing Up Nisei: Race, Generation, and Culture Among Japanese Americans of California, 1924-49* (Chicago: University of Illinois Press, 1999).

These examples about the heritages of the six largest Asian American ethnic groups provide just a sketch of what we are dealing with. Now, we turn to the idea of cultural archetype as a tool to handle the various dimensions of Asian heritage in the Asian American experience of our global and multicultural world.

Cultural Archetypes and Interculturality

Dealing with Asian heritage in concrete lives, we need to be adroit in multiple cultural narratives, describing, critiquing, and reimagining them in light of the gospel. For this task, we need to avoid essentialist outlooks about these divergent narratives and employ cultural archetypes instead of stereotypes. Moreover, we need to analyze currents of interculturality, by which I mean all the ways in which cultures interact with each other, especially their dissonances and confluences. My goal here is proficiency and clarity in our theological discourse when dealing with multiple and divergent cultures. I hope to evaluate current concepts and practices, pushing for greater precision.

In his take on an Asian theology and working from the grassroots ecclesial experience, Simon Chan begins by eschewing "the habit of describing different patterns of thought in terms of Eastern and Western ways of thinking."[37] Chan argues that "[s]ometimes the antithesis between the East and West is no more than a way of expressing certain value judgments," such as using "the West" to represent oppression whereas "the East" means empowerment.[38] Examples of this binary approach might include individualistic-communal, direct-indirect, guilt-shame, and so on.

Such a bifurcation between the East and West is common in books about cultural intelligence and it functions as a sort of shorthand when dealing with cultural complexities. It can be allowed, if used with caveats.[39] However, as Chan is hinting at, they can also be highly problematic and even

---

[37]Simon Chan, *Grassroots Asian Theology: Thinking the Faith from the Ground Up* (Downers Grove, IL: IVP Academic, 2014), 10.
[38]Chan, *Grassroots*, 10.
[39]Geert Hofstede's Cultural Dimensions Theory and Kluckhohn and Strodtbeck's Values Orientation Theory can easily become categories for essentializing binarism. Geert Hofstede, *Cultures and Organizations: Software of the Mind*, 3rd ed. (New York: McGraw-Hill, 2010); F. R. Kluckholn and F. L. Strodtbeck, *Variations in Value Orientations* (Evanston, IL: Row, Peterson, and Company, 1961).

oppressive if their immediate limitations are not clearly stated, and if there are no other more sophisticated tools at hand. Then these categories or stereotypes become shallow abstractions of real life, grotesque caricatures, or essentialized portrayals.

Namsoon Kang dissects this binarism and avers how this dichotomizing fails to "accurately reflect how different and diverse the Asian cultures are."[40] The diversity and the specificity of ethnic cultures and heritages become all lumped together in amorphous generalizations about the East. For example, how much do Japanese, Indonesians, and Indians share in common? These binaries are directly connected to Orientalism, where the East is "conceptualized by . . . its strangeness, difference, exotic sensuousness, eccentricity, backwardness, silent indifference, feminine penetrability, uncivilized nature, and the like" as well as being "static, frozen, and fixed eternally."[41] Thus, the attitude toward the East often becomes broad demonization or romanticization, neither of which recognizes the cultural specificity of actual people.

It is important to note that, in reacting against negative stereotypes, Asians' own "attempt to increase their self-esteem" offers an analogous response.[42] This turning of the tables, however understandable, merely aggravates the essentialism that "represses the recognition of Asia's internal diversity and potential for endogenous transformation."[43] Instead of this essentialism, what Kang and other postcolonial theologians offer are "ever-changing . . . hybrid, decentered, multiple" ways to being and representing Asians.

Even though Kang is discussing the Asian context, this kind of hybridity applies to Asian Americans, as well as to everyone in a sense. As Kathryn Tanner notes, postmodern insights have taught us how cultures all feature "change, conflict, and contradiction," with no sharp boundaries to delimit them.[44]

---

[40]Namsoon Kang, "Who/What is Asian?: A Postcolonial Theological Reading of Orientalism and Neo-Orientalism," in *Postcolonial Theologies: Divinity and Empire*, ed. Catherine Keller, Michael Nausner, and Mayra Rivera (St. Louis, MO: Chalice Press, 2004), 103.

[41]Kang, "Who/What is Asian?," 102.

[42]Kang, "Who/What is Asian?," 103.

[43]Kang, "Who/What is Asian?," 105.

[44]Kathryn Tanner, *Theories of Culture: A New Agenda for Theology* (Minneapolis: Fortress Press, 1997), 53.

Given this hybridity and the dangers of essentialism and stereotypes, how do we proceed in engaging culture? Instead of the problematic generalizations and stereotypes, I propose *cultural archetypes* as a tool for engagement.[45] Carl Jung conceptualized his view of the collective unconscious and the hidden archetypes as universally relevant, beyond the boundaries of any particular culture.[46] Whether these Jungian archetypes as "universal images" exist is not relevant for my argument.[47] What I am proposing is more limited and particular.

A cultural archetype is an element of influence with a conceptual specificity and a historical rooting. It can be a practice, value, ideal, pattern, connection, or trajectory, to name a few of the many possibilities. Moreover, it can arise out of religious, communal, sociological, and philosophical origins or even out of historical events. However, a cultural archetype must have conceptual and historical concreteness. For example, a generalized stereotype about Eastern sensibilities of hierarchy and authoritarianism can be attributed to a cultural archetype of Confucian filial piety, which has distinct conceptual features and historical rootage. This key tenet of Confucianism has a long history of development and has broad impact on and conceptual connections to identity, politics, and ethics.

A cultural archetype's influence can be conscious or unconscious.[48] However, in order to analyze and engage it critically, the archetype must be named and its features described. Without an adequate vocabulary to lay hold of and contemplate it, a cultural archetype remains an undeveloped

---

[45]Isolated reference to cultural archetypes reveals that this term is used similarly to *stereotypes*. For example, Kochman and Mavrelis use the term cultural archetype to "describe patterns of difference that ethnic group insiders would agree are true, authentic, and representative of the culture of the group." Thomas Kochman and Jean Mavrelis, *Corporate Tribalism: White Men/ White Women and Cultural Diversity at Work* (Chicago: University of Chicago Press, 2009), 5-7. The significant feature in their definition is the emic perspective and description based on salience, or a bell-shaped curve. However, in its function, this definition of cultural archetype functions similarly to stereotypes in its generalizations. As I will present below, my definition differs from theirs, especially in its interpretative function.

[46]See *The Collected Works of C. G. Jung*, ed. and trans. Gerhard Adler and R. F.C. Hull, vol. 8, *Structure and Dynamics of the Psyche* (Princeton, NJ: Princeton University Press, 1970) and *The Collected Works of C. G. Jung*, ed. and trans. Gerhard Adler and R. F. C. Hull, vol. 9, part 1, *Archetypes and the Collective Unconscious* (Princeton, NJ: Princeton University Press, 1981).

[47]*The Collected Works of C. G. Jung*, 9:1:5.

[48]In this aspect, cultural archetypes are similar to Jung's definition: "We can therefore speak of an unconscious only in so far as we are able to demonstrate its contents. . . . The contents of the collective unconscious . . . are known as *archetypes*." *The Collected Works of C. G. Jung*, 9:1:4.

stereotype. Not every East Asian person has studied Confucian filial piety, nor can everyone explicitly articulate its effect on his or her life. However, this knowledge provides the ability to see and to name the ghosts and spirits in their lives.

Its influences might be wide, but how communities, families, and individuals appropriate a cultural archetype could vary significantly in degree and in either a positive or negative trajectory. Because of their distinct characteristics, some families might value and practice Confucian filial piety in its almost traditional expression, while others react against it and adopt a more progressive stance. The key point to recognize is that the archetype still influences even negative appropriations, reactions against that archetype.

Therefore, a lack of respect for elders does not only or necessarily imply the adoption of Western values. Rather, the ready adoption of Western egalitarianism might be explained by a rejection of the filial piety archetype. Of course, the converse might be true as well. In this sense, the postcolonial idea of mimicry, if understood pejoratively as self-erasing assimilation, can be misleading if it does not include room for cultural exchange and adoption that occur universally.[49] Similarly, cultural appropriation with its real problem of power, privilege, and commodification, still needs to consider the fluidity and dynamics of every cultural context. Within every context and community, "there are conservatives and there are reformers" in an endogenous sense as its natural feature.[50] Unless we mean to deploy tests of cultural authenticity, defined by essentialism, we must carefully discern and limit accusations of mimicry.

Ultimately, the power and significance of a cultural archetype resides in its heuristic capacity to make sense of life. Of course, it is possible that certain East Asian contexts are no longer influenced by any particular historical tradition, lost through diminishment and decay or replaced by another more compelling archetype.

---

[49]Generally, mimicry is seen as assimilation that capitulates to the normativity of the colonial culture, suffering violence to a person's selfhood, although Bhabha suggests that it also possesses a subversive dimension that undercuts the oppressive powers. Homi K. Bhabha, *The Location of Culture* (New York: Routledge, 1994), 130.

[50]Lesslie Newbigin, *The Open Secret: An Introduction to the Theology of Mission*, rev. ed. (Grand Rapids, MI: Eerdmans, 1995), 144.

In any context, there are multiple cultural archetypes that we could be negotiating. In their interactions, the familiar can be underscored or a new possibility arise. Interculturality—the manner of the interaction between different cultural archetypes—can lead to dissonance or confluence. *Intercultural dissonance* occurs when two or more cultural archetypes conflict with each other, whereas *intercultural confluence* refers to when they overlap and affirm each other.

Now to see how all these tools operate together, we can analyze the idea of a Tiger Mom.[51] Through her satirical memoir, Amy Chua describes a parenting style that she attributes to Chinese mothers. This idea of seemingly superior Asian parenting touched a raw nerve in America, given the academic successes of some Asian American students in the country's top educational institutions.[52] Chua offers that there is some truth to this stereotype given the statistics. But—and she confesses to speaking loosely—when she uses "the term 'Western parents,' of course, [she's] not referring to all Western parents—just as 'Chinese mother' doesn't refer to all Chinese mothers."[53] While Chua is trying to articulate something real, her limited conceptual lexicon leads her and her readers toward crude essentialism and racist stereotypes.

Of course, we must remember that Chua's discussion is not technical in any sense of the word. Still, instead of using stereotypes with caveats, the proposed archetypes would have equipped her with more precise tools for this discussion. One of the most influential Chinese mother archetypes is found in the mother of Mencius, one of the greatest Confucian scholars in early China.[54] A popular story tells how she moved three times to ensure that Mencius' environment would be conducive to his formation. Along with the extent of her commitment to his education, we observe the mother's identity and thus her worth being found in the accomplishment of her child. In many historical sources, she is nameless, only identified by her relationship to her famous son.[55]

---

[51] Amy Chua, *Battle Hymn of the Tiger Mother* (New York: Penguin Press, 2011).

[52] Chua's posture is oblivious to oppressive systemic forces of orientalism and model minority myths, and lacks awareness of how she might be abetting them. However, this is beside the point.

[53] Chua, *Battle Hymn*, 4.

[54] Anne Behnke Kinney, ed. and trans., *Exemplary Women of Early China: The Lienü Zhuan of Liu Xiang* (New York: Columbia University Press, 2014), 18-19.

[55] In Kinney's translation, Mencius's mother remains nameless as well.

Given this ideal of a mother, this cultural archetype, Chinese and Chinese American mothers who grew up under its influence would have to negotiate its relevance for them. Some would appropriate these values positively, while others react negatively, all doing so in varying degrees and manners. This archetype would also conflict with various American archetypes of scientific approaches to parenting, or double up with the authoritarian parenting styles of some fundamentalist Christians.[56] The bottom line here is clearing the fog of influences, naming the spirits, and excavating the subterranean forces, while focusing on communal or personal negotiation or appropriation. Thus, essentialism and reductive generalizations are avoided as well as an elusive hybridity that remains inarticulate and seemingly incomprehensible.

I have offered this idea of cultural archetypes as one contribution toward a more dynamic, perceptive, and nimble approach to a thick description of culture in a globalizing context. In the next sections, I explore the ways in which we theologically discern this new tool.

THE DIALECTICAL NATURE OF CULTURAL ARCHETYPES

In the same genus with crosscultural binaries and essentialism are moral assessments of culture or cultural elements as good, bad, or neutral. The problem with these assessments is that they often derive from a simplistic perspective. Analogous to the tension in creation's goodness and its pervasive fallenness, culture and its archetypes are dialectical.

Chuck Kraft, along with others, has described human culture *in and of itself* as theologically neutral, neither good nor bad.[57] Kraft acknowledges that humanity is "pervasively infected by sin" and that our use of culture is therefore also "always affected by sin."[58] However, he separates out the sinfulness of humanity from the neutrality of culture because he wants to affirm that God "chooses to use culture and at major points to limit himself to the

---

[56]See, for example, some very popular but controversial works of Gary Ezzo: Gary Ezzo, *Growing Kids God's Way: Biblical Ethics for Parenting* (Louisiana, MO: Growing Families International, 2007); Gary Ezzo and Anne Marie Ezzo, *Preparation for Parenting: Bringing God's Order to Your Baby's Day and Restful Sleep to Your Baby's Night* (Chatsworth, CA: Growing Families International, 1990), some of which has gone through multiple revisions to respond to criticisms of medical and other errors.

[57]Charles H. Kraft, *Christianity in Culture*, 25th anniversary ed. (Maryknoll, NY: Orbis, 2005), 89.

[58]Kraft, *Christianity in Culture*, 89.

capacities of cultures in his interaction with people."[59] This neutral view fails to account for sin in its systemic or structural sense.

On the other hand, Lingenfelter proposes that culture as a rubric for human existence is "created and contaminated by human beings; culture is the pen of disobedience from which freedom is possible only through the gospel."[60] This total fallenness of culture is why Newbigin describes conversion as a "paradigm shift," because human sinfulness is comprehensive and all-encompassing.[61] Moreover, Hendrik Kraemer advocates for a total discontinuity between gospel and culture for the very same reason.[62] Here, sin is more robustly accounted for; however, more nuancing is needed.

Sin should be understood here as a theological category rather than a moral one. Sin is always against God, first and foremost. Rather than simply an expression of immorality, sin is our separation, rejection, and independence from God revealed in Jesus Christ. Theologically speaking (in the presence of God, *coram Deo*), human culture is totally lost and apart from God in Christ in its apparent goodness and wickedness.[63] There is no doubt that there are good works being done in human cultures; however, this is speaking from a moral or worldly perspective (in the eyes of the world, *coram mundo*).

But again, even if we accept the total fallenness of the world, including all humanity and culture, we cannot deny God's gracious presence in the most unexpected places. Kevin Vanhoozer summarizes the four doctrinal reasonings for God's presence in culture: the incarnation, general revelation, common grace, and the *imago Dei*.[64] Each of these doctrines supports the possibility of the Spirit's work in the world of culture so that we can discern

---

[59]Kraft, *Christianity in Culture*, 90.

[60]Sherwood Lingenfelter, *Transforming Culture: A Challenge for Christian Mission* (Grand Rapids, MI: Baker, 1998), 17.

[61]Lesslie Newbigin, *Foolishness to the Greeks: The Gospel and Western Culture* (Grand Rapids, MI: Eerdmans, 1986), 62.

[62]See Hendrik Kraemer, *The Christian Message in a Non-Christian World* (New York: IMC, 1947).

[63]See Luther's usage of the distinction between *coram Deo* and *coram mundo*. Martin Luther, "Two Kinds of Righteousness, 1519," in *Luther's Works*, vol. 31, *Career of the Reformer I*, ed. Jaroslav Pelikan, Hilton C. Oswald, and Helmut T. Lehmann (Philadelphia, PA: Fortress Press, 1957), 307-26.

[64]Kevin J. Vanhoozer, "What is Everyday Theology? How and Why Christians Should Read Culture," in *Everyday Theology (Cultural Exegesis): How to Read Cultural Texts and Interpret Trends*, ed. Kevin J. Vanhoozer, Charles A. Anderson, and Michael J. Sleasman (Grand Rapids, MI: Baker Academic, 2007), 14-60.

that "part of what culture says is true, good, and beautiful; other parts, however, are false, bad, and ugly."[65]

This task of cultural exegesis and discerning between the good and bad parts is complicated in crosscultural or intercultural situations fraught with a long history of binarism and essentialism. Also, in our "multicultural" zeal to find the specific "gift" of every culture and people, we can fall right back into stereotypes and generalizations.[66]

To navigate this task of cultural exegesis in our globalized hybrid context, I offer three guiding reflections regarding how the proposed cultural archetypes should be handled.

First, we must not make a priori judgments about cultural archetypes. The problem with an a priori evaluation is that it uses an abstract moral criterion instead of the concrete action of God in the lives of people. In *Creation and Fall*, Dietrich Bonhoeffer notes that in the beginning Adam "knows neither what good nor what evil is and lives in the strictest sense *beyond good and evil*; that is, Adam lives out of the life that comes from God."[67] The tree of the knowledge of good and evil was forbidden because it symbolized a departure from living out this relationship. Such innocence is not possible for us; however, thinking analogously, our criteria for good or evil could be in this same sense, with an abstract morality apart from God. Again, Bonhoeffer notes that with moral discernments apart from God, our existence becomes not a gracious gift but an oppressive commandment.[68] In that vein, a priori judgments are legalistic, not of the Spirit. Returning to God in Christ means that we live out of a new center where we are "set free from the knowledge of good and evil."[69]

We must attend to the Spirit's work in terms of how a cultural archetype functions in life before we can make judgments about its goodness or

---

[65]Vanhoozer, "Everyday Theology," 44.

[66]On how popular literature on the Asian American context defines their unique gifts, see Jeanette Yep et al., *Following Jesus Without Dishonoring Your Parents* (Downers Grove, IL: InterVarsity Press, 1998), 159-75; Soong-Chan Rah, *The Next Evangelicalism: Freeing the Church from Western Cultural Captivity* (Downers Grove, IL: InterVarsity Press, 2009), 164-99. Rah (10-27) also points out the dangers of cultural discernment among Asian theologians.

[67]Dietrich Bonhoeffer, *Dietrich Bonhoeffer Works*, vol. 3, *Creation and Fall: A Theological Exposition of Genesis 1-3*, ed. John W. de Gruchy, trans. Douglas Stephen Bax (Minneapolis: Augsburg Fortress, 1997), 87-88, italics included.

[68]*Dietrich Bonhoeffer Works*, 3:90.

[69]*Dietrich Bonhoeffer Works*, 3:92-93.

wickedness. Rather than abstract or transcendental, our judgments must be theologically and dynamically informed in our interaction with God. In *Fear and Trembling*, Kierkegaard introduces the idea of the "teleological suspension of the ethical" and warns against a priori judgments about God's Word and actions.[70] Kyle Roberts explains how according to Kierkegaard "a universal ethical principle cannot usurp the primacy of the God-relationship and cannot be the primary criterion of a person's religious life,"[71] and I would add of cultural discernment as well. This "suspension," however, is not "an abrogation of ethics,"[72] but rather a deconstruction of morality as an idol.

Going back to the example of Confucian filial piety, when seen through the lens of moral categories it might be evaluated as good given that it resonates so closely to the fifth commandment. That was the evaluation of Matteo Ricci and the Jesuit fathers. Ricci concluded "that Confucianism in its earliest manifestations was a nearly perfect expression of the 'natural law' and that it served as a natural foundation for Christian teaching in China."[73] Of course, such conclusions ignore the oppressive potentiality of Confucian ethics in general and filial piety in particular.

Second, this example points to the dialectical nature of cultural archetypes. Martin Luther in his *theologia crucis* asserts that although "the works of man always seem attractive and good they are nevertheless likely to be mortal sins."[74] Luther wanted to highlight how seemingly good works might be full of arrogance and enmity toward God from a theological perspective. Gerhard O. Forde, commenting on this very Lutheran distrust of human goodness per se, declares that "[d]eadly sin lurks at the most pious places."[75] Cultural archetypes as human products reflect "simultaneously just and sinner (*simul iustus et peccator*), a fundamental tenet of Luther's doctrine of

---

[70]Søren Kierkegaard, *Kierkegaard's Writings*, vol. 6, *Fear and Trembling / Repetition*, ed. and trans. Edna H. Hong and Howard V. Hong (Princeton, NJ: Princeton University Press, 1983), 54-67.

[71]Kyle Roberts, *Emerging Prophet: Kierkegaard and the Postmodern People of God* (Eugene, OR: Cascade, 2013), 93.

[72]Roberts, *Emerging Prophet*, 93.

[73]Douglas Lancashire and Peter Hu Kuo-chen, translators' introduction to *The True Meaning of the Lord of Heaven (T'ien-chu Shih-i)*, by Matteo Ricci (St. Louis, MO: The Institute of Jesuit Sources, 1985), 9.

[74]Martin Luther, "Heidelberg Disputation, 1518," in *Luther's Works*, 31:43.

[75]Gerhard O. Forde, *On Being a Theologian of the Cross: Reflections on Luther's Heidelberg Disputation, 1518* (Grand Rapids, MI: Eerdmans, 1997), 37.

sin and grace" in that, when God uses it for good, it is by grace and not of its own doing.[76]

If what appears as good could be working as evil, the converse could be true as well. A cultural archetype that is seemingly evil could become a manifestation of *felix culpa* (blessed fall), where God brings good out of evil for divine glory. Lesslie Newbigin opines that it is

> . . . the central paradox of the human situation, that God comes to meet us at the bottom of our [ethical] stairways, not at the top; that our real ascent toward God's will for us takes us further away from the place where he actually meets us. "I came to call not the righteous, but sinners."[77]

Third, beyond this dialectical nature, God in divine freedom can commandeer cultural archetypes to speak and to be a source of revelation. In his creative formulation, Karl Barth articulates a supralapsarian and christological universal election and shows how all creation is in Christ.[78] While unpacking these moves is beyond our scope, Barth summarizes thusly:

> Before the world was, before heaven and earth were, the resolve or decree of God exists in view of this event in which God willed to hold communion with man, as it became inconceivably true and real in Jesus. And when we ask about the meaning of existence and creation, about their ground and goal, we have to think of this covenant between God and man.[79]

There is a real de jure participation of creation in Christ. However, because this participation is an eschatological reality, this de facto participation retains its event character, meaning God is sovereign over how culture can function theologically.[80] This participation is hidden, but Christ is present in creation because of election, and he can summon and unveil any part of

---

[76]Forde, *On Being*, 38.

[77]Newbigin, *Open Secret*, 181.

[78]See McCormack who has masterfully argued this very point about election. For Barth's theological methodology, the doctrine of election became for Barth "a 'regulative principle' which 'stands at the beginning of and behind all Christian thinking.'" Bruce L. McCormack, *Karl Barth's Critically Realistic Dialectical Theology: Its Genesis and Development 1909–1936* (Oxford: Clarendon, 1995), 460.

[79]Karl Barth, *Dogmatics in Outline* (New York: Harper & Row, 1959), 63-64. Barth is aware of the temporal perplexity that this move causes. Barth's solution affirms Jesus Christ as "the centre of time."

[80]McCormack describes *Realdialektik* as an actualistic, indirect identity within Barth's doctrine of revelation, which is critical to the whole of Barth's theological project. Bruce L. McCormack, *Orthodox and Modern: Studies in the Theology of Karl Barth* (Grand Rapids, MI: Baker, 2008), 109.

it to witness to himself. Given God's implicit presence in all creation, Barth argues that "God may speak to us through Russian Communism, a flute concerto, a blossoming shrub, or a dead dog."[81] Later in his *Church Dogmatics*, Barth develops this participation in his doctrine of lights, which states that even though Jesus Christ is *the* one and only light of life, there are other lights that witness to that living Word, besides that of the Bible and the church. In fact, we "not only may but *must* accept the fact that there are such words and that it *must* hear them too, notwithstanding its life by this one Word and its commission to preach it."[82]

In sum, cultural archetypes must be evaluated using a dialectical imagination.[83] Seemingly good archetypes possess shadow sides, the evil inherent within; the seemingly bad archetypes hold the possibility of silver linings of divine repurposing. Put differently, the *simul* reality means that even though these archetypes are limited per se, these archetypes can embody or point to goodness in God. Furthermore, divine freedom and the doctrine of election grant revelatory significance to cultural archetypes.

This section developed a view for a theology of culture that is nimble, dynamic, multidirectional, and multi-perspectival, empowering us to take on our world in its full diversity. In the final section, I continue this agenda by incorporating Richard Niebuhr's Christ-Culture types into Karl Barth's doctrine of reconciliation.

TRIPLEX GRATIA AND THE RECONCILIATION
OF CULTURAL ARCHETYPES

One of the critiques of Richard Niebuhr's presentation of the five Christ-Culture types (Christ against culture, Christ of culture, Christ above culture,

---

[81]Karl Barth, *Church Dogmatics*, vol. 1, part 1, *The Doctrine of the Word of God* (Edinburgh: T&T Clark, 1936), 55.

[82]Karl Barth, *Church Dogmatics*, vol. 4, part 3, *The Doctrine of Reconciliation* (Edinburgh: T&T Clark, 1956), 115, my italics.

[83]Tracy admits that in cultural engagement, the dialectical and analogical dimensions must both be affirmed. In fact, he argues that the absence of the dialectic "produce[s] not a believable harmony among various likenesses in all reality but the theological equivalent of 'cheap grace': boredom, sterility and an atheological vision of a deadening univocity." David Tracy, *The Analogical Imagination: Christian Theology and the Culture of Pluralism* (New York: Crossroad, 1981), 413. However, the advantage of beginning with the dialectic like Karl Barth is that the analogical is never presupposed, never inherent to culture or nature. Instead, the analogical always remains an expression of God's active freedom and present grace.

Christ and culture in paradox, and Christ as Transformer of culture) has been his partiality for the transformation type against others.[84] If culture is recognized as hybrid and dialectical as it really is, various stances toward culture are required. The idea of affirming the need for and the use of multiple types of cultural engagement is not new.[85] Lesslie Newbigin provides an illustration from missiology of how these types work together where the gospel-culture interaction involves at least two cultures, that of missionary and that of the mission field.[86] This interaction here is not static but dynamic, changing through the generations.

The "Christ against culture" posture of first-generation Christians receives the gospel and reacts strongly against their own culture by believing in a total discontinuity between their former religious and spiritual worldview and that of the Bible. The elements in their old cultures are perceived, "even if not evil in themselves (such as music, drama, and visual arts) . . . [as] evil because of their association with the rejected worldview."[87] The second or third generations, however, seek to recover the cultural heritage that had been rejected wholesale. This recovery process mirrors the "Christ of culture" type. Since these cultural elements no longer possess a direct relationship with their pagan roots, the church begins to reflect on the Christ of the traditional culture. The need then occurs for a reform movement, or the "Christ the transformer of culture" type, which seeks to change the culture in light of the gospel.

Niebuhr himself actually has a very similar idea about the historical process of the church and its cycles of different interactions with the cultural context.[88] This history of the church's relationship with its context is "marked by periods of conflict, of alliance, and of identification" only to lead to "a new withdrawal followed by a new aggression."[89] If we were to use this

---

[84]John Howard Yoder, "How H. Richard Niebuhr Reasoned: A Critique of Christ and Culture," in *Authentic Transformation*, ed. Glen H. Stassen, D. M. Yeager, and John Howard Yoder (Nashville: Abingdon, 1996), 42.

[85]See for example Brad Harper and Paul Louis Metzger, *Exploring Ecclesiology: An Evangelical and Ecumenical Introduction* (Grand Rapids, MI: Brazos Press, 2009), 207-26.

[86]Newbigin, *Open Secret*, 148.

[87]Newbigin, *Open Secret*, 148.

[88]H. Richard Niebuhr, "Toward the Independence of the Church," in *The Church Against the World*, H. Richard Niebuhr, Wilhelm Pauck, and Francis P. Miller (Chicago, IL: Willett, Clark and Co., 1935), 123-56.

[89]Niebuhr, "Toward the Independence of the Church," 123.

essay, written in 1935, as a framework to understand Niebuhr's Christ and culture types, we would end up with a very different picture of how to interpret each of their significance. Rather than attempting to evaluate a most compelling type, we would use them to discern the state of the church and where it must head next. Even then, because Niebuhr theorizes with broad strokes with the majority culture in the West in mind, he can talk about the stages of a cycle for America. Timothy Keller clarifies that because of the diversity of our contemporary situation, rather than discerning the cycle stage, it is better to use the "tool kit" of a type that is appropriate for the task at hand.[90]

This idea of using the range of Niebuhr's types as interpretative patterns is fitting given the complexity and the diversity of our cultural context and it would apply to cultural archetypes as well. However, a simple collection of tools offers no coherent and unified model to bring these various approaches together, nor gives any insights into the possible relationships between them. I seek to organize these tools by using the doctrine of reconciliation as articulated by Karl Barth. Barth's three christological movements of reconciliation—justification, sanctification, and vocation—provide a valuable order and structure to how cultural archetypes can be theologically interpreted.

Barth identifies three forms of the conversion of humanity to God. Like Calvin's *duplex gratia*, these three graces are what we experience through our union with Christ through faith. This reconciliation is first and foremost an event that occurs in Jesus Christ. Thus, the *munus triplex* of Jesus is the basis of the three forms:

> In all three developments we must ensure that Jesus Christ is constantly known and revealed as the One and All that is expounded. He is the One who justifies, sanctifies and calls. He is the High-Priest, King and Prophet.[91]

Thinking analogously, reconciliation of cultures begins with the divine judgment of them as sinful human institutions. Every aspect of culture is wholly sinful and wholly lost. In light of Christ's righteousness, even the good and most transcendent aspects of cultures are condemned as filthy

---

[90]Timothy Keller, *Center Church* (Grand Rapids, MI: Zondervan, 2012), 238.
[91]Karl Barth, *Church Dogmatics*, vol. 4, part 1, *The Doctrine of Reconciliation* (Edinburgh: T&T Clark, 1956), 147.

rags along with their base and immoral depravities. This judgment of cultures is a theological statement based on faith in Jesus Christ, not a conclusion based on our moral observations. The total judgment also means a possibility of transformation and witness. Even elements of culture that might be negative could be transformed and/or serve to point to the gospel. This justification dimension might be implicit; however, even when hidden, it serves as the basis of sanctification and vocation. Of course, often the ultimate transformation and witnessing role of all culture and its archetypes are hidden eschatological realities as well. This is the dialectical nature of culture and cultural archetypes that I explored above.

Sanctification or transformation of culture begins as the old plausibility structure is demolished and the new paradigm of the upside-down kingdom is embraced.[92] The gospel is not simply reasonable or logical knowledge, like moral standards that can be accepted without a radical paradigm shift in frame of reference. Only when you have a conversion, a paradigm shift in your worldview, does the scandal of the gospel become a thing of beauty and the object of adoration.[93] Sanctification means that the paradoxical nature of the gospel transforms various cultural elements into aliens within their own home environments.

When commandeered by God, cultural archetypes can point beyond themselves to their Redeemer. God's reconciliation establishes the possibility of archetypes' witness to the Word, but it does not assert or guarantee their continual reality as a static given. Only by God's grace and in his wisdom do the transformed and called cultural elements actually function as witnesses.

The beauty and power of employing Barth's movements of reconciliation become immediately clear in its ability to incorporate all three categories in unity-in-distinction. These three movements are in dialectical union and cannot be divided just as Christ cannot be divided.[94] You cannot have one without the others, although they might not always be expressed explicitly. Moreover, this unity means that there is relative freedom as to what comes first in practice. Barth notes Calvin as an example of how there can be

---

[92]Newbigin, *Foolishness to the* Greeks, 148.
[93]Newbigin, *Foolishness to the* Greeks, 64.
[94]Adam Neder, *Participation in Christ: An Entry into Karl Barth's* Church Dogmatics (Louisville, KY: Westminster John Knox, 2009), 51.

freedom in practice because all three forms are ways to see the whole, all benefits of *participatio Christi*.[95]

In regard to the example of Confucian filial piety as a cultural archetype, the significance of the justification aspect might mean that it stands under divine judgment, God's "No," even with its possible ethical merits. This "No" could be the way in which God uses this archetype to draw people toward great revelation. For example, a rejection of oppressive hierarchy can lead to a different kind of a parent, a different imagination of a "king." Put differently, this divine "No" might be in service of a "Yes" toward a transformed vocation.

The sanctification of this cultural archetype would mean the purification of shadow sides, casting out oppressive and legalistic expressions of an archetype through the transformation of its inner logic. No longer driven by contractual relational dynamics and shame, Confucian filial piety could become an expression of covenantal submission out of joy and freedom.

Superficially speaking, this archetype can appear good, even godly. However, Kierkegaard's distinction of the unassuming "knight of faith" from the ostentatiously "knight of infinite resignation" might elucidate the matter.[96] The "knight of infinite resignation" describes the act of someone who does not yet understand the nature of the gospel but yet tries to live rightly and morally *in and of* himself. The paradox of the gospel is that the knight of faith "is continually making the movement of infinity, but he does it with such precision and assurance that he continually gets finitude out of it, and no one ever suspects anything else."[97] Even with similar appearances, these two knights are vastly different. Sanctification of a seemingly good archetype would have a similarly important internal transformation.

In that fashion, the vocation of filial piety, truly understood, will practice supernatural acts of faith, but in the hidden guise of the natural. Like prayer, fasting, or acts of righteousness done in secret, the true vocation is hidden and yet, because of this hiddenness, truly and faithfully witnessing to the

---

[95]Karl Barth, *Church Dogmatics*, vol. 4, part 2, *The Doctrine of Reconciliation* (Edinburgh: T&T Clark, 1958), 510-11.

[96]*Kierkegaard's Writings*, vol. 6, *Fear and Trembling/Repetition* (Princeton, NJ: Princeton University Press, 1983), 40.

[97]*Kierkegaard's Writings*, 6:41.

Word (Mt 6:1-18). The power of its witness resides in God and not in itself. Also, we cannot assume that it would work the same way for everyone. Incidents of its witness are testimonies and not proofs of God's ways.

As I noted early in this chapter Michael Amaladoss, C. S. Song, and Kosuke Koyama all in their different approaches affirm the place of constructive theological engagement with Asian heritage. Drawing from my own theological formation and commitments, I have sought to press into the *simul* nature of culture in its fallen as well as its redemptive dynamics, describing how to make sense of such an engagement. The internal dialogue that Amaladoss notes looks different in my living in the US compared to him, my Asian heritage functioning in a much more subterranean and implicit manner.

Any tool's worth is found in its usefulness. Like the rest of the AAQ, cultural archetypes must be evaluated based on their heuristic efficacy and interpretive power. Does this methodological apparatus allow us to articulate our reality more accurately or precisely? A methodology and its corresponding vocabulary function like a paradigm, evaluating what is relevant and filtering out the rest; "[i]ndeed those that will not fit the box are often not seen at all."[98] Our way of theology is a language and a worldview.[99] Thus, these tools have the power to bring unconscious elements to the surface, enabling us to behold them. Conversely, if we lack the words to describe them, even conscious elements can be rendered invisible.

Beyond the incorporation of these tools into the discipline of theology of culture, we must wonder what other shifts, perhaps even more fundamental transformations, must be made in light of globalization. Instead of Christ and culture, Lesslie Newbigin used a trialogue between gospel, church, and culture.[100] In Newbigin's mind, each of these categories is complex and dynamic, as we have been discussing throughout. Incorporating these insights into our theology of culture would be another way to proceed. When you

---

[98]Thomas Kuhn, *The Structure of Scientific Revolutions*, 4th ed. (Chicago: University of Chicago Press, 2012), 24.

[99]Lindbeck made this cultural-linguistic function of theology explicit. See George A. Lindbeck, *The Nature of Doctrine: Religion and Theology in a Postliberal Age* (Louisville, KY: Westminster John Knox, 1984).

[100]See Hunsberger for a well-presented summary of Newbigin's triangle. George R. Hunsberger, *Bearing the Witness of the Spirit: Lesslie Newbigin's Theology of Cultural Plurality* (Grand Rapids, MI: Eerdmans, 1998), 235-79.

accept the hybridity of our culture, the pressing question is not only *what* or *whether* but *how*, as in, how do we describe, critique, and engage this culture adequately, avoiding the problematic stereotypes that very well could be seen as racist or colonialist? The promise of cultural archetypes as a tool should be evaluated in light of these difficulties.

5

MIGRATION AND LOSS

When one leaves one's country of origin—voluntarily or involuntarily—
one must mourn a host of losses both concrete and abstract.

DAVID L. ENG AND SHINHEE HAN

DURING THE TRANSPACIFIC FLIGHT that brought our family to the
States, I cried for hours because of terrible toothaches. Apparently, the air
trapped in my rotten teeth could not deal with the increase in cabin pressure,
resulting in hours of excruciating pain for a ten-year-old boy. In the coming
weeks, I would lose a number of my remaining baby teeth. During those first
hours of being in the States, although I was disappointed to see that American
cars did not float and glide in the air as I had somehow imagined, I believed
that our new life in the US held new opportunities and much more possibilities. And later, except for those teeth, I never thought that I had lost much
in this migration journey. However, decades later now, I have come to reflect
on the losses, both concrete and abstract, that I never saw. For example, with
my slow English acquisition and mastery, I lost my early love and enjoyment
of literature, only to finally recover it fully after my seminary years.

Asian Americans are not alone in our migration experience to the States.
Except for Native Americans, Americans of every heritage have migrated
here. However, as I argue throughout this book, the interaction of migration
with the other themes of the Asian American Quadrilateral, namely, Asian
heritage, American culture, and racialization, creates a unique trajectory of

Epigraph: David L Eng and Shinhee Han, *Racial Melancholia, Racial Dissociation: On the Social
and Psychic Lives of Asian Americans* (Durham, NC: Duke University Press, 2019), 48.

history and experience. Also, like the theme of Asian heritage, Asian American migration experience is much varied.

For example, the first Asians who landed in North America were Filipino sailors shipwrecked from a Spanish galleon that touched land at Point Reyes, Marin County, California in 1587.[1] Of course, the Filipino sailors did not settle there, and this land belonged to Spain. The territories of New Spain included the Philippines, Mexico, Florida, and practically everything west of the Mississippi river. Later, beginning in 1763, Filipino sailors would settle on various areas of this territory, including New Orleans and Acapulco. We should also remember that the Philippines was an American colony for about fifty years (1898–1946). So, many Filipino Americans did not come to America, but rather America came to them. This is true of many Mexican Americans as well, who became American through land acquisition and the resulting border changes. As I contemplate this bit of Asian American history while living in Southern California, it strikes me how Asian migration to this land, which successively belonged to Native American tribes, New Spain, Mexico, and later the United States, is much more layered and complex than any one single narrative.

The first significant Asian immigrants to the United States in modern history were poor and desperate Chinese men from Guangdong province in the mid-1800s. They came with dreams of California gold, becoming miners and railroad workers. Along with them, there were others from Japan, Korea, and South Asia who came and established their communities, suffering racial trauma from everyday experiences to state sponsored injustices like the Chinese Exclusion Act of 1882 and similar legislation like the Immigration Act of 1924 and the incarceration of Japanese Americans during World War II (1942–1946). My own family's immigrant story, like so many other Americans, can be traced to the impact of the 1965 Immigration and Nationality Act, also known as the Hart-Celler Act, which lifted some of the previous racist quota policies. This important piece of legislation, inspired and driven by the civil rights movement, has changed the face of America.

---

[1]Carl Nolte, "400th Anniversary of Spanish Shipwreck / Rough First Landing in Bay Area," *San Francisco Chronicle*, November 14, 1995, www.sfgate.com/news/article/400th-Anniversary-Of -Spanish-Shipwreck-Rough-3019121.php.

Throughout at least the last 170 years of American history, multiple waves of Asian "immigrants," including Filipinos, Chinese, Japanese, Indians, Koreans, Vietnamese, Hmong, and so many other national and ethnic groups, have come and made their home here. We must take care that these so-called immigrants include indentured workers, colonial subjects, refugees, and a stream of often invisible transnational adoptees as well. Many works, like Ronald Takaki's classic *Strangers from a Different Shore* or Erika Lee's more recent *The Making of Asian America*, raise our collective memory about this history.[2] Of course, the idea of an Asian American history only resonates with those who are aware of the racio-political panethnic Asian American identity. We will address that issue of race in chapter seven.

The concern of this chapter is migration experience as a source of theological inquiry. What pressing questions about God and divine presence and work arises out of this experience of migration? As before, we go about our theological project mindful of the diversity, complexity, and dynamism of Asian American migration. We must strive to avoid essentialism, stereotypes, and the temptation of a single story. The categories of analysis introduced in the last chapter, that is, a dialectical imagination that acknowledges both the good and the shadow sides, as well as the triadic modes of reconciliation (justification, sanctification, and vocation), will also be useful here.

The rest of the chapter is organized thusly: First, the various biblical and theological themes that are often used to interpret this migration experience will be laid out. Concepts like exile, promised land, and hybrid identity inform how to perceive Asian American identity as well as the American context. Of course, in our hermeneutical spiral, Asian American experiences highlight and provide insights to our biblical interpretation as well. Second, the modes of trauma and loss in migration are outlined. The loss of our heritage, of our families, and ourselves, which stems from migration and post-migration trauma, results in losses in our past, present, and future. In conjunction with the articulation of these losses, the process of recovery and healing will also be proposed. Finally, I will offer some creative ethical and missional possibilities that can arise out of this migration experience. These possibilities are not logical benefits of suffering,

---

[2]Ronald Takaki, *Strangers from a Different Shore* (Boston: Little, Brown and Company, 1998); Erika Lee, *The Making of Asian America: A History* (New York: Simon & Schuster, 2015).

but rather openness to God's surprising grace and divine redemption in the midst of disruption and pain.

INTERPRETING MIGRATION

Depending on our interpretative framework, how we understand and process the migration experience varies significantly. Our narratives organize the raw material of our experience into some sense of a coherent whole and help to guide what we alternately celebrate or mourn, recognize or ignore. Given that their migration experience was so formative for so many Asian Americans, they naturally seek to make sense of it by framing it within a broader story and meaning, often within the story of God. This search for spiritual meaning can be true for Christians as well as non-Christians. Here I present three themes that resonate closely with the experience of migration and are referred to by Asian American ministers and theologians.

First, America as the promised land is the most basic national mythology that frames the experience of Asian Americans, as it has for so many migrants to the US. This historic trope began with the spiritual vision of William Bradford, the founder of Plymouth Colony, who believed that America was the promised land and the Pilgrims were the chosen people escaping religious persecution.[3] Of course, in his view of the Promised Land, the Native Americans became the ungodly Canaanites, the wild savages whose removal was necessary. This spiritual vision continued in John Winthrop's American exceptionalism, casting the country as a "city on a hill" for all the world to see, and later in the notions of manifest destiny and American imperialism.

This narrative is what America propagates, and many Asian Americans have been drawn toward this vision of a better and prosperous life. In James Turslow Adams's definition, the "American Dream" means "a better, richer, and happier life for all our citizens of every rank," as opposed to the various rigid classes of the Old Country.[4] Adams takes care to note that this dream was never simply about material wealth, but a spiritual ideal as well. We will

---

[3]William Bradford, *Of Plymouth Plantation 1620-1647* (New York: Random House, 1981), 70. The reference to "the top of Pisgah to view from this wilderness a more goodly country" is a reference to Deuteronomy 34:1 when Moses views the Promised Land that he would never enter.

[4]James Truslow Adams, *The Epic of America* (Boston: Little, Brown and Company, 1931), viii.

critique this dream in time, but we should note that for many migrants from Asia, America did mean a better life not only materially, but also spiritually, in terms of religious freedom and the resources to follow Christ. If we do not affirm the positive, life-giving experiences of many, our critique will ring hollow.

Indeed, Asian Americans might see their experience of migration to the US as one of divine deliverance away from devastating poverty, war, genocide, and death. As Adams notes, in the American Dream there was hope for a better life for citizens of *every rank*. No one is stuck in their own station in life. Within this narrative, Asian Americans might, like Ruth, say "Where you go, I will go; where you lodge, I will lodge; your people shall be my people, and your God my God" (Ruth 1:16). This trope of a promised land guides a hyper-assimilationist trajectory, a conservative political stance, and even a dismissive view of our pre-American past, our life before entering the so-called land of God. This theological vision of a promised land fuels the model minority striving of so many Asian American Christians. For example, theologian Kirsten Oh recalls how in her earlier years of upward mobility she did not want to be like Lot's wife, looking back and mourning her pre-immigration life. Rather, she sang, "I have decided to follow Jesus . . . No turning back, no turning back," choosing "to forsake all—the old land, the old ways, the old relationships and choose to follow Jesus in this new land in order to flourish," only realizing much later what she had lost.[5]

To be sure, especially as Christians in America, there is great beauty, liberty, and opportunity, in comparison to parts of Asia. However, even the elect people of God in the Promised Land do not remain morally pure or spiritually exceptional. Great injustice and oppression have always existed, and persist, in this so-called godly nation. The problem of the American Dream and the vision of a promised land lie in its ideological hypocrisy and political pharisaism. Imbuing the American national myth with an element of divine election has allowed the co-opting of Christianity for the purposes of ideological machination. Thus, Asian American migrants who come to accept this spiritual propaganda become complicit in this national iniquity.

---

[5]Kirsten Oh, "Irit Redeemed: Casting My Lot with Lot's Wife," in *Mirrored Reflections: Reframing Biblical Characters*, ed. Young Lee Hertig and Chloe Sun (Eugene, OR: Wipf and Stock, 2010), 45; see also 43-54.

Viet Nguyen states that whereas immigrants are "the story of the American Dream, of American exceptionalism," refugees are "the reminder of the American nightmare," referring to the concrete and real collateral damages of American imperialism and war.[6] In her book *America for Americans*, historian Erika Lee shows how malignant xenophobia from the nation's founding continues to this day.[7] With this kind of historical root, xenophobic and nativist racism will continue for the foreseeable future. With the election of Donald Trump and the rise of White Christian nationalism, as well as the complicity of White evangelicalism, this idea of an American nightmare has again come to the forefront of our mainstream cultural awareness. The American Dream is only available for some, and for others living under structural oppression it remains a lie or a fantasy. Facing this nightmarish reality in the form of Japanese American concentration camps, the destruction of the Los Angeles riots, the torturous drops of daily microaggressions, rampant invisibility in popular cultural media, and the deeply and historically embedded nature of great racial inequalities, Asian Americans have looked to another narrative to make sense of their migration and post-migration experience.

A second theme is that of exile or pilgrimage, which has become a dominant narrative within Asian American reflections. This exile or pilgrimage theme arose as Asian American migrants did not find their home in the promised land. In an influential essay, Sang Hyun Lee invokes Abraham's obedience to God's call and the biblical injunction for God's people to be aliens and strangers (1 Pet 2:11) as a paradigm for Asian American life.[8] Although Lee's pilgrimage leans more on the first-generation experience of migration, the idea of turning perpetual foreigner stereotypes into the role of a resident alien continues even in later generations. In his autobiography, Russell Jeung draws from his Chinese *Hakka* (which translates literally as "guest people") ethnic heritage, and his experience of living with Southeast Asian refugees, to actively embrace his spiritual status as a resident alien.[9]

[6]Viet Nguyen, "April 30," *Viet Thanh Nguyen*, April 30, 2016, https://vietnguyen.info/2016/april-30.

[7]Erika Lee, *America for Americans: A History of Xenophobia in the United States* (New York: Basic, 2019).

[8]Sang Hyun Lee, "Pilgrimage and Home in the Wilderness of Marginality: Symbols and Context in Asian American Theology," in *New Spiritual Homes: Religion and Asian Americans*, ed. David K. Yoo (Honolulu: University of Hawai'i Press, 1999), 220.

[9]Russell Jeung, *At Home in Exile: Finding Jesus Among My Ancestors and Refugee Neighbors* (Grand Rapids, MI: Zondervan, 2016), 81.

Studying with Sang Hyun Lee almost two decades ago, I believed that he was overstating this idea of exile and marginalization. Looking back, there were a number of reasons why this exile motif did not resonate with me and many of my friends: modern individualism made it hard to see societal and structural forces. The support and belonging that I received from my ethnic community actually blinded me to the harsh racist realities in mainstream America. I believed that my marginalization was a temporary immigrant experience and not a part of a historic racism. I accepted White normativity as an unquestioned de facto trait of America. As a 1.5-gen Korean American, my most vivid experiences of oppression came mostly from the first generation and not from White America. I was still too young and too far from centers of power to experience the bamboo ceiling and institutional racism. And overall, my immigrant church was too deeply entrenched in the American Dream narrative to guide me toward a deeper critical awareness.

This theme of exile, while it frees one from the idolatry of the American Dream, is not without dangers. Whereas the promised land theme might encourage White assimilation, conservative politics, and rejection of Asian heritage, this exile theme can produce the opposite reaction. In the stories of Daniel and Esther, their faithfulness depended on them remembering and asserting their identity against the prevailing cultural forces. Following Daniel or Esther in their own fashion, Asian Americans can look to their ethnic identity, enclave, and church as a refuge. Within this interpretative framework, there can be a conflation of ethnic identity and covenantal identity for God's people. Thus, instead of America being God's country, our ethnic heritage becomes infused with spiritual significance.

There are at least two expressions of this problematic direction. One issue is an essentializing and glorification of ethnic identity. While the affirmation of our ethnic and racial identity in reaction to the forces of White assimilation is beneficial, the specific problem lies in its reactive and defensive protection of authentic identity. This drive toward authenticity or true identity leads to an idolatrous essentialism that easily becomes suffocating. The reason why I proposed the Asian American Quadrilateral was to avoid this idolatry. When we review Helen Lee's seminal article on the silent exodus and the reasons for later generations leaving the ethnic church, the suffocating danger of this essentialist ethnic identity becomes evident.[10]

The other temptation is the political quietism that can arise from viewing ourselves as resident aliens. In a democratic system, what is our responsibility as Christians? While we should not put our hope in political power or seek to gain Christian influence through the political process, our commitment to Christ guides us to seek a just society that is hospitable for the beauty of the gospel to be revealed. Without this political activism, we ghettoize our understanding of discipleship, justifying this attitude with talk of being visitors. The kingdom of heaven is not primarily advanced through the political process, but we also cannot abdicate our responsibility to protect minorities and the vulnerable through the democratic system. This is a much-needed word to the Asian American Christian community, who must learn to bring our politics under God's rule, like every other aspect of our lives. Thus, Sang Hyun Lee warns of an escapist nationalism where we fail to take seriously the task of Asian American discipleship in America.[11] Russell Jeung, recalling Jeremiah 29, further develops this truth of how we must invest and work to bring about justice and peace in the midst of exile.[12]

The last theme is one of bicultural identity, especially for the purpose of ministry and mission. Within this framework, the purpose of migration can be found in the raising of people like Moses and Paul, bicultural and specifically positioned and nurtured for God's kingdom work. The core idea is that God redeems the often-onerous complexities of Asian American identity with missional import. We will look more closely into the creative potential of Asian Americans later in the chapter; however, here we just note some issues with this interpretive framework.

The most obvious issue in this bicultural theme is that even for Paul, Moses, Esther, and Daniel, their ethnic identity had covenantal import. Their remembrance and affirmation of their ethnic heritage and identity equated to spiritual faithfulness. This is simply not the case for Asian Americans. The multicultural proficiency that many migrants and even later generations

[10]Helen Lee, "Silent Exodus: Can the East Asian Church in America Reverse the Flight of Its Next Generation?," *Christianity Today*, 40, no. 12 (August 12, 1996).

[11]Sang Hyun Lee, *From A Liminal Place: An Asian American Theology* (Minneapolis: Fortress, 2010), 128.

[12]Jeung, *At Home in Exile*, 142-43.

have is definitely a great benefit in crossing boundaries and building relationships. However, there are no spiritual or even moral imperatives for us to retain our ethnic identity as the fundamental core of our lives. Of course, in many contexts and likely even more than we are aware of, Asian Americans have little choice but to own our ethnic and racial identities. Still, the affirmation of this identity is not rooted in divine command in the same way that the Jewish identity was throughout Scripture.

Negatively speaking, our ethnicity is not eternal, but rather fluid and dynamic over time.[13] Through redrawn national boundaries and ethnic intermixing, what we consider to be our ethnic identities are not exactly the "every nation, from all tribes and peoples and languages" of Revelation 7:9. The issue here is more about human particularity, and not some version of multiculturalism. Like so much of the book of Revelation, this figure of speech is symbolic, like the "pearl" gates and the "gold" and "glass" streets (Rev 21:21). If we hold these distinctions too technically, we will begin to create another set of problems by idolizing ethnic purity and leaving no room for mulatto, mestizo, multiethnic, and multiracial heritages.

Asian American ethnic heritage would fall into general Gentile identities that have no covenantal significance, except for the fact that God's Spirit is not limited to Jewish flesh. Following this line of Gentile diversity and the movement of the Spirit, Amos Yong argues that Pentecost in Acts 2 affirms a kind of global theology that values cultural, ethnic, and language differences.[14] However, given the hybridity and multiplexity of the global context and the significance of racial or phenotypical categories, neither of which are well covered by the concepts of cultures, nations, peoples, or language groups, this pneumatological move still appears limited. Also, this emphasis on culture, ethnicity, language, and nations, while not without relevance, reduces Asian Americans to "Asians living in America" and retains the presumption of America as a White pseudo-European nation. This is one of the limitations of using a global or diasporic framework for the Asian American context; they reinforce the perpetual foreigner stereotype. These

---

[13]See my engagement of this issue from a Barthian perspective in *Double Particularity: Karl Barth, Contextuality, and Asian American Theology* (Minneapolis: Fortress Press, 2017), 11-17.

[14]Amos Yong, *The Future of Evangelical Theology: Soundings from the Asian American Diaspora* (Downers Grove, IL: IVP Academic, 2014), 136-37.

commonly used missiological categories do not do justice to the full range of Asian American experience.

Positively, our bodies in their full particularities are the sites of God's call and our response. Instead of an eschatological grounding of ethnicity, our human particularities are contextually relevant to the divine calling at hand.[15] The idea of human particularity in our theological anthropology will be developed in chapter seven as an Asian American takes on a theology of "race."

These three themes, while not exhaustive, display the ways in which a biblical and theological framing of migration and post-migration interprets and guides our identity, ethics, and outlook. In the next two sections, we will focus on the loss experienced in migration, as well as the creative possibilities that can come from it.

LOSSES VISIBLE AND INVISIBLE

In chapter one, I noted that one of the reasons for theological inquiry from the Asian American vantage point was to address the particular pains of Asian Americans. Without the language to express or identify the locus of suffering, we struggle to know how God's work of reconciliation makes any difference in our lives. Of course, divine action is not limited to our knowledge, nor is it always tangible. However, given that God invites our supplications and cries for help and justice, as the psalmists have taught us, it behooves us to know the places of our pain. Also, because triumphalistic themes like America as the promised land hamper the mourning process, this journey of enumerating and taking stock of our losses is critical.

The loss suffered varies widely depending on the circumstances and details of migration. The experiences of early migrant individuals with no means to travel back and forth, communicate with their family, enjoy cultural products of the homeland, or find a large community of co-ethnics are worlds apart from the lives of recent transnational families who exist in a globalized world and can settle in a majority ethnic neighborhood. Also, generational distance from the migration experience will determine both the intensity and kind of loss experienced.

---

[15]Karl Barth, *Church Dogmatics*, vol. 3, part 4, *The Doctrine of Creation* (Edinburgh: T&T Clark, 1961), 288.

Because roughly three quarters of the Asian American population were born overseas, migration and its losses are personal for many. The same can even be said for many who are one generation removed. However, even if one's family is now up to the fifth or sixth generation living in the US, this migration experience and its losses still matter. The reasons for this also apply to how our cultural heritage, described in the last chapter on Asian heritage, can be transferred through the generations as well.

First, the experiences and losses of the first generation, and even the pre-migration generation, impact later generations when understood through the lens of family systems theory. According to family systems, we are all interconnected, even beyond our immediate family.[16] A particular symptom or a neurosis can express itself in a person, but its source can reside in a different person and even in an interpersonal dynamic further removed from this person. Through concepts like "the *identified patient,* the concept of *homeostasis* (balance), *differentiation of self, the extended family field,* and *emotional triangles*" from Bowen theory, Edwin Friedman breaks down how individuals function within an interconnected system. Patterns, attitudes, and life philosophies can and do transfer through the generations even from distant members of the family who are back in the motherland. There are various ways to interpret biblical texts about generational sins visiting the later generations (Ex 20:5-6; Lev 26:39), many of which can be more superstitious and fatalistic and inadequately account for Christ's work. However, family systems theory can provide a way to account for that kind of inter-generational human reality without falling into superstitious legalism.

The second way to understand the continuing influence of migration loss is by understanding the familial *scripts* that we live by.[17] In the introduction, I mentioned that after I married, I was surprised by the power of the inter-generational scripts that I had seen in my parents and had discovered were internalized in my own newlywed life. Embedded within these scripts are our presupposed and unspoken gender and spousal roles, fears, logical connections, and even hopes. Scripts even function as plausibility structures,

---

[16]There are a number of family systems theories, but I draw primarily from Bowen theory as applied to church contexts in Edwin H. Friedman, *Generation to Generation: Family Process in Church and Synagogue* (New York: Guilford Press, 1985).

[17]Margaret Kornfeld, *Cultivating Wholeness: A Guide to Care and Counseling in Faith Communities* (New York: Continuum, 1998), 161-62.

with their own internal logic and coherence. For example, what a normal good father does from my family script guides my actions and orders my self-evaluation. This paternal script corresponds to what I believe a normal good child should be as well, defining how I see my kids. Within my familial framework, the father-child relationship makes perfect logical sense *to me* as I apply them for everyone. Of course, the fact that these scripts remain unconscious and unarticulated makes them all the more potent and dangerous for relational strife.

Third, transgenerational epigenetics provides another explanation for the persistence of these influences. In interpersonal and psychological fashion, the impact of loss and trauma through later generations can be explained through family systems and the presence of family scripts. However, transgenerational epigenetics is a way that these influences and traumas impact us in our body and then move on to our children. Epigenetics refers to the process by which gene expressions are controlled. Our DNA, the genetic material, is not impacted by our experiences, but their expression, whether a certain gene gets turned on or off, can be influenced through trauma and other factors. The latest epigenetic research shows that such biological memory can be passed down through the generations.[18] While there is still much research needed on this new field of science, we do know that trauma can reside in our brains and in our bodies.[19] Thus, this idea of transgenerational epigenetics is not beyond the realm of possibility.

All these possible reasons reinforce the idea that formative and deformative experiences linger, haunt, and reside with us for generations. Of course, it is important to acknowledge that positive experiences can also be passed down as well. However, I am taking pains to expand on the role of losses because the migrant mentality can often focus on pressing forward and downplaying the pains of the past. Again, if we see the US as the promised land, then acknowledging our loss could be considered grumbling against God like the ungrateful Israelites in the desert. However, we have

---

[18]See, for example, Rachel Yehuda et al., "Holocaust Exposure Induced Intergenerational Effects on FKBP5 Methylation," *Biological Psychiatry*, 80, no. 5 (2016): 372-80, and Natan P. F. Kellermann, "Epigenetic Transmission of Holocaust Trauma: Can Nightmares Be Inherited?," *The Israel Journal of Psychiatry and Related Sciences*, 50, no. 1 (2013): 33-37.

[19]Bessel van der Kolk, *The Body Keeps the Score: Brain, Mind, and Body in the Healing of Trauma* (New York: Penguin, 2014).

already noted the theological problems with this interpretative framework. What we do not know, disregard, fatalistically resign ourselves to, or see as irrelevant, can and does hurt us profoundly. Setting aside these parts of our lives limits our full discipleship to Christ, where we are called to bring all of ourselves under the reign of God. Thus, I outline three areas of loss that occur in migration and in post-migration.

The first loss is the loss of our past and heritage. Migration is a disruption, a traumatic discontinuity in our life journey. We must look beyond just the concrete disruption and also recognize the abstract ones too. For some of the more recent and well-off transnational immigrants, there might be a temptation to see this disruption as a minor inconvenience. However, slowing down to sit with the grief and account for it in our lives is crucial. The loss of homeland, extended family, language, social status, and others vary widely, but it is real, even when or especially when life circumstances in the US are so much better than in the country of origin. This is true even in a life transition that is filled with joy. In getting married, we can mourn the loss of our singleness. With the birth of a first child, we grieve the passing of couple life and life without a dependent. Acknowledging the losses amid these joyous transitions without shame or guilt is important for our own well-being and for finding healthy passage through this life stage. Agency and volition are significant factors in the nature and impact of our loss. Whatever the circumstance, the goal is the same: to present all of our selves to God, not just the selves we would like to present.

This loss is immediate for the first generation, extracted from the cultural context in which to understand themselves and their lives. If they do not or did not have a chance to return back soon or regularly to their homeland, it is possible that they would lose the homeland through time, because in their absence it would continue evolving, changing like all living things. This experience of a lost homeland is relevant to transnational adoptees or even later generations of migrants as well. Returning to the country of origin might not feel like coming home for a myriad of reasons. Thus, this loss of past or heritage is elusive.

However, the importance of recalling and learning our historical heritage in order to acquire language and concepts for our life today has already been noted in the previous chapters. We must recover this loss, working hard to see through the fog of nativism, Orientalism, and racism, all of which discredit and marginalize it as worthless baggage better forgotten. Mourning this loss and seeking to recover what we can does not make us less American, as the perpetual foreigner trope would claim. Rather, it makes us more human, more deeply rooted in our bodies and our histories.

The second loss is the loss of our family: for parents, the loss of their children, and for children, loss of their parents. Obviously, despite stereotypes to the contrary, many migrant families are close and enjoy their relationships. However, the forces and pressures on the family in the migration process are immense, and when compounded by the stresses of raising children, dissonant acculturation can occur where family members lose each other.

For parents, as their children become socialized into American life through schools and media, they often find that they can no longer communicate or connect with them. Also, as children continually absorb Orientalist portrayals of Asians in the media, embarrassment and rejection can result from these portrayals being projected on their parents.

For children, parental loss is suffered as their parents are absent, busy providing for the family. Whether professionals, blue-collar workers, or entrepreneurs, these parents are overwhelmed with the stresses of "language difficulties, financial uncertainties, and downward social mobility"[20] and "incidents of racial prejudice, glass ceiling effect, and misunderstandings that stemmed from cultural and language barriers with supervisors, co-workers, and customers."[21] As many parents succumb to stress, abuse and neglect occur, they become toxic parents as well as abusive spouses.[22]

An important point about parents is that they serve as a de facto embodiment of Asianness for many Asian Americans. This is why rejecting Asian heritage also aggravates the relationship with parents, and dysfunctional parental relationships can lead to wholesale rejection of ethnic identity. This is a particular problem for the later generation who lacks

---

[20]Grace J. Yoo and Barbara W. Kim, *Caring Across Generations: Linked Lives of Korean American Families* (New York: New York University Press, 2014), 17.
[21]Yoo and Kim, *Caring Across Generations,* 34.
[22]Susan Forward and Craig Buck, *Toxic Parents: Overcoming Their Hurtful Legacy and Reclaiming Your Life* (New York: Bantam, 1989); Carlos E. Sluzki, "Migration and Family Conflict," *Family Process* 18, no. 4 (1979): 379-90.

direct access and broad experience with their ethnic context. Even later on, if they are exposed to their culture in their family's country of origin, they will have to overcome the prejudices that they have harbored as a result of their relationship with their parents. Of course, this parental or grand-parental embodiment of ethnic culture can also be positive, serving as an emotional and psychological home base and a cultural mentor. However, given the Orientalist and racial pressure from mainstream American society and even White American Christianity, it is more often the case that American-born generations of Asian Americans end up rejecting their ethnic cultures and instead favoring an assimilative Americanness. With these interconnections, in losing their parents, Asian Americans lose their past and a part of themselves as well; this relational loss is really a triple loss. Along with this relationship between parental attachment and ethnic attachment, there is a cross-generational pendulum swing as well, where one generation's ethnic rejection is followed by the next generation's ethnic recovery. This idea of third generation return, which is not an exact science, explains these reactive dynamics.[23]

We should note that the process of negotiating the American context, whether through full assimilation, segmented assimilation, acculturation, or enculturation, can be a place of conflict not only between generations, but among various family members as well, especially if they diverge politically or move to different parts of the country. In all these incidents, the result is the loss of family.

Third, through migration and continuing in post-migration, we struggle with the loss of ourselves. Du Bois's concept of "double consciousness" describes African Americans with "two souls, two thoughts, two unreconciled strivings; two warring ideals in one dark body, whose dogged strength alone keeps it from being torn asunder."[24] For many Asian Americans, the popular notion of biculturality or being a bridge between cultures fails to account for societal forces that often make "Asian" aspects of ourselves undesirable and disposable, such as our accents, our smelly food, our embarrassing parents,

---

[23]See Marcus Lee Hansen, *The Problem of the Third Generation Immigrant* (Rock Island, IL: Augustana Historical Society, 1938).

[24]W. E. B. Du Bois, *The Souls of Black Folk: Essays and Sketches* (Chicago: A. C. McClurg and Co, 1903), 3.

and so on. I will expand on this theme of the double or fragmented self in chapter eight.

The migration and post-migration marginality experienced by Asian Americans is that liminal space of betwixt and between. This loss cannot be solved, and so creates a context of racial melancholia.[25] Mourning these losses is a luxury. The migrant's survivalist mentality has no margin to recall the past or even linger in the present. Rather, it pushes toward the future, toward survival and hopefully closer to the dream. Even to talk about the past or the present can feel like opening the Pandora's box of pain, regret, and loss that appears to have no hope of healing given their limited resources. This survivalist mentality can continue into later generations as well, in its attitudes and drivenness even when survival is no longer in question. In this place of survival, even the practice of lament can be beyond their capacity.

Lament is a struggle, a baring of the soul, and a wrestling with God for healing and blessing. The question is, Do the people or community have enough energy required for this task? If not, the mourning and healing process can be stillborn. I will go on to outline the process of integration and healing in chapter eight. At this moment, what we need to consider is how taking account of these losses is a critical part of the Asian American theological task.

A migrant's financial predicament is one of the more significant factors in how they experience the disruptive loss and transition of migration. While migration losses cannot be done away with altogether, class often dictates the outcome of questions such as what neighborhood to live in, how much racial privilege they are seen to possess, finding protection from societal vulnerabilities, and amassing the resources to see relatives more often.

For Asian American women, migration can mean more freedom from patriarchal forces, but can also spell out vulnerability and added suffering under multiple patriarchies.[26] Adjusting to a new country, women often

---

[25]David L. Eng and Shinhee Han, "A Dialogue on Racial Melancholia," *Psychoanalytic Dialogues* 10, no. 4 (2000): 667-700.

[26]Yen Le Espiritu, "Gender and Labor in Asian Immigrant Families" in *Gender and U.S. Immigration: Contemporary Trends*, ed. Pierrette Hondagneu-Sotelo (Berkeley: University of California Press, 2003), 95.

carry a double load of wage-earning work as well as housework and childcare due to traditional divisions of labor. Also, as immigrant men lose the social status they enjoyed in old-world patriarchies, mounting pressures on family systems can fall on women, "leading to resentment, spousal abuse, and divorce."[27]

Creative Possibilities for Discipleship and Witness

These losses of migration can be overwhelming, yet there are also creative possibilities. I have already noted that, even though the ideology of America as the promised land is fraught with idolatries, for many there are life-giving aspects of living in the US that bear some resemblance to the mythical American Dream. Along with the loss and trauma that gets passed down because of various factors listed above, the later generation also benefits from the positive and constructive characteristics of the migrant generation. It is important to be reminded that these creative possibilities are not logical conclusions, as though all migrants will enjoy all of these benefits. Similar to the distinction between cultural archetypes versus stereotypes, this language of possibility stresses the ambivalence and divergence within Asian American circumstances and experiences.

Sang Hyun Lee, who develops his thinking from Victor Turner's categories of liminality and Everett Stonequist's marginality, points to these creative dimensions.[28] Lee summarizes the three elements in Turner's concept of liminality: openness to the new, the emergence of *communitas*, and the creative space for prophetic knowledge and action.[29] While Lee wisely reflects on the limitations of these positive traits given the destructive powers of racism and marginalization, others tell a more sanguine story.

These creative possibilities have been labeled positively as the "immigrant mentality or mindset" in the business world. The idea is that the survivalist drive to take care of your family and make it in America can be packaged into six principles like: "1. Look for Opportunities Everywhere, 2. Stay on Your Toes, 3. Unleash Your Passion, 4. Live With an Entrepreneurial Attitude, 5. Work With a Generous Purpose, and 6. Focus on

[27]Espiritu, "Gender and Labor," 95.
[28]Lee, *From A Liminal Place*, 1-11.
[29]Lee, *From A Liminal Place*, 7-9.

Leaving a Lasting Legacy."[30] Correspondingly, there are Christian versions of this upbeat narrative as well. Immigrants are characterized as creative, hardworking and sacrificial, able to reach other marginalized peoples, adaptive for missional encounters, and able to serve as "bridge people." The process of migration can be a time of transition and search, not only for a new home but a new meaning, identity, and hope. In turn, these immigrants and refugees become impact ministers, bringing fresh vision and practices to renew and stimulate their host nation.[31] Jehu Hanciles points out the long history of immigrant waves having a profound impact on the church in the US, arguing for the missionary function of immigrant congregations.[32] Indeed, Asian American churches have produced many leaders who bring cultural proficiency and spiritual fervor to create new kinds of ministries for diverse communities and to energize White Christian institutions.[33]

There is definitely some sense of truth to these ideas. However, what is often ignored are the hidden costs, the shadow side of these amazing characteristics. Unless we acknowledge the loss and trauma that migrants and their later generations carry, as well as the structures that have and continue to hinder them, this narrative is a version of the model minority myth that will ultimately be unhelpful and even destructive. Hope is not inherent in the experience of migration per se, but rather the migrant God who travels with us.

In the life of Jesus, we see the refugee fleeing terror, a migrant whose family relocates to another country (Mt 2:13-23), someone who is politically marginalized in their own country under occupation. In all the biblical narratives, we can know that our Savior knows and empathizes with migrants of every kind (Heb 4:15). Divine migration is at the heart of the gospel.

---

[30]Glenn Llopis, "Adopt an Immigrant Mindset to Advance Your Career," *Harvard Business Review*, August 24, 2012, accessed February 4, 2018. https://hbr.org/2012/08/adopt-an-immigrant -mindset-to.

[31]Stephen B. Bevans, "Migration and Mission: Pastoral Challenges, Theological Insights," in *Contemporary Issues in Migration and Theology*, ed. Elaine Padilla and Peter C. Phan (New York: Palgrave Macmillan, 2013), 168.

[32]Jehu Hanciles, *Beyond Christendom: Globalization, African Migration, and the Transformation of the West* (Maryknoll, NY: Orbis, 2008), 248-79. Also, Jehu Hanciles, *Migration and the Making of Global Christianity* (Grand Rapids, MI, Eerdmans, 2021).

[33]For some of these examples, see Helen Lee, "Asian Americans: Silent No More," *Christianity Today*, 58 (2014): 38-43.

Incarnation is the "way of the Son of God into the far country."[34] This biblical allusion to the parable of the prodigal son has migration resonances.[35] In the incarnation, God takes up the migration experience into the divine self. God in Christ "goes into the far country, into the evil society of this being which is not God and against God" in the incarnation, concluding on the cross with the death of divine life, the "familial" Father-Son relationship, and the divine self.[36] Of course, while there are analogies, this divine loss is not like our loss, in that God takes these losses within the divine life and never ceases to be God in all this. Thus, categorical differences remain.

Recalling his Hakka heritage as a "guest person," Russell Jeung imagines Jesus as a Hakka, a marginalized traveling person having no homeland.[37] Following this Hakka Jesus means that we not only tread lightly on earth apart from the empires, but also show our solidarity with the poor and the powerless. Seeing Jesus as an immigrant, a refugee, and a Hakka challenges our grasp of false security and worth. Racist and nationalistic forces make these statuses or familial histories undesirable and can pressure us to develop self-hatred as well as an aversion to others with this same identity. Passing as model minority, immigrants who assimilate into Whiteness, or at least claim a White-adjacent location, can lose the Hakka Jesus and radical discipleship in exchange for the idol of social status and nationalist identity.

Several years ago, during the Obama administration, I attended the historic first-ever White House briefing for AAPI religious leaders.[38] During our numerous meetings with various departments, I learned that recent refugees from Asia are some of the most vulnerable and needy Asian Americans. I wondered, with all the rhetoric about outreach and mission in many East Asian American churches, do they ever think about the needs of Asian

---

[34]Karl Barth, *Church Dogmatics*, vol. 4, part 1, *The Doctrine of Reconciliation* (Edinburgh: T&T Clark, 1956), 158.

[35]Daniel G. Groody, "Homeward Bound: A Theology of Migration," in *Migration as a Sign of the Times: Towards a Theology of Migration*, ed. Judith Gruber and Sigrid Rettenbacher (Leiden: Brill, 2015), 137-38.

[36]Barth, *Church Dogmatics*, IV/1, 159.

[37]Jeung, *At Home in Exile*, 80-81.

[38]The historic event in 2014 was hosted by Korean Churches for Community Development (KCCD), which later become Faith and Community Empowerment (FACE), with the innovative leadership of Hyepin Im.

refugees. The more conservative churches mostly focused on overseas missions, and the more progressive congregations seemed to focus on Black and Brown communities. While I deeply believe in both of these kinds of outreach, I believe Asian American churches are missing out on the unique gifts that we can bring to these Asian refugees. How much of this disconnect is Asian American invisibility and ignorance about our own community? How much is the result of internalized nativism, where Asian Americans avoid association with "FOBs" so as to earn White approval?[39]

As we grow in our capacity to articulate the various aspects of migration and post-migration from the Asian American perspective, we will be empowered toward theological construction. And as we do so, the particular pains, challenges, redemption, and healing coming out of this experience will be used for God's kingdom work.

The ways in which we theologically and biblically frame our migration narrative have a profound impact on how we perceive and digest these complex experiences of migration and post-migration. Avoiding ideological pitfalls like American exceptionalism helps us to own all dimensions of our experience, even those that do not fit the narrative of America as a promised land.

---

[39]FOB means "Fresh off the Boat," as in a recent immigrant unfamiliar with American cultural norms.

6

AMERICAN CULTURE AND REPRESENTATION

This is narrative scarcity—the lack of characters who looked like us, and when they looked like us, were not really human.

VIET THANH NGUYEN

IN HOMER'S ODYSSEY, the twists and turns of Odysseus's journey home and his son Telemachus's longing for the long-lost father in the face of a mounting domestic crisis stirred my soul, resonating with my own struggle to find home as an Asian American, and my longing for a better father than the abusive one with whom I grew up. The novels of Tolstoy and Dostoyevsky have also been my life-long companions since my days in high school when I learned what good literature should be. I also grew up on sitcoms like *Friends, The Office, Parks and Recreation*, and so many other portrayals of multifaceted American life.

Education and various forms of mass media consumption are powerful socialization processes. Through years of socialization, we learn what distinguishes the classics, which then define our imagination of the good, the true, and the beautiful. They form what we consider to be our own personal tastes and preferences. TV shows and our education offer a particular take

Epigraph: Viet Thanh Nguyen, "Asian-Americans Need More Movies, Even Mediocre Ones," *New York Times*, August 21, 2018, www.nytimes.com/2018/08/21/opinion/crazy-rich-asians-movie.html.

on understanding our world with their selections, inclusions, exclusions, interpretations, and affirmations. These processes are difficult to see and grasp because they are perceived to be normal *to those who have been socialized by them,* to those who have been programmed to think that these images accurately represent our world.

For Asian Americans, our Asian aspects, like Asian cultural heritage or the migration process, stick out especially if you do not live among many other Asian Americans. We can be otherized because of these features, so we are more aware of them. However, the "normal" American aspects of ourselves can be much more subversive, because they are shared with everyone around us.

Along with education and mass media, many Asian American Christians have also been formed through the lens of White American evangelicalism, following luminaries like Billy Graham, John Piper, and Tim Keller. For much of my own evangelical spiritual formation, I soaked in every bit of wisdom from books by C. S. Lewis, Eugene Peterson, and Henri Nouwen. I encountered God in the worship ministries of Hillsong and Jesus Culture. While I do not doubt that we have experienced God through these various ministries, we must realize that they all embody the gospel in a particular contextual manner while they simultaneously assume a universal and normative stance as discussed in chapter one.

The AAQ framework incorporates these so-called American, or more accurately mainstream or White American cultural, aspects as a part of who we are. Within our hybrid concepts of ourselves, this mainstream American socialization can be authentically as much a part of us as our Asian cultural heritage. However, this mainstream American culture also possesses many highly problematic aspects like White normativity, racism, Orientalism, and a lack of Asian American representation. These aspects are so deeply entrenched in this American culture that it will not easily be distinguished from what we consider to be positive aspects. If we remember that gospel mediums are like jars of clay, we can still affirm and accept God's work in, through, and especially in spite of American culture, as with every culture.

Even though I am more critical of this culture, especially post Trump, I would be remiss if I didn't recognize that I am a product of this evangelicalism along with much of my American formation. The gospel embodiments of American evangelicalism did help me understand the gospel and know God, particularly the sides of myself that overlap with mainstream American experience.

Trying to find some pleasure reading a couple of years ago, it suddenly occurred to me that I had not read any Asian American novels for pleasure, but only for my academic work. Throughout my life, I had been so indoctrinated to think of great literature as Western and White that I could only contemplate a decision between a Dickens novel or the short stories of Chekhov, only thinking of Asian American literature as suitable for cultural study. There was nothing wrong with my enjoyment of these works of Western literature, but there was a problem with how I understood literature in a White normative way, excluding Asian American works as among the classics. My tastes and discernment had been formed to exclude Asian American works and lives.

I saw that I still had such a deep sense of self-hatred, not so much in rejecting my body or heritage, but in denigrating and devaluing Asian American voices and works. The lack of Asian American representation in TV shows and movies was easier for me to recognize, because I didn't love them like I loved literature growing up. I felt embarrassed and saddened that even as I taught my students about their own colonialized minds, I still had much more room to grow. I write this as someone still on a journey and who will continue on just like all of you.

As noted in chapter three, every theme of the AAQ serves as a mental category in which to gather and organize information regarding the Asian American experience. The themes of migration and racialization are more focused and narrower, whereas what we consider Asian heritage can be quite broad, including religious and philosophical traditions and movements, as well as significant historic events. Our present theme, American culture, can appear to be a bin containing rather disparate ideas and concepts. Both of these terms, *American* and *culture*, are highly contentious and rather amorphous. However, for our purposes, I will present what I am calling American culture in four aspects: Western intellectual tradition, missionary and colonial history, White mainstream American evangelicalism, and Asian American representation. The first half of this chapter will cover the first three aspects, critiquing and appropriating their insights from an Asian

American perspective. Given the limits of this chapter, my goal is to simply outline some key ideas to consider in this very broad survey of themes.

The second half of the chapter will pick up on the fourth aspect, Asian American representation, for constructive theological engagement. I propose an outline for a theology of cultural representation, articulating the idea of culture-making as a divinely given vocation that serves humanity. This human criterion of culture-making as it relates to the *imago Dei* is the crux of my argument.

INFUSION AND CO-OPTION OF THE GOSPEL

Missiologist Andrew Walls believes that gospel-context interaction can be described with the double idea of "indigenizing" and "pilgrim" principles. The gospel "indigenizes" and makes a home in a context.[1] However, it must keep its own sense of integrity and be a "pilgrim" so as not to become domesticated by any context. In this section, I would like to discuss the complex dynamics of gospel-context interaction in the Western tradition, missionary and colonial history, and American evangelicalism. As we have done in chapter four on Asian heritage, we must take up a dialectical approach when we evaluate these traditions. The seemingly constructive and positive dimensions often are closely connected to co-opted and negative dimensions of the gospel-context interaction. Thus, all critical reflections are tentative and open to reevaluation.

Western intellectual tradition. The long historical engagement of the gospel with the West affords a multifaceted witness to God's grace and to biblical imagination, infused into many different aspects of Western culture including mainstream American culture. Whether it be Western literature, the arts, music, politics, and even languages, everywhere there lay remnants of Scripture and Christian motifs. Without a working knowledge of the Bible, it would be difficult to understand many of the great authors of Western literature such as Milton, Shakespeare, Dante, Melville, and Faulkner, as well as the many others they have influenced. In art and music, whether Bach's *Mass in B Minor* or *The Last Supper* of Leonardo da Vinci, or in political theory and historiography, that is, checks and balances in the US

---

[1] Andrew F. Walls, "The Gospel as Prisoner and Liberator of Culture," in *The Missionary Movement in Christian History: Studies in the Transmission of Faith* (Maryknoll, NY: Orbis, 1996).

Constitution and apocalyptic visions in movies, it would be difficult to tease out all the Christian influences in Western society. In fact, this long engagement has led to a christening of pagan sources so that they are now received as though they are Christian as well. This baptizing dynamic is especially true of Greco-Roman sources, such as Plato, Aristotle, the Stoics, and Roman law, to name a few. It is important to recognize this constructive aspect of gospel interaction in the West and in the US, and there are many works that describe it in depth.[2] However, this one-sided positive review of history and culture is incomplete and simplistic.

Our family spent a recent summer reading through all the Harry Potter books. Along with falling in love with this fantasy world, I came away thinking how much Christian themes and values were infused and embodied in the characters and the plots, which was surprising given all the fundamentalist hoopla about its witchcraft and paganism. Did they read the same books that our family read? By the end of the series, the seventh book was overtly making connections with Christianity in its themes of sacrifice, resurrection, and salvation. Of course, the Harry Potter series doesn't quite bear the explicit Christian overtones of Lewis or Tolkien, but this was definitely a contextualized retelling, or at least appropriation, of the gospel story. After some Google searches, I wasn't surprised to find that Rowling confessed to being a Christian. Indeed, there were Christian themes scattered throughout the series, but she believed that these themes were especially explicit in the last book.[3] Does the global fan base hear the echoes of the gospel in the Harry Potter world? Of course, in this case, the author consciously incorporated Christian themes, but in so many other seemingly Christless incidents and places, Christ haunts the creativities, narratives, and sentiments as Flannery O'Connor has once articulated.[4]

---

[2]See, for example, Jonathan Hill, *What has Christianity Ever Done for Us?: How It Shaped the Modern World* (Downers Grove, IL: InterVarsity Press, 2005); Alvin J. Schmidt, *Under the Influence: How Christianity Transformed Civilization* (Grand Rapids, MI: Zondervan, 2001); Rodney Stark, *The Victory of Reason: How Christianity Led to Freedom, Capitalism, and Western Success* (New York: Random House, 2005). The weakness of these books and others like it is that they often minimize, ignore, or whitewash the evils that have been perpetuated in the name of Christianity.

[3]Jonathan Petre, "J K Rowling: 'Christianity Inspired Harry Potter'," accessed March 12, 2018, www .telegraph.co.uk/culture/books/fictionreviews/3668658/J-K-Rowling-Christianity-inspired -Harry-Potter.html.

[4]Flannery O'Connor, *Mystery and Manners: Occasional Prose* (New York: Farrar, Straus and Giroux, 1970), 44.

The hijacking of the gospel in the so-called Christian West has its infamous historical examples, like the Crusades, the Spanish Inquisition, con-
quistadors in the Americas, chattel slavery, Nazi Germany, South African
apartheid, and the Ku Klux Klan. In all these cases, Christian rhetoric was
distorted and hijacked for nefarious ends. In one sense, they were using the
Lord's name in vain and have nothing to do with the gospel of grace. But in
another sense, Christianity cannot be so easily exonerated. Theologically
speaking, the church and "Christianity" as a human religion are always ca-
pable of great evil, not just in their moral failures but especially in their
"righteous devotion." Again, in the good, bad, and ugly, gospel "witnesses"
are all around Western culture, from Disney and Pixar movies to NRA ads,
and even atheistic secularism.

So far, the salutary and deleterious sides of the gospel-context interaction
are quite explicit and conscious. However, besides these examples, invisible
dynamics mostly unconscious and implicit must also be named. This invisible dimension is the conflation of society and church in what we call
Christendom, where faith was a socialization process for much of Western
Christianity history.[5] Within Christendom, the church could wield worldly
power with wealth and prestige. The witness of the desert mothers and fathers, and the monastic orders throughout history, bring a counter witness
against this worldly church. The amalgamation of the gospel with Western
society began with the church gaining worldly legitimacy and power through
Constantine and the Christianizing of the Roman Empire, and it continued
with medieval Christendom up to our present day.[6]

Missionary history. These positive and negative, explicit and implicit dimensions apply to missionary and colonial history as well. The fact that we
must discuss missions and colonialism together in one historical narrative
already betrays the nature of this problem. Christianity's first encounter with
Asia is quite early in certain places. For example, according to strong tradition, the apostle Thomas introduced the gospel to India as early as the first

---

[5]Jehu Hanciles, *Beyond Christendom: Globalization, African Migration, and the Transformation of
the West* (Maryknoll, NY: Orbis, 2008), 84.

[6]Narrow arguments by Leithart, for example, about the authenticity of Constantine's conversion
and his well-meaning intentions miss the forest by focusing on a tree. Peter J. Leithart, *Defending
Constantine: The Twilight of an Empire and the Dawn of Christendom* (Downers Grove, IL: Inter-
Varsity, 2010).

century. Alexandrian scholar Pantaenus, acknowledged as "the greatest Christian teacher of his age" with Clement and Origen as his disciples, visited India in the second century.[7] In China, a Nestorian missionary first reached the capital in 635, although Jesuit missions in the sixteenth century found no Christians there and had to start over, so to speak.[8] Thus, except for the Mar Thomas church in South India with its apostolic origin, Asian Christianity found its roots with Western missionaries—although the significance of Asian ministers and evangelists, who are often erased and sidelined, must be fully affirmed.

The faith of Western missionaries was infused with the cultural foundations of their Western context. Particularly, the Christendom mindset identified the church with society and thus also with a particular geography, that is, the idea of a Christian land and its civilization. Even though David Livingston was a missionary to Africa, his argument for the inseparability of the "two pioneers of civilization—Christianity and commerce" represents the kind of mindset that I am highlighting.[9] To be sure, Livingston was seeking the benefit of the Africans in arguing that development of commerce will fight the slave trade. The problem lies not with his intentions, but the presuppositions of Christendom with its colonizing mentality. And their gospel work was done under the shadow of colonialism, which promoted a particular kind of Christianity that could not be easily delineated from power, privilege, culture, so-called civilization, and commerce.

We can highlight some of the high and low points of the Western missionary movement, especially around the introduction of Christianity. However, more than these particular details, which are significant, the overall presupposition of Christendom is what we should keep in mind. That does not take away from the profound commitment and devotion of these missionaries, but it does remind us of the broader systemic and cultural waters in which they were formed and had to navigate.

The Jesuit missionaries of the sixteenth century working in China and Japan are well-known for the innovative ways in which they adopted

---

[7]Samuel Hugh Moffett, *A History of Christianity in Asia*, vol. 1, *Beginning to 1500* (Maryknoll, NY: Orbis, 1998), 25, 266.

[8]Moffett, *History of Christianity in Asia*, 1:288.

[9]David Livingston, "Lecture I," in *Dr. Livingstone's Cambridge Lectures*, compiled by William Monk (London: Bell and Daldy, 1858), 21.

indigenous customs over ecclesiastical tradition for their evangelism. However, on closer study there are many troubling realities of their mission. Their accommodationist attitude in Japan and China were more out of ex- pedience and not out of deeper theological principles. Believing that "Af- ricans, Indians and the people of Indonesia were inferior to Europeans," they made those converts adopt Portuguese names and Western clothing.[10] The Japanese and Chinese were "White," and therefore commanded a level of respect for what was deemed their intellectual and spiritual capacity.[11] These Jesuits worked out of a racial imagination that was pervasive to their world. Matteo Ricci's work, in all its achievements, must also be understood within this framework of expediency and racial ideology. Of course, given the po- litical strictures of the time, their endeavors toward a non-European faith in China are still worth affirming. Even this accommodationist mission was an anomaly in greater Christendom, and we see the later rejection of it from a Catholic magisterium in the Rites Controversy, where Confucian ancestor veneration was declared incompatible to Christian faith.

In the Philippines, the harsh Spanish conquistador approach to Christian presence stands in contrast to the voice of Dominican bishop Domingo de Salazar, who was named "the de las Casas of the Philippines."[12] Salazar accused Christian Spanish rulers for being even more oppressive than the Muslim ones who controlled the southern islands of the Philippines. In this case, both colonizers and missionaries are so-called Christians, one oppressing and the other protesting the oppression.

We find a similar juxtaposition in Vietnam. The French Jesuit Alexander de Rhodes, like his Jesuit compadres, worked within the political limits in China and Japan, incorporating principles of inculturation, pushing for in- digenous clergy, and respecting local cultures and customs.[13] Rhodes's work on perfecting the Vietnamese alphabet (*quốc ngữ*) later helped empower the Vietnamese against French colonialism. However, though we may single him out as an exemplar, we must also acknowledge the complicity of later French

---

[10]Andrew C. Ross, *A Vision Betrayed: The Jesuits in Japan and China, 1542–1742* (Maryknoll, NY: Orbis, 1994), 204.

[11]Ross, *A Vision Betrayed*, 205.

[12]Moffett, *History of Christianity in Asia*, 1:154.

[13]Peter C. Phan, *Mission and Catechesis: Alexandre de Rhodes and Inculturation in Seventeenth- Century Vietnam* (Maryknoll, NY: Orbis, 1998), 193.

missionaries with colonial powers. Even as these missionaries sometimes questioned the encroachment of the state on their work, the idea "that Catholic missions and colonial rule were complementary parts of a single French endeavor to bring the benefits of Western civilization to the less fortunate" were a common understanding of not just the French, but even some Vietnamese Catholics as well.[14]

The extent of the problem with Christendom lies in the Eurocentric and missionary-centric narratives of Christian history, where Asian Christian leaders are marginalized or rendered part of the nameless indigenous masses. Sebastian and Kirsteen Kim, who go beyond the commonly presupposed Western missionary-centric view of Korean church history, speak to this problem. They point out that the "early recorded history of Korean churches is colonial mission history, that is, the story of Western missionary initiatives towards Korea rather than about Korean reception of the gospel and agency in its spread."[15]

American evangelicalism. I now turn to White mainstream American evangelicalism, where a majority of Asian American Christians have grown up. In the US, even with its separation of church and state, the qualities of Christendom have persisted. Darrell Guder talks about a functional Christendom in the US where "traditions, attitudes, and social structures" worked together to privilege the church and its moral influence in society.[16] Consequently, we now find widespread support for Christian nationalism as a fearful reaction to the demise of functional Christendom. The heritage of Christendom conflates faith and European culture, or White culture, giving it privilege, universal legitimacy, and power. In the discussion below, while we discuss evangelicalism in the US, the global influence that this movement has beyond its borders should be kept in mind as well.

We have seen above why the positive/negative contribution approach to the influence of Christianity is misguided and myopic. In describing the structural or implicit features of American evangelicalism, Soong-Chan Rah

---

[14]Charles Keith, *Catholic Vietnam: A Church from Empire to Nation* (University of California Press, 2012), 65.

[15]Sebastian C. H. Kim and Kirsteen Kim, *A History of Korean Christianity* (New York: Cambridge University Press, 2015), 2-3.

[16]Darrell Guder, *Missional Church: A Vision for the Sending of the Church in North America* (Grand Rapids, MI: Eerdmans, 1998), 6, 49.

diagnoses a condition of "western White cultural captivity" with individualism, consumerism, and racism as its defining features.[17] Amos Yong further explicates the methodological aspects of evangelicalism as its presumably "a-historical, a-cultural and even a-contextual" commitments.[18] Evangelicalism's modernist delusion of universalistic and objective theology above the fray of history, culture, and context is rooted in its historical beginnings. As a reaction to liberalism's capitulation to modernism's challenges to what they understood to be scriptural authority, fundamentalism ironically cozied up to modern arguments such as inerrancy and reasonability of faith. In a sense, by playing the modernist game to defend the faith, evangelicals became captive to it. Because of this oxymoronic unawareness that they are captive to modernism even as they try to fight it, Gary Dorrien describes early evangelicals as "Antimodern Modernizers."[19] Of course, to these Antimodern Modernizers, postmodernism looked like the devil, not because of the gospel but because of their modernism. Along with this complicated relationship with modernism, evangelicalism was born out of a search to recover intellectual respectability and cultural relevance and prestige.[20] We might understand this fixation over implicit modernism and relevance as, in a sense, the DNA of evangelicalism and the reason why it fails to see how it is repeatedly complicit with aspects of the majority culture, whether individualism, consumerism, or racism as Rah has noted. Our current evangelical failure to resist White normativity and the rise of Trumpism should be understood in light of these dynamics, along with the Christendom mentality that it inherited and had no critical lens to identify.

Whether it be historical Christendom in Western culture and how this tradition has impacted Christianity as it was introduced in Asia, or evangelicalism's functional Christendom and modern captivities, the majority of Asian American Christians have been raised ingesting these influences one way or another. Like the elements in the previous chapters,

---

[17]Soong-Chan Rah, *The Next Evangelicalism: Freeing the Church from Western Cultural Captivity* (Downers Grove, IL: InterVarsity Press, 2009).

[18]Amos Yong, *The Future of Evangelical Theology: Soundings from the Asian American Diaspora* (Downers Grove, IL: InterVarsity Press, 2014), 114.

[19]Gary Dorrien, *The Remaking of Evangelical Theology* (Louisville, KY: Westminster John Knox, 1998), 13.

[20]Dorrien, *Remaking of Evangelical Theology,* 49.

all these have been in our waters and have become a part of who are. Thus, Asian Americans join all other Americans in needing a greater awareness of these historical American realities that continue to distort the faith that we all share.

The three themes of Western intellectual tradition, missionary history, and White American evangelicalism could all be a focus of a much longer discussion. My goal here is to introduce some ways for us to name and own them as part of Asian American Christianity. There is a particular way in which Asian Americans uniquely experience the broader American culture, namely the concerns of nonrepresentation or an Orientalist misrepresentation. In the second half of this chapter, we turn to this critical concern of cultural presentation and seek to develop a theology to address it.

A THEOLOGY OF CULTURAL REPRESENTATION

While watching Korean American celebrity chef David Chang's Netflix show *Ugly Delicious*, I felt impressed, inspired, and stimulated by how Chang raised global, transnational, multiethnic, and multicultural questions about authenticity, appropriation, identity, and racism all through the lens of delicious food. It didn't hurt that Chang, a Korean American man who hails from Northern Virginia like me, especially stressed an Asian American perspective. I felt so visible, so seen, and so affirmed in my Asian Americanness.

Asian Americans have now been part of American culture and history for a long while. Over the years, to name just a few, there have been the first Asian American astronaut Ellison Onizuka, novelist Amy Tan, fashion designer Vera Wang, architect I. M. Pei, figure skater Kristi Yamaguchi, cellist Yo-Yo Ma, and Pulitzer-winning writers Jhumpa Lahiri and Viet Nguyen. Before them, we may talk about Anna May Wong, the first Asian American actress in Hollywood, or Sammy Lee and Victoria Manalo Draves, the first Asian American male and female gold medalist Olympians. And we must remember Kamala Harris, the first Black, the first Asian American, the first female vice president! This is just a tiny sample of the many Asian American contributions to American cultural history. On the one hand, these significant contributions are often invisible even to Asian Americans, because we were taught not to see them through our White-normative education and mainstream culture. At times, because Asian Americans have often been so thoroughly socialized to White normativity, we do not want to see ourselves like them, as Asian Americans, lest we break the illusion of being honorary Whites. On the other hand, while there are all kinds of cultural contributions, we also recognize that Asian Americans are misrepresented or not represented at all.

Media theorists George Gerbner and Larry Gross argue that a lack of cultural representation means "symbolic annihilation."[21] This symbolic erasure has real-life consequences for the perception and understanding of people of color. With protests like #OscarsSoWhite, people of color are resisting their symbolic annihilation in mainstream popular media. And along with the years of alternative programming created for digital spaces like YouTube, more recent inclusion of diverse bodies and voices in network TV shows and Hollywood movies offer promising signs of changes to come. This concern of cultural representation has largely been limited to the sociopolitical sphere, lacking explicit theological underpinnings or implications. In the rest of this chapter, I will gesture toward a theology of cultural representation. Given the limited space here, only a rough outline of what this could look like will be presented.

There is a long history of racist representation or misrepresentation of Asian Americans in Hollywood and other mass media. At the root, Orientalism, which conceptualizes the East by "its strangeness, difference, exotic sensuousness, eccentricity, backwardness, silent indifference, feminine penetrability, uncivilized nature, and the like," as well as being "static, frozen, and fixed eternally," ideologically fuels anti-Asian and anti-Asian American racism.[22] A common and broad expression of this racism is the concept of yellow peril, posing Asians and Asian Americans as "threatening to take over, invade, or otherwise negatively Asianize the US nation and its society."[23] This fear of the unassimilable horde from Asia was the basis of the Chinese Exclusion Act of 1882, the first piece of legislation to single out a specific nationality for exclusion. What began with just Chinese nationals was later

---

[21]George Gerbner and Larry Gross, "Living with Television: The Violence Profile," *Journal of Communication* 26, no. 2 (Spring 1976): 172-99.

[22]Namsoon Kang, "Who/What is Asian? A Postcolonial Theological Reading of Orientalism and Neo-Orientalism," in *Postcolonial Theologies*, ed. Keller et al. (St. Louis: Chalice Press, 2004), 102.

[23]Kent A. Ono and Vincent N. Pham, *Asian Americans and the Media* (Malden, MA: Polity, 2009), 25.

applied to all Asians until its full repeal in 1965. This historic period includes one of the largest mass lynchings in US history, the Chinese massacre of 1871, where seventeen to twenty Chinese immigrants were hanged.

In terms of popular media, the logic of Asian American misrepresentation is yellowface. Kent Ono and Vincent Pham articulate two different versions of this logic, the explicit and implicit. Explicit yellowface is when a non-Asian or non-Asian American plays the role of an Asian or an Asian American, wearing heavy makeup and speaking some imagined Asian accent. One of the more notorious examples is Mickey Rooney's Mr. Yunioshi in *Breakfast at Tiffany's*. Hank Azaria playing Apu in *The Simpsons* is another, although in this case with voicing an animated character, there is no face per se. Implicit yellowface is the essentializing and typecasting of Asian and Asian American performances to some stereotypical standard of racial authenticity, which is a mocking caricature. Long Duk Dong in *Sixteen Candles* is a well-known example, although there are many others. Besides yellowface, another kind of toxic practice is whitewashing, where a White actor is cast for an Asian or Asian American character. Examples include *Ghost in the Shell* with Scarlett Johansson as Major, in *Aloha* with Emma Stone as Allison Ng, or in *Star Trek: Into Darkness* with Benedict Cumberbatch playing Khan Noonien Singh.

Racist representations of Asian Americans or any other people of color cannot be a case of "equal opportunity racism," as some comedians like to argue, the reason being that there is such a limited and narrow representation of them in general.[24] Racist and stereotypically grotesque portrayals are not balanced out by the hundreds of fair and humanizing roles that White people receive in the media. Through the forces of socialization and cognitive framing, these popular cultural representations, especially in movies and TV, create, reproduce, and sustain racial ideologies, specifically that of White normativity.[25]

I would like to lay out three main explanations for Asian American invisibility, namely the perpetual foreigner trope, the model minority myth, and the Black/White binary paradigm. I will return to these concepts again in the next chapter on race.

---

[24]Michael Morris, "Standard White: Dismantling White Normativity," *California Law Review* 104 (2016): 955.

[25]Michael Omi, "In Living Color: Race and American Culture," in *Signs of Life in the USA: Readings on Popular Culture for Writers*, 7th ed., ed. Sonia Maasik and Jack Solomon (Boston: Bedford; St. Martin's, 2012), 628.

First, the *perpetual foreigner* or *forever foreigner* trope lies at the root of Asian American invisibility.[26] Ignoring the one hundred and seventy years of Asian American history, Asian Americans are asked incessantly where they are from. Neither Temple City, California, (where I live now) nor Annandale, Virginia, (where I grew up) is apparently the right answer. For generations, Asian Americans have been represented as Asians living in America rather than Americans of Asian descent. When discussing the lack of Asian American representation in popular culture, one is often countered by the protestation that "in China, they make movies with all Chinese actors. So what is the problem with making American movies with all Americans?" The assumption, of course, is that Americans are White, or perhaps Black, but certainly not Asian. If Asian Americans are precluded from ever being true Americans, the question of Asian American representation is a non-starter.

Second is the *model minority myth*, which imagines Asian Americans as well-assimilated, successful racial minorities, unlike Black Americans or Hispanic Americans. Created and propagated during the Cold War by the White establishment, this myth helps to proclaim the United States as a racial meritocracy, touting Asian Americans as hard workers achieving the American Dream through their diligent labor.[27] In this line of thinking, being accepted as true Americans means becoming *honorary Whites*, or *pseudo-Whites*, or "one of us." And if you have membership in Whiteness then you do not need further representation, because as a human being you are already included in White representation.

Third, the *Black/White binary paradigm* of race in America renders Asian Americans invisible, along with Hispanic Americans and Native Americans. The Black/White binary paradigm will be discussed at length in the next chapter, but for our purposes here, it means that racial realities in the US are simplified and distilled to the Black and White master categories.[28] If the *forever foreigner* trope labels Asian Americans as simply Asian and never

[26]Mia Tuan, *Forever Foreigners or Honorary Whites? The Asian Ethnic Experience Today* (New Brunswick, NJ: Rutgers University Press, 2005).

[27]See Ellen D. Wu, *The Color of Success: Asian Americans and the Origins of the Model Minority* (Princeton, NJ: Princeton University Press, 2015).

[28]Juan F. Perea, "The Black/White Binary Paradigm of Race: The 'Normal Science' of American Racial Thought," *California Law Review* 85, no. 5 (1997): 1213-58, https://lawcat.berkeley.edu/record/1115988.

American, and the *model minority* myth states that Asian Americans are represented by White people, the *Black/White binary paradigm* reasons that when Black Americans are represented, all people of color are represented as well. The reasoning here is that race is split along a binary between Black or White, and the experiences of people of color can all be reduced to various understandings of Blackness.

In light of this structure of misrepresentation and lack of representation, Asian American invisibility is the struggle of Asian Americans to be represented in our full humanity. In terms of doctrinal locus, a theology of cultural representation could be rooted in theological anthropology, with the question of the *imago Dei* in defining humanity. Here I propose three elements that much be included and developed in theological anthropology for our purposes.

First, we have the question of the common dignity and worth of all human beings. In that regard, *imago Dei* must be identified as something more basic to our humanity than a feature that can be narrowly defined by one culture. In the history of doctrine, the *imago Dei* has been defined as morality, religiosity, intellect, or reason, all of which are culturally defined. The history of colonialism and racism reveals the ugly record of dehumanization leading to subjugation and even genocide.

In her book *What It Means to Be Human*, Joanna Bourke shows in the Western imagination how humanity or mankind "never included all humans. At various times, slaves, women, religious minorities, Jews and actors (on the grounds that they pretended to be someone else) were set outside" of this category.[29] Bourke explains that humanity, a highly volatile and highly policed concept, often applied only to well-off heterosexual men with white skins and Western bodies.[30] We might naively assume that the common and shared humanity of all people on earth is a basic given. However, given recent incidents where Mexicans have been deemed "animals," Black Americans (including children) demonized by police officers, and Muslims being regarded as less than fully human by many Americans, our complacency can easily transform into complicity.[31] During the coronavirus pandemic, those

---

[29]Joanna Bourke, *What It Means to be Human: Historical Reflections from the 1800s to the Present* (Berkeley, CA: Counterpoint, 2011), 136.

[30]Bourke, *What It Means to be Human*, 136.

[31]Vann R. Newkirk II, "The Real Risk of Trump's Dehumanization of Immigrants," *Atlantic Monthly*, May 19, 2018, www.theatlantic.com/politics/archive/2018/05/the-real-risk-of-trumps

with East Asian phenotypes were reduced to a virus, waking up many to the reality of dehumanization and the importance of activism.

Sidestepping these landmines, we might look to Karl Barth's relational understanding of the *imago Dei* as fellow-humanity or humanity-with.[32] Though his idea of human unity and gender difference is grounded in some patriarchal reasoning, we may still follow the general features of his proposal. For Barth, the relational divine image is not a static substance, but rather an activity, a task, and a responsibility to fellow humanity.[33] In the encounter among humanity, there is a "mutual recognition that each is essential to the other."[34] It is this recognition that we are interested in. This dynamic understanding of the *imago Dei* is not dependent on any particular human traits. Human dignity and worth are still afforded those who lack any sense of morality, religiosity, or intellect.

Second, we must recognize human difference or particularity. Specifically, for the sake of our current argument, we must acknowledge bodily difference. In the history of doctrine, the doctrine of the *imago Dei* often did not include the body. The divine image in humanity has often been located in a disembodied morality, religiosity, or reason. Within the Reformed tradition, John Calvin in his *Institutes* (I.XV.3) states rather passively that he "shall not contend too strongly" if anyone wishes to include the body, as long as "the image of God, which is seen or glows in these outward marks, is spiritual."[35] In a later development, Dutch theologian Herman Bavinck affirms the whole person as the image of God, including the human body as "an essential component of that image," reasoning his view on the incarnation.[36] Furthermore, extrapolating the logic of humanity in male and female and further human multiplication through history, Bavinck believes:

-dehumanization-of-immigrants/560762/; Damien Cave, "Officer Darren Wilson's Grand Jury Testimony in Ferguson, Mo., Shooting," *New York Times*, November 25, 2014, www.nytimes.com/interactive/2014/11/25/us/darren-wilson-testimony-ferguson-shooting.html; Nour Kteily and Emile Bruneau, "Americans See Muslims as Less than Human," *Washington Post*, September 18, 2015, www.washingtonpost.com/posteverything/wp/2015/09/18/americans-see-muslims-as-less-than-human-no-wonder-ahmed-was-arrested/.

[32]Karl Barth, *Church Dogmatics*, vol. 3, part 2, *The Doctrine of Creation* (1960), 317.

[33]Barth, *Church Dogmatics*, III/2, 269.

[34]Barth, *Church Dogmatics*, III/2, 271.

[35]John Calvin, *Institutes of Christian Religion* (Philadelphia: Westminster John Knox, 1960), 186.

[36]Herman Bavinck, *Reformed Dogmatics*, vol. 2, *God and Creation* (Grand Rapids, MI: Baker, 2004), 560.

Not the man alone, nor the man and woman together, but only the whole humanity is the fully developed image of God, his children, his offering. The image of God is much too rich for it to be fully realized in a single human being, however, richly gifted that human being maybe.[37]

Bavinck's affirmation of the unity and diversity of humanity, and specifically his inclusion of the body in his doctrine of the *imago Dei*, helped fund B. B. Keet's argument against apartheid in South Africa.[38] Thus, we can see the ethical implication of including the body in our understanding of the *imago Dei*. Yet Bavinck, as with Abraham Kuyper before him, used a cultural Darwinism to denigrate colonized people of color.[39] For Bavinck, race was technically not the issue. Rather it just happened that non-Europeans were not developed culturally or civilized like Europeans.

So, the problem can be not just our bodies, but the specific aspect of our embodied and encultured existence that we are dealing with. What I mean by this is that the categories with which we identify ourselves, and other categories we use, change over time. Two hundred and fifty years ago, there was no American identity, because the United States did not exist. Fifty years ago, there was no panethnic Asian American identity. While we often look to Pentecost for inspiration about how the Holy Spirit can overcome racial division, race, as we understand it in terms of color oriented toward Whiteness or non-Whiteness, did not exist at that time. However, to assert that race does not exist because it does not have a basis in Scripture would miss the point, which is to apprehend faithfulness given the particular situation in which we find ourselves.

With that question in mind, lastly or crucially, this embodied *imago Dei* should be thought of dynamically or situationally, meaning that instead of an eternally fixed sense, we need to attend to our experience and identity as features in God's presence. Again, looking to Karl Barth, we can think of our human particularity in terms of our particular context as having "the

---

[37] Bavinck, *Reformed Dogmatics*, 2:577.

[38] George Harinck, "Wipe Out Lines of Division (Not Distinctions): Bennie Keet, Neo-Calvinism and the Struggle against Apartheid," *Journal of Reformed Theology* 11 (2017), 81-98.

[39] Abraham Kuyper, *Lectures on Calvinism: Six Lectures from the Stone Foundation Lectures Delivered at Princeton University* (Grands Rapids, MI: Eerdmans, 1970), 22-23. For Bavinck and Keet, culture still becomes a euphemism for a thinly veiled racism. Harinck unfortunately misses this point in his understanding of the nature of racism. Harinck, "Wipe Out Lines of Division (Not Distinctions)," 84-85.

character of an allotted framework in which [we have] to express [our] own distinctive obedience."[40] Barth affirms regarding these particularities that "it is not accidentally or in vain but meaningfully and purposively that God has called himself and . . . his people to serve Him in this determination and with this outlook, background and origin."[41] Within the context of the divine command, the particularity of humanity is "not mere disposition of nature or fate," but "really is important, and has therefore to be honoured and loved."[42] This discipleship-orientation means that in our particular time, place, bodies, culture, and context, we are to seek to be Christ followers.

However, Barth sets two caveats. First, every aspect of our humanity must be submitted to divine lordship and dealt with critically.[43] They must not be a *telos* in themselves.[44] Second, all aspects of our human particularity should be understood as *reversible, fluid,* and *removable.*[45] For Barth, our particularities are not part of the created order, and therefore there is no essence at the core of our differences. While these human features are all significant in our situations, the categories themselves are not eternal. Barth would say, historically speaking, that nationalities, ethnicities, languages, and even racial categories are reversible, fluid, and removable.

We should not be too idealistic about this dynamic idea of a *reversible, fluid,* and *removable* human particularity in the short term and be misguided into supporting naive post-racialism or simplistic colorblindness. However, Barth's actualistic view of human particularities assists us in avoiding the trap of authenticity. Kwame Anthony Appiah explains how a politics of identity and recognition could produce existential straitjackets, what he calls the "Medusa Syndrome," as it could turn you into stone.[46] In a similar line of thought, Victor Anderson critiques a totalizing ontological Blackness as idolatrous.[47] Especially for Asian Americans, where identity involves

---

[40]Karl Barth, *Church Dogmatics*, vol. 3, part 4, *The Doctrine of Creation* (Edinburgh: T&T Clark, 1961), 288.

[41]Barth, *Church Dogmatics*, III/4, 292.

[42]Barth, *Church Dogmatics*, III/4, 293.

[43]Barth, *Church Dogmatics*, III/4, 287.

[44]Barth, *Church Dogmatics*, III/4, 290.

[45]Barth, *Church Dogmatics*, III/4, 299-303.

[46]Kwame Anthony Appiah, *The Ethics of Identity* (Princeton: Princeton University Press, 2005), 110.

[47]Victor Anderson, *Beyond Ontological Blackness: An Essay on African American Religious and Cultural Criticism* (New York: Continuum, 1995), 15.

complexity, dynamism, and hybridity, Appiah's concerns resonate. For Asian Americans, an essentialistic identity means an Orientalist stereotype.

More practically speaking, while historic and systemic forces of racism, sexism, classism, and others will persist, the particular witness for justice will vary depending on the situation and context. Forces of oppression and marginalization are protean, lying, killing, and destroying in ever-new forms. While Native Americans, Black Americans, Hispanic Americans, Asian Americans, and others struggle under systemic forces, there are those groups who suffered in the past but no longer face the same kind of racialized oppression, including German and Irish Americans for example. Dynamics of gender, sexuality, and class are also ever evolving. Interestingly, Barth's approach not only allows but forces us to discern with God's wisdom the particular lines of dehumanization in a context or situation. Even in concerns of representation, an actualistic identity means that we must be attentive to God's voice and command, lest our struggle become an abstract ideology, a different lord in the guise of justice.

In my particular context, characterized by the historical and structural forces of symbolic annihilation of people of color in popular culture, my Asian American identity matters. This conclusion is a discernment of God's command in my particular situation of discipleship. With Barth's actualistic insights and nuances in mind, struggle for cultural representation is believing that God has created all humanity in the divine image.

Given this understanding of humanity, this issue of cultural representation for people of color in the US is about resisting the powers and principalities of this world. In the next chapter, we will address why it is important to have a robust understanding of evil and sin that goes beyond the personal to the communal, structural, and societal when we address racism. How we must name, understand, and resist these evil forces will be covered in the larger context of kingdom life and witness.

On the one hand, we must name and resist the ideologies within our culture that symbolically annihilate anyone within our society. Our consumption of media must be critical and reflective to see what is erased or distorted. On the other hand, we must take up the creation of culture that is characterized by humanity in the complexity that we have articulated above. Our task of culture should be "specifically human in character," meaning that doing the work should affirm our own humanity as well as serve others in their humanity.[48] Beyond humanity, our work should serve all creation as well.

While I am arguing for Asian American representation here, there is a direct connection between properly seeing ourselves and the ability to see our neighbors who we are called to love. During World War II, Japanese Americans (not only foreign-born Japanese, but even American-born citizens of Japanese descent) were put in concentration camps and given loyalty tests. The excuse given was one of military necessity, which was later fully debunked as a mere cover for hysteria and racism. After the camps, those who did not seek to escape their Japanese heritage, but sought peace with it, become vigorous advocates for civil rights and justice. Japanese American voices have especially advocated for Muslim Americans post-9/11 and up through the recent Muslim ban enacted by the Trump administration. Because they did not ignore or repress aspects of themselves that they didn't feel presentable, they did not avert their gaze from the parallel struggles of Muslim Americans facing racial profiling and violent attacks.

During the First World War, German Americans were racially profiled and discriminated against. Some of them were lynched. The German American community had to repress and abandon their Germanness for the sake of their Americanness. Without conspicuous phenotypical markers, they were able to abandon distinguishing features for safety. What if Americans of German descent remembered and saw themselves in their more recent immigrant neighbors, those who are marginalized and targeted?

There is a direct correlation between how we see ourselves in God's presence and how we see our neighbors. Becoming reconciled to all aspects of who we are has deep consequences for our ability to see our neighbors, our vocation as God's ambassadors, and our calling to serve as instruments of God's peace.

Our identity and self-understanding are a product of our interaction with the world around us. In the next chapter we will see how forces of racialization must be acknowledged and engaged to make full sense of ourselves and our experiences.

---

[48]Barth, *Church Dogmatics*, III/4, 527.

7

RACIALIZATION AND NAVIGATING THE BINARY

Race is a master category—a fundamental concept that has profoundly shaped, and continues to shape, the history, polity, economic structure, and culture of the United States.

MICHAEL OMI AND HOWARD WINANT

"I DON'T UNDERSTAND how early Chinese American experience has anything to do with me," remarked a Cambodian American student whose family came as refugees in the 1980s. Before their arrival in the US, her family, like the majority of Cambodian Americans, traced their background to Cambodia. What connection do the experiences of Chinese Americans or Japanese Americans in this country have to her own history, especially given the Japanese occupation of Cambodia during World War II? I have heard different versions of this same question from Asian Americans of different ethnic heritages.

On a related note, I have also heard many Asian Americans and others generalize Asian America as a community of first- and second-generation immigrants. This stereotype is often employed to excuse the lack of Asian American history. I also often hear people ask why Americans of many different Asian ethnicities are all lumped together as Asian American. How is the Asian American label not simply a crude Orientalist stereotype, or at

---

Epigraph: Michael Omi and Howard Winant, *Racial Formation in the United States*, 3rd ed. (New York: Routledge, 2015), 106.

best a grouping monopolized by Chinese or Korean Americans and ignoring the particularities of other ethnic groups? The specific cultural and colonial histories of, for example, Filipino Americans are often rendered invisible among the larger Asian American grouping, despite being the third largest Asian American ethnic group after Chinese Americans and Indian Americans.[1] This just will not do.

I confess that I too have shared similar sentiments and concerns in the past. However, I have come to realize that this line of thinking ignores the reality of racialization in the United States. While my family's history in the US begins in the 1980s, the history of Asian America goes back one hundred and seventy years. This racial reality does not ignore specific ethnic histories, but without it our lives as Asian Americans are difficult or impossible to comprehend. This racialization is more readily accepted for White and Black Americans. Donald Trump, as a third-generation German American on his father's side and second-generation Scottish American on his mother's side, is still allowed to claim the full history of the United States as his own. This is the dynamic of racialization: we are categorized and share a common history with others in that racial category, despite personally or even culturally sharing little with them.

During my MDiv years at Princeton Seminary over twenty years ago, I remember protesting to Professor Sang Hyun Lee in his Asian American theology class. I complained that he was making too much of racism in general and anti-Asian American racism in particular, because his whole theological approach was based on racism and the liminal experience of Asian Americans. My critique back then was based on the seemingly diminishing presence of racism and also the limited role of racism in the struggle of many Asian Americans. Indeed, unlike the immigrant generation, the felt struggle of my more assimilated generation was a cultural tension with the power dominance of the first generation in immigrant churches, not White people in society.

In the past, there were those who too believed that discrimination is more a problem of the immigrant generation, with their heavy accents and assimilation struggles. Roy Sano describes how over fifty years ago, early second- and third-generation Asian Americans believed that if they assimilated well,

---

[1]Kevin L. Nadal, "The Brown Asian American Movement: Advocating for South Asian, Southeast Asian, and Filipino American Communities," *Asian American Policy Review* 29 (2019): 2-11, 95

they would be fully accepted as Americans, unlike the first generation.[2] However, they were mistaken. Instead of transitioning from immigrants to Americans, meaning White Americans, they would become racial minority Americans, or Americans of color. When later waves of Asian immigrants came not knowing the lessons of the past, they again hoped to become full Americans after shedding their immigrant status.

For some second-generation Asian Americans, their immediate pressure points might come from Asian culture and their interaction with the first-generation, but our whole Asian American experience is still grounded and framed in race and structural racism. Racism is in the water of American culture just like other aspects of the AAQ. We might simply have been overlooking it all along because we did not have the lens to see it. Through years of working in a predominately White institution and also specifically representing Asian Americans, I have seen, experienced, and learned much about how anti-Asian racism works, much of which could be described along the lines of microaggression themes that I describe below.

A couple of years ago, a senior administrator in higher education who was a person of color said that people of color face more racism as they move up in rank in a predominately White institution. The idea is that White structures are okay with inclusion of people of color as long as they can mentor or support those people. When those people of color become supervisors and high-level administrators, these structures begin to treat them very differently. Along these lines, theologian Jung Young Lee points out that it is when marginal people try to move centers of power that they will experience the most marginalization.[3] Those who stay in ethnic enclaves do not experience as much racism because they remain in the margins. Similarly, those who suppress, reject, or abandon marginalized parts of themselves might experience less racism at the centers of power as well. Of course, the question is, What is the cost of this "success"?

In any case, I was becoming more racially aware when the Black Lives Matter movement began to rise. With report after report of dead Black

[2]Roy Sano, "Shifts in Reading the Bible: Hermeneutical Moves Among Asian Americans," in *Semeia 90/91: The Bible in Asian America*, ed. Tat-siong Benny Liew and Gale A. Yee (Atlanta: Society of Biblical Literature, 2002), 107.

[3]Jung Young Lee, *Marginality: The Key to Multicultural Theology* (Minneapolis: Fortress, 1995), 45.

people, even young children, there was no room for lengthy contemplation and a laissez faire approach to learning about racialization in the US. In this case, maintaining neutrality meant being okay with a damaging and violent status quo. Furthermore, the Trump era has been a rude awakening to anyone who shared my early naiveté regarding race in the US. The White supremacy and nationalism that came out of the shadows, prodded by Trump's ideological rhetoric and policies, reflected the deeply held convictions and fears of many.

Returning to our Asian American Quadrilateral, as with all the previous dimensions like Asian heritage, migration experience, and American culture, by *racialization* we are simply naming what's in the water we swim in, a set of assumptions that we breathe in and out every single day that, in fact, has become a part of our being. Like the previous three factors, how and in what sense this dimension of the AAQ impacts us in our experience and personal history varies widely. Also, like other dimensions, though this racial reality is always present in every situation, the degree to which it is salient must be discerned. There could always be other factors that are more pressing and immediate to an issue at hand. In any case, the key is to make sure that we are aware and conscious of this dimension like others, to have race as one of the tools in our toolbox for understanding our lives, identity, and experiences.

As I mentioned in the previous chapter about Asian American invisibility, the reason why racialization is often ignored when discussing the Asian American experience is that often we are not even considered Americans, but rather Asian foreigners living in America. This is termed the perpetual foreigner or forever foreigner myth. In this line of thinking, Asian Americans cannot really have a racial experience because that's reserved for racial minorities like Black Americans. Therefore, our entire experience—our economic success, our mental health, our intergenerational conflicts, and so on—must be interpreted through our cultural heritage. This is quite reductionistic and leads to a distortive reality.

In this chapter, I focus on Asian American experiences of race, racism, and racialization and what it means to seek God's kingdom of justice and righteousness. First, I will briefly lay out the history of the racialization of Asian Americans, along with the various ways we have and continue to experience racism. Second, I will explain and critique the Black/White binary paradigm that Asian Americans, along with Hispanic and Native Americans, must navigate. Finally, I will argue that Asian American Christians, as they pray for God's kingdom to come and they learn to embody that prayer in their lives, will be called to a path of resistance and solidarity in the face of racial oppression.

RACIALIZATION AND RACISM

While race as an identifier has played, and continues to play, a role around the world, it has a uniquely prominent place in the development and organization of American political, economic, and social structures. By race, I mean that socially constructed category that frames our identity based on our phenotype, meaning our bodies' skin color and other physical features. Racialization is the process in which our identity is defined by the corporeal dimension. While racial thought developed for the purpose of structural oppression, various communities in organized resistance have in turn later used these racial categories as a way of recognizing and affirming their own sense of identity in response.

To clear some initial ground, we must first address two common misconceptions regarding this issue: to see race as essence, or race as illusion.[4] Both positions have been supported by appeals to the Bible and theology, although this reasoning is demonstrably faulty. On the one hand, although not as prominent recently, race as essence means that race is considered a fundamental core aspect of who people are, often based on biological arguments, with implications for one's mental, physical, and moral traits. Biblically, Christians have pointed to the three sons of Noah (Shem, Ham, and Japheth) in the Genesis 10 table of nations to ground this ideology. While the text does not indicate phenotypical traits of these sons, Ham with his son Canaan, who was cursed by Noah, has been connected with the Black race and used to justify slavery.[5]

On the other hand, often as a reaction to racial genocide, slavery, Jim Crow laws, and the pseudoscientific racism of the past, race is often regarded as an

---

[4]Omi and Winant, *Racial Formation in the United States*, 110.
[5]Benjamin Braude, "The Sons of Noah and the Construction of Ethnic and Geographical Identities in the Medieval and Early Modern Periods," *The William and Mary Quarterly* 54, no. 1 (1997): 103-42.

illusion that should have no place in our consideration. The idea is that, as a socially constructed concept created for the purpose of oppression with no basis in science and the Bible, we should ignore race. We should all be color-blind, especially Christians. To discredit race, biblical appeals are made to Galatians 3:28, about there being neither Jew nor Greek in Christ, and Ephesians 2:14, where Christ breaks down divisions. Looking to the early church, we also find cases about how Christians thought of themselves as a new people distinct from Jews, Romans, and Greeks, a new universal race that can be formed out of other racial heritages.[6] These texts and ideas are used to support the basis of multicultural churches, which are often colorblind. However, this idea of transcending human divisions ignores the reality of race in our society and personal lives and its concrete consequences.

In affirming the reality of race, we can contrast it to ethnicity to clarify our understanding. The transcending logic of race is often affirmed alongside the vision of eschatological ethnic diversity (Rev 7:9). Contrasted against race, ethnicity is believed to be a more theologically stable concept. Although some use race and ethnicity interchangeably, and there are close connections, what I mean by ethnicity refers to national, cultural or linguistic ancestry or markers, rather than physical appearance.[7] A friend stated that race is a social construct and therefore temporal, whereas ethnicity is eternal because God made us this way and the book of Revelation affirms it. However, this belief ignores that fact that ethnic and cultural identities and distinctions are themselves created, maintained, and re-created over time by humanity.

Culture as a whole is socially constructed. Racial categories are simply a particular instance of this. Just as we take culture and context seriously in ministry and theology, so we must with race as well. In a sense, the table of nations or eschatological vision of diversity do not directly and neatly correlate to modern-day national and ethnic identities in terms of how we label ourselves. What would those distinctions mean in our world with mixed, hybrid, and multiple identities? A better way of thinking about this is that

---

[6]Denise Kimber Buell, *Why This New Race: Ethnic Reasoning in Early Christianity* (New York: Columbia University Press, 2005).

[7]For further discussions on the concept of ethnicity, see Steve Fenton, *Ethnicity*, 2nd ed. (Cambridge; Malden, MA: Polity, 2010).

human particularities in all different ways are all, in differing degrees, a part of who we are. All these approaches to identity are ultimately to be reconciled in Christ. The eschatological vision of the nations is just that, a diverse and symbolic picture of human particularities. Of course, this symbolic fashion is how the book of Revelation as apocalyptic literature communicates in general, even in its picture of the new Jerusalem with giant pearl gates and glass-like gold streets (Rev 21:21).

By race and racialization, we are not chiefly concerned with interpersonal experiences of racism, although we will address them a bit later. These categories are historically and structurally embedded from the very origins of the US. The "discovery," conquest, and colonization of the "New World" and the transatlantic slave trade became a racial template for European civilization, including the Western church and theology.[8] Ian Haney López notes that the first document on US citizenship written in 1790 applied to Whites only, but not Native Americans who would be mostly excluded from American culture, nor African slaves who must remain subhuman to justify their oppression.[9] From then on, the limits and boundaries of what it means to be White was continually questioned, challenged, and changed to perpetuate a form of White supremacy. For example, only over the course of time did later immigrants from eastern and southern Europe began to be considered White. Hispanic and Asian immigrants, on the other hand, still do not easily fit into the White or Black binary categorization. We will address this binary paradigm later. For Asian Americans, our history gradually moves from an absolute rejection and complete exclusion from Whiteness in the late nineteenth century to the status of honorary Whites after World War II. A number of excellent works on Asian American history present a full history of Asian Americans, from early Filipino sailors shipwrecked in North America to the last two decades of transnational wealthy immigrants from a more self-assertive China.[10]

---

[8] Omi and Winant, *Racial Formation in the United States*, 106. Also, Willie Jennings, *The Christian Imagination: Theology and the Origins of Race* (New Haven: Yale University Press, 2010).

[9] Ian Haney López, *White by Law: The Legal Construction of Race*, 10th Anniversary ed. (New York: NYU Press, 2006), 1.

[10] Erika Lee, *The Making of Asian America* (New York: Simon & Schuster, 2016) and Shelley Sang-Hee Lee, *A New History of Asian America* (New York: Routledge, 2013) are two of the best Asian American histories at the present moment.

Another useful approach begins with a number of history-making incidents that were catalytic in the creation of the Asian American people.[11] The first marker is the Civil Rights Act of 1964. Through the leadership of Martin Luther King Jr., the US acknowledged the White supremacy embedded in its culture and laws. With the passing of the Civil Rights Act, racial minority groups and the discrimination that they faced had to be recognized and addressed.

The second marker is the 1968 Third World Liberation Front minority student protest at San Francisco State University and the University of California, Berkley, where Asian American students joined others in expressing a newly found self-conscious panethnic racial identity. Influenced by the Black Power movement, they protested for Yellow Power. Their protest for the establishment of Asian American studies programs and more broadly Asian American racial recognition, as well as others during that time, was a critical step for this community to accept racialization in the US on their own terms. For example, no longer accepting the term *Oriental* with its history of colonialism and denigrating racism, student activist Yuji Ichioka coined the term *Asian American* as a racial and activist moniker for political coalition, representation, and power. Not born but awakened as Asian Americans, these activists chose to declare and collectively own this identity. The 1970s saw the founding of all kinds of Asian American institutions and organizations.

The third marker is the 1977 division of the US population into five racial categories, including "Asian or Pacific Islander," in the Office of Management and Budget's Statistical Directive 15. These categories would help the government gather information to support the enforcement of affirmative action stipulated by Title VII of the Civil Rights Act.[12] Thus, a self-referential activist term became legally established by the federal government through a rather pedestrian bureaucratic process.

By addressing the questions and concerns at the beginning of this chapter, we can see how this new panethnic identity progressed through these three historical markers and how the idea of Asian American history as the

---

[11]I am indebted to Neil Gotanda for this idea of historic markers. Also, see Yen Le Espiritu, *Asian American Panethnicity: Bridging Institutions and Identities* (Philadelphia: Temple University Press, 1992).

[12]David A. Hollinger, *Postethnic America*, rev. ed. (New York: Basic, 2005), 33.

history of a particular racial group was eventually accepted. Now looking back, the Chinese Exclusion Act of 1882 and Executive Order 9066 to incarcerate Japanese Americans can be received as elements in the history of Asian America, shared by the group as a whole.[13] The murder of Vincent Chin in 1982, the Los Angeles riots of 1992, and the discrimination against many South Asians that arose after 9/11 are all a part of our collective history as well.

The racialization of Americans of diverse Asian heritages into a panethnic people called Asian Americans has a number of ramifications. Here we will discuss some of the more significant ones.

First, Asian American identity promotes an interethnic community that often goes against national and cultural divisions within Asia. Japanese Americans and Korean Americans, Indian Americans and Pakistani Americans, or Cambodian Americans and Vietnamese Americans all share a common racialized Asian American experience and find support and solidarity with each other despite their history of conflict and aggression in Asia. These kinds of friendships and connections are not always the rule, but they are fairly common as Asian Americans share a common racialized fate as minorities.

Second, Asian American identity can fall victim to ethnic monopolizing and the invisibility of Asian Americans with certain ethnic heritages. In her classic article on intersectionality, Kimberlé Crenshaw notes that whenever a minority group is represented, the most privileged members within that group often become its representatives.[14] This results in a repetition of marginalization within this population. In Asian American studies, Chinese and Japanese Americans can be overrepresented, whereas in Asian American theology and ministry, especially in evangelical circles, Korean and Chinese

---

[13]The incarceration of Japanese Americans should not be softened with the label of "internment." Legally, internment is the practice of detaining citizens of an enemy state. What the US did was to imprison its own citizens. Seventy percent of the individuals incarcerated were American citizens. See Roger Daniels, "Words Do Matter: A Note on Inappropriate Terminology and the Incarceration of the Japanese Americans," in *Nikkei in the Pacific Northwest: Japanese Americans and Japanese Canadians in the Twentieth Century*, ed. Louis Fiset and Gail Nomura (Seattle: University of Washington Press, 2005), 183-207.

[14]Kimberlé Crenshaw, "Demarginalizing the Intersection of Race and Sex: A Black Feminist Critique of Antidiscrimination Doctrine, Feminist Theory and Antiracist Politics," *University of Chicago Legal Forum* 140, no. 1 (1989): 139-67.

Americans take up space. Of course, Asian American men can frame and define Asian American issues to the exclusion of Asian American women, and wealthy well-educated Asian Americans can also overrepresent their concerns. The most common problem is the monopolizing of the Asian American category by East Asian Americans. Unless this problem of intersectionality and different axes of privilege, such as ethnicity, skin color, class, gender, sexuality, education, and such are addressed, panethnicity can be highly problematic and only lead to further marginalization for many.

Third, with the rise of identity politics and liberal multiculturalism, the conflation of race and culture becomes prevalent. For example, the five racial groups or the ethnoracial pentagon as David Hollinger calls it (White, Black, Asian or Pacific Islander, Hispanic, and Native American) become a simplified shorthand for representing cultural diversity.[15] This race-culture link is responsible for the racial stereotypes and essentialism that we've rejected above as problematic for all racial groups. However, given its broad diversity even compared to the other four racial groups, this is particularly problematic for Asian Americans. For example, I have heard many Asian American worship leaders fret about the overwhelming challenge of trying to put together an Asian American worship night in partnership with other racial groups. Lacking a common language, musical tradition, or spirituality, these worship leaders felt doomed to fail. Their inability to live up to the impossible responsibility of representing all Asian American culture often results in self-blame or pity, in other words: "What's wrong with us Asian Americans, that we have no gifts to offer to the greater church?" Attempting to resolve the complexities of racial representation, they may also fall prey to ethnic monopolization and the presentation of cultural stereotypes, for example: "To represent 'Asian American worship,' we'll sing a song in Korean and then spend time in silent and contemplative prayer."

Lastly and most importantly, this racialized Asian American identity enables and empowers Asian Americans in their solidarity to identify, understand, and fight racism. Asian Americans experience many different kinds of racism. Here are four categories to consider: blatant racism, microaggressions, systemic or structural racism, and internalized racism.

---

[15]Hollinger, *Postethnic America*, 23.

Blatant acts of racism. These acts manifest as physical or verbal assaults directed against Asian Americans because of their identity and what that represents to the assailant. Examples of this kind of racism perpetuated against Asian Americans litter our history. Here are some significant examples, among the many others. The California Supreme Court Case *People v. Hall* (1854) made the testimony of Chinese witnesses against Whites inadmissible, like those of Blacks, mulattoes, and Native Americans against Whites, making anti-Asian violence much easier to commit without penalty. Later, the Chinese Massacre of 1871 in Los Angeles stands as one of the largest lynchings in US history. Seventeen men and boys were murdered, yet many of us have never heard of it. In another tragic example, known as the Bellingham Riots of 1907, a mob of White men from the lumber mills beat and drove Indian American workers from their housing units right out of town. Similar riots occurred to Indian Americans in other towns in Washington state and British Columbia, Canada.

One of most infamous cases of anti-Asian violence is the murder of Vincent Chin, a Chinese American man killed by two White auto workers who were laid off because Japanese imports were hurting US auto companies. They killed him for no reason other than his Asian race. The lenient judge sentenced the murders to no jail time, only three years of probation, and a fine of $3,780 each. This grave injustice kicked off numerous protests across the country from Asian Americans fed up with the racism that they had seen and experienced. In its aftermath, this became a federal civil rights case, the first time the Civil Rights Act was used in a case involving an Asian American victim. This tragedy became a rallying cry for pan-Asian American activism for years to come.

While blatant acts of racism are less frequent, our post-9/11 era has created particular dangers for brown Asian Americans, especially for those who, like many Indian Americans, look remotely Middle Eastern. The fact that Islamophobia can lead to racial attacks on Indian Americans, many of whom have nothing to do with Islam, exemplifies the reality of racialization in the US. We may also recall the 2012 Wisconsin Sikh temple (*Gurdwara*) shooting, where a White supremacist Army veteran killed six people and wounded four others. Disturbingly, there have been other Gurdwara and mosque attacks in the US as well as in Europe.

The latest research on bullying shows that Asian American students face the highest percentage of racial harassment.[16] In terms of overall bullying, however, Asian American students experience less than other racial groups. There is something about their Asian Americanness that makes them exposed and vulnerable to verbal and physical attacks. Particularly, because later generations encounter less racial harassment, it seems that being perceived as more Asian or more foreign is a liability.[17] Racial bullying can also turn deadly. In 2011, Danny Chen, a nineteen-year-old Chinese American US Army soldier serving in Afghanistan, committed suicide after being racially harassed and beaten repeatedly by fellow American soldiers.

Microaggressions. While these kinds of attacks continue, in everyday life Asian Americans more often experience microaggressions, "brief and commonplace daily verbal, behavioral, and environmental indignities, whether intentional or unintentional, that communicate hostile, derogatory, or negative racial slights and insults to the target person or group."[18] Derald Sue and others break down eight themes of microaggressions directed toward Asian Americans:[19]

Theme 1: Alien in Own Land: *All Asians are foreigners. They are all immigrants. They can never be real or fully American. Asian Americans are just Asians living in America.*

Theme 2: Ascription of Intelligence: *Asians are all good at math. They are like robots.*

Theme 3: Denial of Racial Reality: *Asians are the new Whites. They do not experience racial discrimination or attacks although they can be very racist.*

Theme 4: Exoticization of Asian American Women: *Asian women make great girlfriends, submissive and obedient. They are great at sex and love White men.*

---

[16]Nellie Tran and Sumie Okazaki, "Bullying & Victimization and Asian-American Students" (fact sheet, Asian American Psychological Association), www.apa.org/pi/oema/resources/ethnicity-health/asian-american/bullying-and-victimization.

[17]Anthony A. Peguro, "Victimizing The Children of Immigrants: Latino and Asian American Student Victimization," *Youth and Society* 41 (2009): 186-208.

[18]Derald Wing Sue et al., "Racial Microaggressions in Everyday Life: Implications for Clinical Practice," *American Psychologist* 62, no. 4 (2007): 271-86.

[19]Derald Wing Sue et al., "Racial Microaggressions and the Asian American Experience," *Cultural Diversity and Ethnic Minority Psychology* 13, no. 1 (2007): 72-81. The italicized examples are mine based on this article.

Theme 5: Invalidation of Interethnic Differences: *All Asians look alike. There really is no difference between Koreans and Japanese, Vietnamese and Cambodians, or Pakistanis and Indians.*

Theme 6: Pathologizing Cultural Values/Communication Styles: *Asians are too passive, too quiet, too introverted to be good leaders. Asian shame is why they are so mentally unhealthy. Their cultural values make them all workaholics.*

Theme 7: Second-Class Citizenship: *Asians and their issues or interests are not as important as others.*

Theme 8: Invisibility: *Racial diversity and concerns are between Blacks and Whites only. Asians are basically White, Black, or not a part of America.*

Theme 9: Undeveloped Incidents/Responses: other experiences that cannot be easily categorized under the previous eight themes.

While these themes offer some generalizations, the experience of different ethnic backgrounds, especially non-East Asian American ones, can diverge from them. For example, Kevin Nadal has researched Filipino American microaggressions, which overlapped with Sue's works but also included two common anti-Black American themes (assumption of criminality or deviance, and assumption of inferior status or intellect) as well as a number of uniquely Filipino American ones (such as exclusion from the Asian American community, and mistaken identity such as being confused as Latino, for example).[20]

These microaggressions can occur anywhere and come from anyone, including other racial minorities and even other Asian Americans. I have personally seen all of them throughout my life, including in churches and seminaries.

There are two significant points to highlight regarding this kind of racism. First, these kinds of slights and insults can be unintended or even offered as a compliment. Thus, the victims are often left wondering what actually happened, second guessing themselves, or feeling like they are crazy. The aftertaste of the experience can linger, making them racially paranoid. Secondly, although these incidents might be dismissed by some as insignificant, psychologists have found them to be "many times over more problematic,

---

[20]Kevin L. Nadal et al., "Racial Microaggressions and the Filipino American Experience: Recommendations for Counseling and Development," *Journal of Multicultural Counseling and Development* 40, no. 3 (2012): 156-73.

damaging, and injurious to persons of color than overt racist acts."[21] In fact, over time these slights can build atop each other toward "*microaggressive trauma*, or the excessive and continuous exposure to subtle discrimination" that results in trauma-like symptoms.[22] I will unpack the impact of microaggressive trauma on Asian American identity in the next chapter.

Microaggressions can occur not only interpersonally, but institutionally as well. For example, a church or school can continually treat Asian Americans as second-class citizens by instituting policies or curriculum that presume Asian Americanness as the domain of foreigners, immigrants, and international students.

Systemic and structural racism. These forms of racism can be microaggressive or unequivocally oppressive. They can be embedded within the government, the media, our educational system, academic structures, theological and spiritual traditions, organizations, and communities. Like a fish in water, it is hard to recognize something if it is everywhere and seems like it has always been there. Many Asian Americans do not ask why we only make up less than six percent of the US population, unaware that the US government kept America White by excluding Asian immigrants through the Chinese Exclusion Acts of 1882 and later the Immigration Act of 1924 with its racist national origin quotas. The White normativity discussed in chapter one is the core operator of this kind of racism. Simply by treating Asian Americans as nonexistent in our American history, culture, communities, or by casting them as not fully American, systemic injustice is done to Asian Americans. Executive Order 9066 and the Japanese American incarceration during World War II is a direct result of the belief in Asian Americans as forever foreigners.

Internalized racism. This form of racism results from soaking and breathing in all these kinds of racism. With all these messages coming directly and indirectly, consciously and unconsciously, Asian Americans begin to believe them. For many reasons, racist presumptions and reasoning becomes a part of them and they come to view it as their truth. Some ways that internalized racism might manifest include

---

[21]Derald Wing Sue and David Sue, *Counseling the Culturally Diverse: Theory and Practice*, 4th ed. (New York: Wiley, 2003), 48.
[22]Kevin L. Nadal, *Microaggressions and Traumatic Stress: Theory, Research, and Clinical Treatment* (Washington DC: American Psychological Association, 2017), 13.

oppressing the choice of Asian partners, purposely denying a job to an Asian American, discouraging Asian Americans who challenge the racial status quo, perpetuating negative Asian American stereotypes, seeking to change physical characteristics to appear white, and denying one's Asian heritage.[23]

Seeking to avoid racial pain, Asian Americans deform themselves to succeed or just to survive. Closely connected to *colonial mentality*, Asian Americans honor what the White majority culture tells them is valuable and worthy and denigrate themselves with *self-hatred* targeted toward their Asianness and their Asian bodies. How to deal with this internalized toxicity will be discussed further in the next chapter on integration.

In general, because many Asian Americans believe the message that we are not supposed to face racism, we lack resources to deal with them. Or even more correctly, sadly many Asian Americans remain ignorant of the plethora of resources in Asian American studies and activism, instead grasping after assimilation and thereby being estranged from their Asian Americanness and communal racial history.

THE BLACK/WHITE BINARY PARADIGM

When engaging race and racism, Asian Americans often find themselves navigating the Black/White binary—meaning the conversation becomes primarily framed between "White privilege" and "Black lives matter." Put another way, with Blacks as the most oppressed and Whites as the most privileged, everyone else must find their place somewhere in-between. In his influential article, Juan Perea breaks down exactly how the Black/White binary functions as a paradigm for understanding the history of race in the US.[24] Using Thomas Kuhn's ideas about how paradigms shape and filter disparate sets of information for the sake of a more digestible and coherent narrative, Perea argues that the "most pervasive and powerful paradigm of race in the United States is the Black/White binary paradigm."[25] This means that we tend to think about race issues in the US as solely concerning the

---

[23]Rosalind S. Chou and Joe R. Feagin, *The Myth of the Model Minority: Asian Americans Facing Racism* (Boulder, CO: Paradigm, 2010), 157.

[24]Juan F. Perea, "The Black/White Binary Paradigm of Race: The Normal Science of American Racial Thought," *California Law Review* 85 (1997): 1213, https://lawcat.berkeley.edu/record /1115988.

[25]Perea, "Black/White Binary Paradigm of Race," 1219.

relationship between Blacks and Whites, allowing this interface to serve as an archetype, a central power of reference, or a prototype that can be generalized for any other White-minority issues. This idea is often implied with the term *people of color* meaning "Blacks and others like them." This binary way of framing race is simply assumed to be true, so ubiquitous in pop culture, academia, theology, and churches that many people wonder if another paradigm is even possible.

There are reasons why this binary paradigm is important and relevant and other reasons why it is quite problematic. Critically assessing the Black/White binary paradigm is fraught and vulnerable to misunderstandings; however, navigating it is crucial not just to Asian Americans, who are rendered invisible by it, but by anyone seeking to dismantle racial oppression at its root.

In terms of its continual saliency, there is an *exceptional* quality to the experience of Black Americans not shared by other racial minorities. For example, calling for Black Lives Matter to be changed into Minority Lives Matter or All Lives Matter just will not do. There is a particular cross that Black lives have borne and still bear in the long history of racial oppression, beginning with chattel slavery and its continual legacy to the present. In highlighting this exceptional quality of the Black struggle, activist Scot Nakagawa avers that anti-Black racism is the fulcrum of White supremacy, and the liberation of all people of color in the US is connected to the liberation of Black Americans.[26] White power leverages Blackness to justify and express its dominance. At its very root, White dominance is inherently intertwined with economics so that there is a concrete financial benefit to being not-Black.[27] Anti-Blackness has been leveraged throughout American history to coerce other racial minorities to defend White power and its interests.

Understood from this perspective, Black Americans are the racial ancestors of all people of color in the US, in the sense that they are all not "White" and hence "Black." Historically, the earliest Asian "coolies" who arrived as indentured servants experienced the same kind of subhuman

---

[26]Francis Reynolds, "Scot Nakagawa: Dismantling the Fulcrum of White Supremacy," *The Nation*, August 24, 2012, accessed on August 17, 2019, www.thenation.com/article/archive/scot-nakagawa-dismantling-fulcrum-white-supremacy/.

[27]See Satnam Virdee, "Racialized Capitalism: An Account of Its Contested Origins and Consolidation," *The Sociological Review* 67, no. 1 (2019): 3-27.

treatment as the African slaves, including a transpacific passage that was as deadly as the transatlantic Middle Passage. Both were stripped naked, flogged, killed like stock animals, and disposed when their usage expired, all for the sake of maintaining White supremacy and its economic base.

Asian Americans can even transpose their intergenerational differences to the Black experience. For example, there is resonating wisdom to be gleaned in the two visions of being African American during the post-bellum Reconstruction outlined by Booker T. Washington and W. E. B. Du Bois, respectively.[28] In a sense, Booker T. Washington was a "first-gen" freeman, freed at nine years old by the Emancipation Proclamation, who grew up and later worked in an American South deeply entrenched in the plantation system. Washington focused on education for real-life jobs and not asking for equality from the Whites. His concern was for Blacks to get help from the Whites and to accept their place as Blacks on earth. His mindset parallels that of recent Asian immigrants, who also accept as a given that the US is a White nation, focusing on their immediate survival and needs, even if that means a hard assimilation into Whiteness. This attitude is especially true if they settle in an area with little-to-no Asian American population. The children of these immigrant communities often share this White assimilationist orientation.

On the other hand, "fifth-gen" W. E. B. Du Bois, whose maternal great-great-grandfather gained his freedom during the Revolutionary War, grew up in a progressive and integrated community in Massachusetts. Du Bois focused on Blacks gaining equality as full Americans, not just job training to survive. Later generations of Asian Americans, who know our long struggle for visibility and justice as well as our solidarity with other minorities, challenge the notion of the US as a White nation. This sensibility is more common on the West Coast with its large population and rich history of Asian Americans, although even here it is not a given.

The work of Martin Luther King Jr. and others in the civil rights movement cannot be overemphasized. All American minorities have benefited from that work. The passing of the Civil Rights Act of 1964 directly influenced the Immigration and Nationality Act of 1965, which finally ceased the racialist

---

[28]Booker T. Washington, W. E. B. Du Bois, and Frederick Douglass, *Three African-American Classics* (Mineola, NY: Dover, 2007).

policies that began with the Chinese Exclusion Act of 1882. Many Asian American communities are here in the US now because of this Immigration Act, for which we can thank these civil rights leaders.

In terms of the Asian American movement and history of activism, whether it be the influence of Black Power for inspiration or Yuri Kochiyama's friendship with Malcolm X, there is no denying the indebtedness of Asian America to the Black struggle.

Summarizing this Black-Asian connection that is lost to many, Gary Okihiro states this:

> We are a kindred people, African and Asian Americans. We share a history of migration, cultural interaction, and trade. We share a history of colonization, oppression and exploitation, and parallel and mutual struggles for freedom. We are a kindred people, forged in the fire of white supremacy and tempered in the water of resistance.[29]

While affirming the reality of solidarity and the need to support the Black community in their particular experiences of societal oppression, there are limitations to using the Black/White binary as a *paradigm* for all minority racial experiences. The exceptional nature of the Black experience is one of kind and not of degree, as it is often assumed to be. Simply put, it is not that non-Black racial minorities suffer less than Blacks, but that they encounter and suffer racism in different forms and expressions.

The Black/White binary paradigm functions out of a single-axis or one-continuum model of oppression/privilege, with Blacks on the bottom and Whites on top. Given this framework, Asian Americans can be seen as "Black" along with other people of color.[30] Given the history and current reality of structural racism, this categorization of Asian Americans has some justification.

However, mainstream media since the 1980s has promoted Asian Americans as "White" or at least an "honorary White" model minority, and many Asian Americans have internalized this myth, happy to enjoy the White

---

[29]Gary Okihiro, *Margins and Mainstreams: Asians in American History and Culture* (Seattle: University of Washington Press, 1994), 60-61.

[30]Janine Young Kim, "Are Asians Black?: The Asian-American Civil Rights Agenda and the Contemporary Significance of the Black/White Paradigm," *Yale Law Journal* 108, no. 8 (1999), 2385-412.

privilege that this brought.[31] This idea of Asian Americans as White misses persistent structural issues.[32] Lacking deeper racial consciousness, under this categorization Asian Americans can only be complicit with the oppressive White dominant system.

If Black and White do not fully describe the place of Asian Americans, the idea of a "middleman minority" who mediates between majority and minority groups describes the experience of many Asian American small business owners in predominately Black and Hispanic neighborhoods, like my parents in southeast Washington, DC.[33] Such a framing locates Asian Americans somewhere in the middle of Black and White, having economic but not political power, and sees them ultimately scapegoated from both sides as we saw in 1992 Los Angeles Riots, also known as the Los Angeles Uprising.

In all this, the internal diversity of Asian Americans is simply ignored, that East Asian (Yellow) versus Southeast and South Asian (Brown) Americans have significantly different experiences on the Black/White continuum. For example, sometimes Filipino Americans are externally lumped in with or they internally associate with other Latin communities, rather than Asian Americans who are assumed to be East Asian in heritage.[34] Similarly, some South Asian Americans can register as Black and experience racism accordingly. When race is seen only as a proximity to Blackness, the issue is that along with phenotype and colorism, other cultural dimensions that complicate the Asian American experience are marginalized, such as having an accent.

Moving beyond the single axis of the Black/White binary, Claire Kim theorizes a two-axis racial triangulation model of Asian American experience.[35] On the privilege/oppression axis that the Black/White binary describes, Asian Americans do have "relative valorization" somewhere

---

[31]The term *model minority* originates from William Petersen, "Success Story: Japanese-American Style," *New York Times Magazine*, 9 January 1966, but the term proliferated in the 1980s as seen in the "Asian-American Whiz Kids" cover story of *Time* Magazine on August 31, 1987.

[32]Min Zhou, "Are Asian Americans Becoming 'White?'" *Contexts* 3, no. 1 (2004): 29-37.

[33]Hubert M. Blalock Jr., *Toward a Theory of Minority-Group Relations* (New York: Wiley and Sons, 1967).

[34]Anthony Christian Ocampo, *The Latinos of Asia: How Filipino Americans Break the Rules of Race* (Stanford: Stanford University Press, 2016).

[35]Claire Kim, "Racial Triangulation of Asian Americans," *Politic and Society* 27, no. 1 (1999): 105-38.

between "superior" White and "inferior" Black. However, Kim offers a second "foreigner/insider" axis, where Asian Americans end up as perpetual foreigners unlike either Black or White. Kim underscores how Black/White parameters for perceiving structural racism are too narrow to accurately encapsulate the experience of non-Black racial minorities.

The Black/White binary suffers from another problem according to Perea. Using this paradigm forces all other racial groups to be understood within its boundaries, often with the impact of rendering other racial groups "invisible" and implicitly characterizing them as "passive, voluntary spectators."[36] Thus, the long history of non-Black struggles for racial justice, including Asian American ones, are disregarded as insignificant. Where are the stories of Wong Kim Ark, Yuri Kochiyama, Grace Lee Boggs, Fred Korematsu, Larry Itliong, and Bhagat Singh Thind, not to mention all the struggles of Latinos/as? White supremacy matured and became more sophisticated legally while oppressing Latinos/as and Asian Americans with cases of naturalization racial prerequisites.[37] Perea points out that this paradigm erases Latinos/as, Asian Americans, Native Americans, and other racial minorities from the race discussion altogether.

Given the prominence of the Black/White binary paradigm and the ongoing exclusion of Asian Americans from our school curricula, it is no wonder that many Asian Americans struggle to enter the race and racial justice conversation at all. It is not simply a matter of being complicit with dominant culture or stuck in Asian passivity. Erasure and invisibility are a significant and active part of how Asian Americans experience racism.

Given the exceptional nature of the Black experience, this paradigm cannot be simply rejected. Consequently, for Asian Americans, navigating this binary means at least three things.

First, it means identifying White supremacy—otherwise known as Whiteness, White privilege, White normativity, White power, or White nationalism—rather than the relationship between Black and White as the culprit. White supremacy might manifest in different ways and to differing degrees against different minority communities, all for the sake of keeping power and privilege.

---

[36]Perea, "Black/White Binary Paradigm of Race," 1222.
[37]López, White by Law.

Second, it means advocating for justice and supporting the struggle for Black lives, as well as acknowledging the privileges that Asian Americans enjoy. Suffering discrimination as perpetual foreigners, many Asian Americans seek to be model citizens, which can take the shape of "honorary White status" with accompanying privileges. In such cases, Asian Americans' silence about Black lives does mean complicity with the systems of racism.

Third, without weakening the first two, it means critiquing this binary as restrictive and dated, unable to deal with the complexity of what American identities have become. Can Asian American identity be affirmed without being understood as something like being White or being Black? Affirming the particularity of the Asian American experience as genuinely American is what is at stake.

THE ASIAN AMERICAN MOVEMENT AND RESISTING LORDLESS POWERS

From the 1990s, multiculturalism had served as the way to frame discussions about racism. Building on the idea of ethnic studies, multiculturalism in the US understood racism as the problem of peoples of different identities and social and cultural backgrounds unable to live in harmony and mutual understanding.[38] When racial conflicts arose, the solution was building relationships across differences and finding reconciliation beyond the personal prejudices. This is the model that American evangelicalism followed with talks of racial reconciliation and the need for multiethnic churches.

The problem with this approach is that it is basically ahistorical and individualistic, thinking that the different people were all on an equal playing ground, functioning as individuals. Differences were explained as cultural without acknowledging the structural and systemic legacies and vestiges. This explains why Black liberation theology did not follow this route but focused instead on liberation and White supremacy. The earliest Asian American theology, which can trace its roots to the Third World Liberation Front protests, had the same orientation as well.[39] The problem is not merely

---

[38] Gary Y. Okihiro, *Third World Studies: Theorizing Liberation* (Durham, NC: Duke University Press, 2016), 6.

[39] Roy Sano, ed., *The Theologies of Asian Americans and Pacific Peoples: A Reader* (Berkeley: Asian Center for Theology and Strategies, Pacific School of Religion, 1976).

that of cultural difference and misunderstanding but the structures of a society deeply engrained in Whiteness.

Given the more accurate understanding of the kind of sin and evil that we are dealing with, the primary mode of faithfulness should be resistance instead of reconciliation. The theological task is to make sure that we can understand the problem and the faithful response in the context of the gospel and not just political ideology. This does not mean that political insights are unhelpful, but to make sure that the logic of the gospel reigns, avoiding ideological co-option.

In this regard, I have found helpful insights from Karl Barth's idea of "lordless powers." In *The Christian Life*, Barth describes human-originated ideas and forces that become alienated from and ultimately oppress us.[40] The powers are "entities with their own right" and while they are in a sense "pseudo-objective" realities, they nevertheless are "real and efficacious."[41] In a tentative list, Barth includes Empire and Mammon ideologies, as well as chthonic or earthly forces such as technology, fashion, sports, mass media, alcohol, sex, transportation, and so on.[42] The powers of White normativity, Orientalism, and the like would fall under this same list of ideologies that seek to reign over us.

In this resistance, proper naming is one of the first steps. There are many words regarding these issues of representation such as diversity, racism, and racial justice, and even Whiteness, White supremacy, or White privilege. However, these are either too general, too abstract, conceptually ambiguous, or lacking clarity for our situation. The proper name of that demon that we seek to cast out is White normativity, and its hegemonic rule operates implicitly and unconsciously, often masquerading as objective science, theological orthodoxy, or credible scholarship. White normativity claims that White people are the racial, cultural, political, economic, physical, and scientific norm.[43] This means that only White people are truly human, and the members of other racial groups are only human to the extent that they

---

[40]Karl Barth, *Church Dogmatics*, vol. 4, part 4, *The Christian Life: Lecture Fragments* (Grand Rapids, MI: Eerdmans, 1981), 213-33.

[41]Barth, *Church Dogmatics*, IV/4, 214-16.

[42]Barth, *Church Dogmatics*, IV/4, 219-33.

[43]Michael Morris, "Standard White: Dismantling White Normativity," *California Law Review* 104, no. 4 (2016): 950.

resemble White people. Failure to mimic Whiteness places one in the realm of "freaks and outliers."[44] As mentioned before, Orientalism perpetually otherizes Asians and Asian Americans, reducing them to exotic anthropological curios, not concrete humanity but some sort of abstraction.

Against these powers, Barth extols us to pray for God's kingdom, which has already come in Christ and which will also come anew in a specific time and space. Moreover, the actions of those who pray for God's kingdom to come should be "kingdomlike."[45] Here, in defining what *kingdomlike* means, Barth applies the criterion of humanity, of human rights and dignity. In line with this criterion of humanity, the church should take sides and "will have to say Yes or No, and say it resolutely, to current ideas of lifeforms" without falling into the danger of ideologies.[46] In our concerns about justice regarding cultural representation, this would mean being and becoming faithful consumers and creators, as well as faithful activists, telling the truth, witnessing to the criterion of humanity and the *imago Dei* in all humanity.

This idea of becoming kingdomlike and seeking justice against the powers and principalities is not something separated from worship. In seeking justice and the well-being of all those around us, especially the marginalized, we are loving God and God's reign. Intimacy with God is part and parcel of serving our neighbors, because in that interaction with "the least of these" we serve, we encounter the living Christ who we adore (Mt 25:40).

The works of justice and our personal growth and development must go hand in hand. The famous activist Grace Lee Boggs, moving beyond her early Marxist convictions concluded:

> A revolution involves making an evolutionary/revolutionary leap towards becoming more socially responsible and more self-critical human beings. In order to transform the world, we must transform ourselves.[47]

In agreeing with her about the importance of personal transformation, I also must affirm that in our relationship with the incarnate God, we learn what

---

[44]Morris, "Standard White," 951.
[45]Barth, *Church Dogmatics*, IV/4, 266.
[46]Barth, *Church Dogmatics*, IV/4, 268.
[47]Grace Lee Boggs, introduction to *Revolution and Evolution in the Twentieth Century*, by James and Grace Lee Boggs, new ed. (New York: Monthly Review Press, 2008), viii.

it means to be human and also to become more human. Because all that we do in the world is vitally connected to who we are within ourselves, in the next chapter we turn to the crucial role that personal integration plays in our discipleship to Christ.

8

FRAGMENTATION AND INTEGRATION

*Integrity is how we know ourselves and choices that sustain
our values in relation with others. It is a complex, evolving
process over time, captured in moments of self-awareness and
self-acceptance—brief interludes of consciousness that appear
within the tossing turbulence of many people and places.*

Rita Nakashima Brock

IN *MEET THE PATELS*, a documentary film about the love life and family
dynamics of Indian American actor Ravi Patel, he explains how he grew up
leading a double life. At home, he was *Indian* Ravi: speaking Gujarati,
hanging with Indians, and watching Indian movies. Outside the house, he
was *American* Ravi: speaking English with American friends and watching
American movies. As an adult, Ravi begins dating a White woman, but he
finds himself unable to bring her home to meet his parents, ultimately
breaking up with her. Did the White girlfriend only date American Ravi and
not Indian Ravi as well? Does American Ravi go home to his Indian parents,
or just Indian Ravi? Ravi grew up being able to navigate both worlds as a
bicultural person, and perhaps even felt quite comfortable in those worlds.
However, it is apparent that he is living two parallel lives, presenting different
selves to each of these worlds. More importantly, these two selves were not
at peace with each other.

Epigraph: Rita Nakashima Brock, "Cooking Without Recipes: Interstitial Integrity," in *Off the Menu: Asian and Asian North American Women's Religion and Theology*, ed. Rita Nakashima Brock et al. (Louisville, KY: Westminster John Knox, 2007), 126.

Various concepts are used to define and understand the hybridity and multiplicity of Asian American identity, including third culture, biculturalism, code-switching, double consciousness, and enculturation/acculturation.[1] Viet Nguyen begins *The Sympathizer* with these lines: "I am a spy, a sleeper, a spook, a man of two faces. Perhaps not surprisingly, I am also a man of two minds."[2] Nguyen comments elsewhere how through the biracial Vietnamese spy protagonist of his novel, he expressed his childhood experience of feeling like a double spy, spying on his White friends for his parents while spying on his parents for his friends. Of course, W. E. B. Du Bois's classic idea of "double consciousness," describing how Black Americans perceive and experience themselves through White eyes as well as their own, resulting in the creation of two souls and minds, resonates with many people of color.[3]

Some of these conceptions of identity do not adequately address the challenge of self-integration, of owning various aspects of self together in divine shalom. For example, biculturality might be a description of adroitly code-switching back and forth while still lacking the consciousness of the systemic forces that necessitate the need for this skill. As a sociopolitical expression of oppression and survival under White normativity, this so-called biculturality reflects fragmentation or even balkanization of various unacceptable selves. An acculturation/enculturation framework could be understood similarly as parallel tracks, being adept at navigating two different worlds with two different lives. The integration that they speak of assumes an ideal, open, multicultural context that does not exist yet in many parts of the US and at many levels of society.

In this chapter, I propose that Asian Americans often have a fragmented self as a result of microaggressive trauma. Pushing past previous language of a "double self," "biculturality," and the like, I draw together trauma theory, interpersonal neurobiology, and attachment theory to describe more precisely the nature of our pain as well as to move toward our healing and restoration into God's shalom. Recalling chapter one where I pointed out God's

---

[1]See, for example, T. LaFromboise, H. L. K. Colman, and J. Gerton, "Psychological Impact of Biculturalism: Evidence and Theory," *Psychological Bulletin* 114 (1993): 395-412.
[2]Viet Thanh Nguyen, *The Sympathizer: A Novel* (New York: Grove Press, 2015), 1.
[3]W. E. B. Du Bois, *The Souls of Black Folk: The Oxford W. E. B. Du Bois* (New York: Oxford University Press, 2007), 3.

call to bring all of our selves into the divine presence, here I stress how all of our selves unites with Christ. In that context of our full union with Christ, this journey of integration is a vital part of our discipleship and vocation.

MICROAGGRESSIONS FROM MULTIPLE FRONTS

In the last chapter on race, we identified microaggressions as one of the most significant ways that Asian Americans experience racism. These everyday experiences of subtle racism demean, drain, irritate, and puzzle Asian Americans. The damage is not tied to any individual microaggression, but an accumulation of them over time, days, months, and years. According to Filipino American psychologist Kevin Nadal's concept of "microaggressive trauma," these everyday indignities, slights, and insults over time add up to manifest trauma-like symptoms.[4] Nadal explains that this "microaggressive trauma" is often misdiagnosed because people suffering from it will inevitably recall their latest microaggression, which, in and of itself, is not traumatic. Their trauma reaction then sounds overwrought, perhaps even a bit neurotic. For many Asian Americans working in predominately White contexts, their work environment becomes toxic because these microaggressive traumas can become debilitating.

While we have been dealing with racial microaggressions, a similar kind of low-grade oppression based on cultural values can happen in Asian or Asian American spaces. For example, in my personal experience as a pastor in a Korean American church as well as in my teaching experience with Korean American seminarians, I have seen stress, trauma, and abuse from "cultural" values. Whether patriarchy, sexism, ageism, classism, legalism, authoritarianism, nepotism, and so on, these oppressions are communicated in the guise of cultural values, such as "being Korean." In chapter four, I described how culture cannot be labeled in such an essentialistic manner and that what deserves the label of "cultural heritage" is highly contentious. Just like everyday racism, this everyday cultural stress can add up to becoming traumatic.

Asian Americans thus face stress and microaggressions on two fronts: in mainstream White contexts and within Asian/Asian American contexts. In

---

[4]Kevin L. Nadal, *Microaggressions and Traumatic Stress: Theory, Research, and Clinical Treatment* (Washington, DC: American Psychological Association, 2018).

White contexts, our appearance and our very bodies are the source of that traumatic pain. In Asian American contexts, our ethnic/cultural identity elicits cultural trauma. On top of these forces, gender-based microaggressions aggravate the situation for Asian American women within both contexts. Asian American men face their own racist tropes that denigrate and emasculate them as asexual and undesirable as mates while, in certain White contexts, Asian American women can experience a particular favor. Of course, this nearly always reveals itself to simply be a patronizing fetishization. As with our discussion on racism, instead of thinking about degrees of oppression and suffering between Asian American men or women, it will be more constructive to focus on the difference in the kind of negative experiences and the source of the oppression. However, overall, the sexism and patriarchy against Asian American women, especially in Christian contexts, must be explicitly acknowledged and actively resisted, especially by men. A myriad of other parameters exists as well that can further multiply the suffering.

In terms of ministry, in whatever context you may serve, negative pressures can make a person be so oriented toward survival, keeping oneself from drowning in negativity, that they lose their effectiveness. Like everything else regarding microaggressions, the loss of ministry capacity might be gradual and accumulative, often escaping attention until it is dire. I highlight three different areas where this corrosive effect appears.

First, microaggressions disturb the leader's sense of presence, being in the moment and fully engaging the person in front of you. Ministry at its core is built on presence, embodying God's grace and love in our own physical and emotional nearness. Whether preaching, teaching, counseling, or just making small talk, being able to truly see the people around us is crucial. This sense of presence, of course, arises out of our own experience of God's presence through various spiritual practices. However, with chronic stress and everyday invalidations from racial and cultural toxicity, the very sense of self can erode.[5] In terms of relationships, the erosion of the self leads in turn to disconnection with others. Neuroscientists talk about our "mirroring neurons" which act in interpersonal encounters to imitate the other person's internal state in our own

---

[5]Bessel van der Kolk, *The Body Keeps the Score: Brain, Mind, and Body in the Healing of Trauma* (New York: Penguin, 2014), 97.

minds and bodies.[6] This means that, at a subconscious level, we sense and feel in our bodies what the other person is feeling. We are sending nonverbal messages and they are being processed by others at a level that neither of us are fully cognizant of. We cannot offer ourselves in relationship when our own sense of being is under attack. In this sense, our relationship with God also suffers unless we can identify and offer up this toxic force to God.

Second, and closely connected to the first point, these beleaguered leaders struggle with sensing and controlling the emotional temperature of the room. Being socially aware, sensing how the group is doing and feeling, is one of the basic skills of leadership.[7] This ability to resonate with a community can then serve as a baseline to operate from, either raising the temperature to challenge and disrupt or lowering the temperature to calm and assure.[8] Microaggressions tax the emotional faculties, overworking awareness about the self and social interactions with lingering questions and disturbances about seemingly minor incidents. Through emotional exhaustion, their thermometer and thermostat degrade in function. As a result, these ministers speak or act in a tone-deaf fashion, sowing confusion and criticism throughout their ministries.

Third, with the emotional and mental drainage of energy, one's creativity is sapped. In any kind of ministry, creativity is essential. Another way of thinking of creativity is that of being open to the Spirit's life-giving prompting and guidance. Existing in the survival mode that stress and toxic environments induce depletes one's ability to be creative. There is a direct relationship between the body's stress responses and creativity, so that when we are most stressed, we are least creative.[9]

Mounting pain and frustration are difficult to contain and process in a healthy manner, leading to emotional leaking. Where, when, and to whom the leaking happens, no one can predict. Often, close family members suffer the brunt of it. This leaking explains the unfortunate, but common interaction between someone with privilege and someone of a marginalized status. For

---

[6]Daniel J. Siegel, *The Developing Mind*, 2nd ed. (New York: Guilford, 2012), 164-66.

[7]See Daniel Goleman, Richard Boyatzis, and Annie McKee, *Primal Leadership: Unleashing the Power of Emotional Intelligence* (Boston: Harvard Business Review Press, 2013).

[8]Ronald A. Heifetz and Marty Linsky, *Leadership on the Line* (Boston: Harvard Business School Press, 2002), 107-16.

[9]Archibald D. Hart, *Adrenaline and Stress*, rev. ed. (Dallas: Word, 1995), 184.

example, experiencing a microaggression from a White man during a chance encounter, an Asian American man might lash out with "I am sick of people like you!" The Asian American man reacts against the White man with the force of all the accumulated pain, even though this pent-up pain is not from this particular White man. Most of it might be from just living in our White-normative society. The White man is confused by the overreaction to his seem-ingly benign comment that, as microaggressions often do, intended no harm. He thus determines that he is experiencing reverse racism and concludes that the minority's obsession with racism is ultimately the problem.

In this scenario, both parties are right and wrong. Yes, microaggressions are destructive regardless of the intent. However, since the level of pain and anger experienced by the Asian American man was not solely caused by this one interaction, the severity of his angry response is incommensurate to the offense. On the other hand, ignorance does not spell innocence. Our actions, cultivated by our society, can and often are complicit with grave injustice and evil. Yet, having someone you barely know label you as "one of those" people from one interaction is rather unfair.

I have seen this script play out repeatedly to no good ends on both sides. In the past, I have been that angry Asian American man, unsympathetic to the confusion that I was causing. I can also provide examples of how, in committing gender microaggression, I have been labeled as "one of those sexist Korean men," in the exact same mold as the pastors, fathers, husbands, and brothers who have hurt them over the years. I believe that I am deeply committed to gender equality and feminism, and yet I do not defend myself, because I know I have hurt women in so many unknowing ways. Because there is no end to the complex ways in which we are privileged and unaware, there can be endless critiques and attacks on each other, all in the name of "justice." Speaking truth to oppressive power is important, but there are times when this "call out" culture of endlessly and ungraciously critiquing offenders, no matter how contrite, grows toxic, a leaking of pain rather than a holy vocation.[10]

Regarding cultural pains, I have met too many second-gen pastors who shake the dust off their feet against first-gen abusers, setting off with visions

---

[10]Loretta Ross, "I'm a Black Feminist. I Think Call-Out Culture Is Toxic," *The New York Times*, August 17, 2019, www.nytimes.com/2019/08/17/opinion/sunday/cancel-culture-call-out.html.

of churches that will not repeat the patterns of our immigrant churches. Inevitably, because the hurt and its residual impact are not fully acknowledged and addressed, they end up repeating abusive ministry practices and relational dynamics. (Of course, many of them run away to White churches, but we now know that this fix is a superficial one.) There are definitely toxic contexts that are not what God wills for us or anyone else to be a part of. I have counseled many, pointing out the distinction between perfect churches, which do not exist, and healthy churches, which do, and the distinction between dysfunctional and abusive ones. Every family is to some degree dysfunctional, but not every family is abusive. Healthy parents will have arguments, but physical or emotional abuse is something different. In the same way, some churches are not just imperfect, but rather they are downright deadly. Those kinds of churches should be avoided.

Even if we are in a good ministry context, cultural and racial microaggressions in our city or family cannot be avoided. Given that hurt and offense are the everyday reality of our lives, without restorative practices and supports we will quickly become a cog in this machine of being hurt and lashing out rather than an instrument of God's peace. Here I list three strategies essential for health.

First, a support system of people can provide safe respite from the barrage, a reality check to discern our experiences, emotional and moral support, and wisdom and strategy so that we do not act foolishly out of anger. No one person, or even a single set of people, can meet all these needs. Over the years, I have had wonderful therapists, who have helped me recover when I was absolutely drained and needed to be slowly nursed back to the land of the living. Good friends with whom I can share a meal and drinks have restored my soul's ability to remember joy and laughter. I have sought out multiple mentors, each of whom provide wisdom regarding a specific area of life and leadership. And my spiritual director has now walked with me for nine years, bearing witness to God's presence when I become overwhelmed with fear and doubt.

Second, bodily practices engage the embodied nature of this accrued pain and trauma. The long-term effect of these microaggressions depletes our bodies. In many ways, we are unaware of this process. Our spiritual practices can be top-down and even disembodying, disconnecting us from our bodies. That is why working bottom-up or "through the back door," as I like to say, can be fruitful. I always remind myself of the most basic and bodily aspects of life: food, sleep, and exercise. I have appreciated the profound wisdom of sleeping as a fundamental spiritual experience of accepting God's lordship and grace.[11] I have found that many Christians miss the corporeal dimension of sabbath, that the rest and affirmation of human life and enjoyment are in and of themselves God ordained. Centering prayer, practice of silence and solitude, breathing prayer and other practices that incorporate the body can all be helpful.

These practices do not have to be "spiritual" per se. Nothing gets me connected to my body like being in nature. Hiking and backpacking have changed my life, grounding me into an earthy life in God. Belden Lane extols the salutary benefits of *Lectio Terrestris*, "a richly interactive reading of the earth itself," which "demands the exercise of all of our senses."[12] I attribute my recovery from workaholism to nature encounters in the Sierra Nevada mountains in the north and the local San Gabriel mountains, both of which my good friend Josh Ritnimit introduced me to. Along with being in nature, rock climbing at my local gym has also become a core practice of connecting and engaging with stress in my body. Bouldering pushes me to overcome my fears, to train for strength and power, to discipline my body for better technique, and problem solve for the workable route. In a sense, climbing has been a body-mind integrative practice, especially for someone like me whose sedentary work mostly involves the mind.

Third, we must find ways to become more and more at peace with our bodies, our troublesome racial features, and our ambivalent cultural and ethnic heritage. In some ways, this is what this book is about, the heart of Asian American theology. The rest of this chapter will discuss this idea of integration and bringing all of our selves into God's presence.

INTEGRATING THE FRAGMENTED SELF

Anyone overwhelmed with stress suffers in these key leadership challenges of presence, temperature awareness and control, and creativity. What sets

---

[11]See Smith's discussion of sleep as a spiritual exercise, James Bryan Smith, *The Good and Beautiful God: Falling in Love with the God Jesus Knows* (Downers Grove, IL: InterVarsity, 2009), 33-36.
[12]Belden Lane, *Backpacking with the Saints: Wilderness Hiking as Spiritual Discipline* (New York: Oxford University Press, 2015), 211-12.

Asian Americans and other minorities apart is that the stress is intertwined with their bodies and identity. As aspects of ourselves are targeted with micro-assaults and associated with pain, they become identified as unwanted liabilities. These internal conflicts lead to a fragmentation.

In trauma studies, children who have suffered abuse or trauma for a long period of time can create a double self, where a good, pure, perfect, over-achieving self—untainted by abuse—balances out the dirty bad self. Judith Herman observes "when it is impossible to avoid the reality of the abuse, the child must construct some system of meaning that justifies it."[13] Along with creating a perfectionist self that is "a superb performer . . . an academic achiever, a model of social conformity,"[14] "fragmentation becomes the central principle of personality organization."[15] Is Asian American identity analogous to having a double self in terms of racial trauma? Our self-hatred and self-blaming along with overachieving tendencies fit the pattern. The concept of double self explains Asian American self-hatred and self-blaming in regard to racial-ethnic identity, along with the overachieving and perfectionistic tendency toward becoming an honorary White or model minority. As a survival or success strategy, one might adopt a bifurcation where the private/communal (*Gemeinschaft*) Asian self operates at home and within ethnic circles, while the public/societal (*Gesellschaft*) American self presents to the White-normative world outside.[16]

Trauma studies also give us the concepts of intrusion and constriction.[17] Intrusion here means that every microaggression carries the accumulated weight of all those prior incidents. This intrusion disrupts life by constricting it, causing one to avoid places and situations where one might be exposed to the risk of microaggressions. However, since these everyday incidents are ubiquitous, physical constriction to safe spaces is difficult, although many Asian Americans might avoid going to rural areas, the

---

[13]Judith Herman, *Trauma and Recovery: The Aftermath of Violence—from Domestic Abuse to Political Terror* (New York: Basic, 1997), 103.

[14]Herman, *Trauma and Recovery*, 105.

[15]Herman, *Trauma and Recovery*, 107.

[16]See how Hurh and Kim use the categories of *Gemeinschaft* and *Gesellschaft* to analyze racial pressures and ethnic affiliation, Won Moo Hurh and Kwang Chung Kim, "The Religious Participation of Korean Immigrants in the United States," *Journal for the Scientific Study of Religion* 29, no. 1 (1990): 19-34.

[17]Herman, *Trauma and Recovery*, 37, 42.

Midwest, or the South. More commonly, this constriction occurs in terms of creating a constricted self for the public—a redacted or truncated self that is more presentable and less visible. This self-editing, where the unpresentable Asian parts are repressed when in unsafe contexts, might be positively considered as code-switching or biculturality. In reality, so-called bicultural competence within this framework is a pathological acquiescing of the two selves, both located separately within their respective worlds.

For many Asian Americans, this discernment of self-editing becomes a skill required for everyday life—unconscious and almost second nature. Furthermore, after years of such practice, the deformed or truncated self becomes one's own self-understanding, leading to dissociation from one's body or a fragmentation of the self into pieces. Moreover, even as almost second nature, this constant self-redaction as a "continually active process" can be taxing, draining well-being and creativity.[18] The idea of a double self presents the possibility of such exhausting dissociation even when Asian Americans might express high levels of bicultural competence, albeit dichotomized.

Along with the psychological costs on the individual, this double life registers a broader impact. Even if they are so-called biculturally competent, the inclusion of Asian Americans in societal and institutional power structures would not contribute to efforts toward diversity and racial justice, but rather aggravate them. They themselves are navigating the systems publicly but at the cost of being less than who they fully are. The model minority myth is an archetype of a self-redacted Asian American suffering from a double self. This complicity in systemic injustices is a byproduct of self-redaction, where non-Whiteness is safely ghettoized, maintaining White normativity. Thus, true integration must be activist, resisting the marginalizing forces of normativity. For this process to occur, new mental categories that question the status quo and normative assumptions of society must be introduced in a safe environment.

Framing Asian American identity as a trauma-induced fragmented self provides a conceptual framework to explain the various tendencies of Asian American experience, such as compartmentalization and code-switching.

---

[18]Sigmund Freud understood repression as an unconscious and yet still active process. See Stephen Frosh, *A Brief Introduction to Psychoanalytic Theory* (New York: Palgrave Macmillan, 2012), 59.

More importantly, the trauma-orientation also provides a trajectory toward wholeness and an integrated self. This integration does not imply that the journey of identity will end. An integrated self will still be complex, fluid, and polycentric as opposed to being centered on just one aspect of our identity. The simplistic assertion of Christian identity as the only true identity or our real identity is insufficient because it presupposes a disembodied, cultureless self. Instead of our identity in Christ as the only true one, integration points to all of our identities being in Christ.

Taking all these insights into consideration, we at Fuller's Asian American Center have found three core components to healing this personal fragmentation: language, narrative, and community.

First, the introduction of mental categories that enable an adequate narration of the nuances of Asian American identity and experience is crucial. The inability to articulate our experience, especially our pain, leaves us helpless. Education and collective wisdom about the full range of Asian American experience is the key that provides the path forward.[19] This is the reason why the Asian American Quadrilateral was theorized with the categories of Asian heritage, migration experience, American culture, and racialization.

Second, using this vocabulary, a coherent narrative of our life must be constructed. With an expanded vocabulary, we can give adequate language to our past experiences, recovering, reframing, and reinterpreting them. New language reframes our present situation and reality, as we noted in chapter three on the AAQ. This process sheds light and gives understanding to the shadowy past, bringing order or structure to the confusion. I draw this idea of a coherent narrative from the Adult Attachment Interview (AAI) research of Mary Main.[20] Main's research showed how adults lacking a good processing of their relationship with their parents displayed poor attachment orientation, and that this poor attachment continued to manifest in all of their ongoing relationships. This processing of the past that Main detailed focused on coherence, meaning that our past and present experiences are fully acknowledged for what they are without making excuses to avoid painful realities.

---

[19]Rosalind S. Chou and Joe R. Feagin, *The Myth of the Model Minority: Asian Americans Facing Racism* (Boulder, CO: Paradigm, 2010), 193-94.
[20]Siegel, *The Developing Mind*, 351-55.

This idea of coherence helps us understand Asian American identity as integrative. In a sense, we lack attachment to our Asian Americanness, a concept closely related to our parents, who often serve as the primary embodiment of that idea during our early developmental stages and throughout the rest of our lives. Parental and racioethnic attachment would apply to multiracial Asian Americans in how their Asian American parent owns Asian Americanness and how they relate to this Asian American parent. For Asian American adoptees, regarding these two attachments, the way their parents affirm or dismiss their racioethnic identity would impact their identity development.

The goal of personal storytelling as a coherent narrative has concrete physiological impacts with bi-hemispheric and vertical integration of various brain processes.[21] Using the left/right model of the brain, this bi-hemispheric integration means that the nonverbalized memories and emotions embedded in our bodies can be given language and logical order. In terms of a triune model of the brain, the lower instinctual reptilian brain and the emotional limbic brain can be brought closer to the rational neocortex.[22] Educator Louis Cozolino explains it this way:

> A story well told contains conflicts and resolutions, gestures and expressions, and thoughts flavored with emotion. The convergence of these diverse functions within the narrative provides a nexus of neural network integration among left and right, top and bottom, and sensory, somatic, motor, affective, and cognitive processes in all parts of the brain.[23]

Third, community plays an important role in the healing process. Judith Herman explains how processing groups can incorporate all the key ingredients of trauma recovery, which includes healing relationships, safety, remembrance and mourning, reconnections to life, and commonality.[24] In our seminary context, we have found that a covenanted small group of four or five persons meeting weekly for one academic quarter is the best context for this coherent narrative to be processed. Our groups are small in number because

---

[21]Siegel, *The Developing Mind*, 383.
[22]For more on these models of the brain, see Siegel, *The Developing Mind*, 15-21.
[23]Louis Cozolino, *The Social Neuroscience of Education* (New York: W. W. Norton and Company, 2013), 21.
[24]Herman, *Trauma and Recovery*, 221.

of scheduling conflicts that made the meetings only an hour long. With a facilitator modeling and setting the bar for vulnerability, safety, mourning, and affirmation, the members are invited to invest in the group. In my experience of leading these groups for the last eight years, I have found that when we create a strong container to hold whatever we are carrying around, people are willing and ready to share. The courage to share and willingness to grow in listening skills are both equally vital for the group to function.

The format of the weekly meetings includes centering prayer, check-in, a designated group member sharing their narrative, a time of reflection and response, and finally closing with a prayer for the sharer. The centering prayer follows guidelines from Thomas Keating, where the goal is being fully present with all parts of ourselves in God's gracious presence, as if God was an old friend.[25] Sometimes, I will ask the members to offer God a different part of their bodies, becoming aware of them one at a time. The check-in is simple, offering an opportunity for self-reflection on the week. Each group member is given a minute or two to briefly share and thus consciously own the feelings that might have been subconsciously driving their lives that week. We have done this with simple question prompts: What were the highest and lowest points of the past week? How are you doing on a scale of one to ten, one being worst and ten being best? It is a rare gift to have a small group of people be so attentive to how I am doing each week.

All members sign up for a week to share their story as a combination of story and reflection—a sequence of experiences and thoughts told through events, people, or other markers in one's life, all in about twenty-five to thirty minutes. There does not need to be a forced closure or moral, but instead I have encouraged members to close by summarizing what they appreciate, what they are struggling with, and what questions they still have. Some members write their narrative and read it or use notes, whereas others simply talk extemporaneously. However, the goal of good personal narrative is a sense of coherence, which I will explain below. Next, we provide a time for the sharer to reflect on how this sharing felt to them, and for the listeners to express words of appreciation as well as share any aspect of the story that resonates with parts of their own lives. Finally, the meeting ends with a

---

[25]Thomas Keating, *Intimacy with God: An Introduction to Centering Prayer* (New York: Crossroad, 2009).

prayer of blessing for the member who generously shared their lives with the group.

Because members share formative, even harrowing events in their lives, and the fact that this process inherently requires vulnerability, every meeting is very carefully facilitated by the leader, usually a Fuller professor. Listeners are warned not to jump to soothing and reassuring after difficult stories just because they feel the urge to resolve tension. For example, after hearing the sharer relate past unresolved trauma, no one should say, "God will redeem all those terrible things and use them for God's glory, so be comforted!" It is not that this has no truth, but this kind of spiritually saccharine response short circuits the long journey of healing and struggle that we must do with God. More often than not, these kinds of responses are more indicative of the listener's inability to bear pain or unresolved tension, rather than concern for the welfare of the sharer.

We have found that hearing another person's coherent narrative is as beneficial as sharing one's own. Often hearing other people's experiences can stimulate our own memories of events thought long-forgotten or safely repressed. This is one of the amazing aspects of hearing the intimate details of another person. Because everyone in the group is Asian American, with the common goal of personal integration in God's presence, these life stories spur each other forward in each of our own journeys.

THE SPIRIT OF INTRAPERSONAL RECONCILIATION

Without a doubt, the cognitive, therapeutic, and neurological initiatives that I have presented above are a part of healing the fragmentation and dissociation within Asian American lives. They can be understood as something akin to spiritual disciplines in the sense that they create space for us to be in God's healing presence. However, the deep and true healing is God's work. In this final section, I present a theological perspective on the divine work of integrating our disparate parts. With the *intra*personal aspects of God's salvific work, I am bearing witness to God as the one who finds and gathers together the fragments of Asian American lives that we have hidden, abandoned, and rejected.

If we use the metaphor of identity as a collection of selves, some favored and some abandoned, we can think of the Good Shepherd who leaves the ninety-nine "found selves" in order to seek and find that one "lost self," bringing it back into divine fellowship. In this vein, I have prayed Psalm 139, asking for the presence of God to be with the various selves throughout my past. God is with the self that is in heaven as well as the self that is down in the depths (Ps 139:8). Over the years, whenever I felt like a stranger to myself, when I could not untangle the emotional and psychological knots within me, I prayed the last two verses, saying

> Search me, O God, and know my heart;
> > test me and know my thoughts.
> See if there is any wicked way in me,
> > and lead me in the way everlasting. (Ps 139:23-24)

I have more recently imagined God searching for my lost selves, with whom I had lost connection. Connecting with this image of God as the one who seeks, finds, and gathers, I propose that the Holy Spirit brings about an *intra-personal* reconciliation as well as interpersonal reconciliation. The Spirit as the integrator of our fragmented self can be understood in three aspects.

First, the Spirit of God is the One that holds together the disparate aspects of Asian American selves. The apostle Paul uses the body as an analogy for the macrocosm of society and the church, all the while interrogating and subverting assumptions about honor and status (1 Cor 12:12-27).[26] What has been considered honorable is not truly worthy of that status, and the seemingly inferior members are in reality indispensable ("our ugly parts have greater beauty, while our beautiful parts have no need," in Martin's rendering of verse 23).[27] The Spirit brings all these members together as one brings about "an actual reversal of the normal, 'this-worldly' attribution of honor and status."[28]

Applying the body analogy psychologically to the fragmented Asian American self, we can discern the Spirit's work as a reassignment of status and honor to the various aspects of the polycentric identity. The immigrant status or being phenotypically Asian, considered ugly in the sight of a White-normative world, could be held in honor. Meanwhile, what is taken

---

[26] I am indebted to Martin's work on the Greco-Roman backdrop of Paul's body analogy. See Dale B. Martin, *The Corinthian Body* (New Haven, CT: Yale University Press, 1995).

[27] Martin, *Corinthian Body*, 95.

[28] Martin, *Corinthian Body*, 96.

as beautiful, the presentable White-assimilated self, should be evaluated more soberly. Especially cogent in the Spirit's work are all aspects of Asian American identity gathered and held together in Christ (Eph 1:10). Where racial trauma pressures the Asian American self toward disconnection and dissociation from the body, cultural heritage, and family lineage, Christ holds all these aspects of ourselves together in every situation and in every way. Of course, this gathering and holding together does not mean dispensing with the strategic code-switching that is necessary to navigate the world in its fallenness. However, the Spirit's presence and work pervade and operate at a deeper level. Relating to and communing with the disparate aspects of the self can be expressed as the perichoretic work of the Spirit, keeping in union the apparently discordant and contradictory.

Second, the Spirit of God helps express the unarticulated pains and hurts that come from these redacted parts of our Asian American selves.[29] The Holy Spirit is the one that "searches everything" (1 Cor 2:10) and guides us to all the truth (Jn 16:13; Rom 8:26-27). With trauma, while the body might remember and keep score, the explicit identification of pain often remains hidden and unnamed.[30] With microaggressive trauma that is essentially accumulative, there will not be a single incident but rather a thousand subtle occurrences that the self has erased in order to survive. In other words, since the racial microaggressions that create the fragmented self are essentially invisible, they can manifest as a frustrating and mentally sapping experience of internal conflict. In this place, the Spirit reveals the hidden nature of the pain and reveals the truth of the matter, that is, the social and structural powers of oppression.[31] The connection between flesh and language at the Pentecostal outpouring is evocative of how the Holy Spirit empowers an embodied and linguistic articulation. The work of naming the reality of racial microaggressions and trauma, as well as the broader forces of colonialism and imperialism, is in that vein a pneumatological work of

---

[29]While my concern is narrower with the idea of a fragmented self, I draw inspiration from Rambo's innovative pneumatology envisioning the Spirit as the persisting and remaining divine presence post-trauma. Shelly Rambo, *Spirit and Trauma: A Theology of Remaining* (Louisville, KY: Westminster John Knox, 2010), 111-41.

[30]Van der Kolk's works underscores how the body knows more than the mind regarding trauma. Bessel van der Kolk, *The Body Keeps the Score: Brain, Mind, and the Body in the Healing of Trauma* (New York: Penguin, 2014).

[31]Rambo, *Spirit and Trauma*, 123-25.

opening the mouths of the oppressed to cry out, making both pain and healing intelligible.

Third, the Spirit integrates all of ourselves in union with Christ and, through Christ, with other people as well. Having all of ourselves united with Christ is the spiritual telos that leads to genuine shalom within ourselves. This intrapersonal dynamic is closely related to the interpersonal work of solidarity, of being reconciled to others who are also united to Christ, and through Christ, united with us as well.

The Spirit's inner work of gathering, uniting, and healing the self extends to Asian American communities that also collectively can be fragmented.[32] The similar dynamics of redaction and dissociation could be ecclesially manifested as well, even often theologically enabled.[33] Incorporating the personal and the communal, the Spirit's movement continues with the outer work of gathering, uniting, and healing our fragmented and divided world. While these inner and outer works might be comprehended as in tension or even conflict, they are united in the Spirit who brings all things together in Christ as the Spirit of participation. Using different terminology, centrifugal integration and centripetal solidarity are both the one work of the one Spirit, participating in the one multifaceted *missio Dei*.[34]

---

[32]See Jeffrey C. Alexander et al., *Cultural Trauma and Collective Identity* (Berkeley: University of California Press, 2004).

[33]Some of the Asian American evangelical churches seeking to be multiethnic for the purpose of inclusivity while denying their Asian Americanness could be understood as fragmented and suffering dissociation. See Russell Jeung, *Faithful Generations: Race and New Asian American Churches* (New Brunswick, NJ: Rutgers University Press, 2005).

[34]Michael J. Gorman, *Becoming the Gospel: Paul, Participation, and Mission* (Grand Rapids, MI: Eerdmans, 2015), 37.

9

EMBODIMENT AND ECCLESIOLOGY

Will non-Asians be able to move past race and
accept Asian American leadership?

RUSSELL JEUNG

ON A PANEL OF SPEAKERS addressing ministry in diverse contexts, a Black lead pastor of a multiracial church described his ministry as "a picture of heaven" because they "had them all: White, Black, Asian, and Hispanic." You can hear the pride in his voice as he described his heavenly church of every "nation, tribe, people, and language" (Rev 7:9) displaying the divine vision of racial reconciliation unlike those other segregated churches. Over the last two decades, it appears the importance of multiracial churches as a solution to the persistent problem of racism in the US has become a self-evident truism. Referencing Martin Luther King Jr.'s dream where our children "will not be judged by the color of their skin but by the content of their character," supporters of multiracial churches talk about the church leading our racist broken world as "People of the Dream," witnessing against the appalling fact that the most segregated hour of Christian America is eleven o'clock on Sunday morning.

What lies beneath this seemingly straightforward reasoning of multiracial ecclesiology is a different story. Not without its ideological underpinnings, this multiracial ecclesiology suffers from a number of problematic presuppositions, resulting in a toxic outlook. Stuck within this framework of the so-called

Epigraph: Russell Jeung, *Faithful Generations: Race and New Asian American Churches* (New Brunswick, NJ: Rutgers University Press, 2004), 156.

multiracial versus monoracial, integrated versus segregated, a Korean American pastor friend relays a question posed by a young college student: Is their predominately Korean American church doing something wrong because it is not able to become more diverse? This question haunts him. His church tries and yet struggles to reach beyond its racial boundaries—non-Asian Americans visit but do not return. Another Asian American pastor shares a moment when he realized that he was actually valuing White families more than recent Asian immigrants, all in the pursuit of trying to reflect the diverse neighborhood, to move his congregation (a recently independent English ministry) out of an immigrant church and toward "the picture of heaven." This pastor confesses how his pursuit of a multiracial church led him away from actually ministering to the people in front of him and made him strangely prejudice. These pastors feel inklings of something awry.

In this chapter, I present the Asian American church as the context of Asian American theology for the purpose of holistic discipleship. In the process of elaborating on Asian American ecclesiology and ministry, I first challenge the supposed orthodoxy of multiethnicity. Specifically, I argue that multiracial ecclesiology functions as propaganda with problematic presuppositions that remain largely unquestioned. While the problems of racism and segregation are real, the multiracial ecclesiology is blind to problems that it creates behind the guise of a heavenly vision of reconciliation. What is lost in multiracial ecclesiology is the possibility and reality of these churches becoming a hydra-like manifestation of the same toxic racism that they purport to address. If the problems and dangers of these multiracial churches are fully acknowledged, then these churches would have a place among others within the mixed economy of diverse churches as they all pursue one mission and kingdom work of God. In humility they need to understand their place within the larger community.

After addressing the issues around multiracial ecclesiology, I will present the theological underpinnings of an embodied ecclesiology. In particular, using the Chalcedonian christological pattern, we can affirm the fullness and particularity of the humanity of the local church community as well as its divine origin. This human element will take account of the broader historical, sociological, and political realities of the US, not just the demographic of the immediate neighborhood.

Finally, in the last section I will propose the kind of challenges and tasks that confront the three main models of Asian American churches, the ethnic-specific, pan-Asian, and multiethnic. For each of these models of ministry, benefits and dangers must be clearly acknowledged and engaged to achieve ecclesiological integrity and ministry faithfulness.

Diagnosing Multiracial Ecclesiology

Multiracial churches definitely have a significant place within the greater ecclesial landscape, but only if they understand that every ecclesial expression comes with their challenges and pitfalls. Here I present four concerns regarding multiracial ecclesiology: Terminological confusion, anachronistic use of *segregation*, shallow antiracism, and generic discipleship.

First, my critique of multiracial ecclesiology begins with its sloppy terminology. A number of labels describe a diverse church. Books like *United by Faith* accurately describe the telos of multiracial ecclesiology as fighting racism, mostly defined in terms of the Black/White binary.[1] However, other books muddy the categories, confusing international, intercultural, multiethnic, and multiracial.[2] All of these terms signify different things, especially to Asian Americans, as well as Latino/a Americans, because we know that race, ethnicity, and culture are interconnected yet different realities.

As I have discussed throughout this book, Asian Americans require various distinct categories to make sense of our experience and the Asian American Quadrilateral can help order the multiple layers of experience. My nationality (American), ethnicity (Korean), race (Asian), culture (Asian American and Korean American) cannot be conflated if I am to be included in this discussion about ecclesiology, diversity, and justice. For Asian Americans, confusing these categories results in anti-Asian racism, as we

---

[1]Curtiss Paul DeYoung et al., *United by Faith: The Multiracial Congregation as an Answer to the Problem of Race* (New York: Oxford University Press, 2003). This work responds to the previous work, Michael O. Emerson and Christian Smith, *Divided by Faith: Evangelical Religion and the Problem of Race in America* (New York: Oxford University Press, 2001). This work describes the chasm between the perceptions of White and Black evangelicals about systematic discrimination against Blacks.

[2]Just to mention a few: Mark DeYmaz, *Building A Healthy Multi-Ethnic Church: Mandate, Commitments, and Practices of a Diverse Congregation* (Minneapolis: Fortress, 2020); David Anderson, *Multicultural Ministry: Finding Your Church's Unique Rhythm* (Grand Rapids, MI: Zondervan, 2004); Douglas J. Brouwer, *How to Become a Multicultural Church* (Grand Rapids, MI: Eerdmans, 2017).

discussed in chapter seven regarding Orientalism and perpetual foreigner tropes. With many works interchanging the use of race/ethnicity and multiracial/multiethnic, their theological arguments become clumsy. This kind of carelessness already displays inaptitude toward handling the complexities of human diversity with the needed nuance and attention to detail, resulting in propaganda-like features, widely promoted yet misleading, such as "our church has all the colors, every one of them."

Second, referring to the diversity of the local churches in our contemporary context as a problem of segregation is anachronistic. Yes, there still exists real segregation in our school systems and neighborhoods.[3] However, we must recall the historical context of King's statement. When in 1963 Martin Luther King Jr. said, "Eleven o'clock on Sunday morning is the most segregated hour in America," over ninety-five percent of the minority population was Black. The historical context of the Black church was slavery and later Jim Crow. However, because of the Hart-Celler Immigration and Nationality Act of 1965, a direct result of the civil rights movement, Hispanics are now estimated at a little under half of all minority population, with the Black community under thirty-three percent and Asian Americans at around fifteen percent.[4] These immigrants brought and formed new congregations. To label this ecclesial diversity as segregation is a misnomer, reducing this reality into a narrow pre-1965 Black/White rubric. In chapter seven on racialization, I analyzed the Black/White binary paradigm with its continuing relevance as well as its limitations. This language of segregation coming out of this paradigm is not appropriate for our current ecclesial reality.

King's words here must be interpreted historically, just like the color-blindness of his "I Have a Dream" speech of 1963, which means two different things before and after the Civil Rights Act of 1964. When King said he dreamed of a day when his kids will "not be judged by the color of their skin, but by the content of their character," he was longing for equal treatment and

---

[3]Erica Frankenberg et al., "Harming our Common Future: America's Segregated Schools 65 Years After Brown," The Civil Rights Project. May 10, 2019. www.civilrightsproject.ucla.edu/research /k-12-education/integration-and-diversity/harming-our-common-future-americas-segregated -schools-65-years-after-brown/Brown-65-050919v4-final.pdf.

[4]"Population Estimates, July 1, 2021, (V2021)," *QuickFacts*, United States Census Bureau, accessed May 2, 2022, https://www.census.gov/quickfacts/fact/table/US/PST045221. This site is updated periodically with new data.

the end of racial oppression. After the Civil Rights Act, in order to address the problem of race, we had to see race and its machinations at the social and systemic levels. Ironically contemporary colorblindness is a White racist reaction against the Civil Rights Act and its efforts to dismantle racial oppression, what Ian Haney López calls "Colorblind White Dominance."[5] If there is no race, there is no racist oppression. When some quote King in support of contemporary colorblindness they either are anachronistically subverting him to the nefarious ends of colorblind White dominance or shutting their eyes to the historical and sociopolitical realities of injustice. Like the Civil Rights Act, in our time, we must see race if we want to follow King's dream.

Third, proposing multiracial churches as a solution to the problem of racism misunderstands racism. Intentional or not, offering a church as a solution to the problem of racism in the US presupposes an ethnic or race relations framework, where the problem is about different kinds of people not getting along.[6] Or from a different angle, the foundation is liberal multiculturalism with discussions of minority rights and representation without full account of the ways in which racism is embedded into the very structures of our society. This liberal multiculturalism assumes a level playing field largely devoid of historical injustices that cripple a minority community's opportunities and efforts. Theologically speaking, the doctrines of original sin and the *imago Dei* as applied to all humanity via an individualist anthropology with no social identities abets this liberal multiculturalism. Evangelicalism's vision of racial reconciliation functions largely within this philosophical rubric of liberal individualism.[7] Martin Luther King Jr. did not march for the lost souls of individuals. Rather he marched for the soul of our nation. Without a critical theological apparatus to handle social identities, the universalizing anthropology leads to colorblindness or ahistorical multiculturalism with a focus on cultural differences that supposedly divides us.

---

[5]Ian Haney López, *White by Law: The Legal Construction of Race*, 2nd ed. (New York: New York University Press, 2006), 147-48.

[6]Gary Y. Okihiro, *Third World Studies: Theorizing Liberation* (Durham: Duke University Press, 2016), 21-22.

[7]Emerson and Smith deftly show this mistake of thinking of racism as purely interpersonal and systemic within White evangelicalism. Michael O. Emerson and Christian Smith, *Divided by Faith: Evangelical Religion and the Problem of Race in America* (New York: Oxford University Press, 2001).

Either way what results is a colorblind White dominance; the status quo is never impacted by these interracial churches.[8] Unable to correctly name the demon, the lordless power of racism discussed in chapter seven roams free, devouring in the shadows.

Multiracial ecclesiology might talk about the neighborhood but ignores the broader society, resulting in narrow congregrationism. An example of this myopia is the 80/20 definition of a multiracial congregation, meaning no one racial group should be over eighty percent of the community.[9] If you have been following the argument so far, the problem with this generic concept should be clear. This definition does not distinguish between a so-called multiracial church that is eighty percent White and twenty percent people of color, and a different one that is eighty percent Black and twenty percent White along with other people of color. Simply looking at the individual congregation, the logic of eighty percent and the "minority" can guide the issue of power and representation without any regard to societal forces.

While advancing multiethnic churches, the homogenous unit principle has been identified and critiqued as the culprit for our divisions. Theorized by missiologist Donald McGavran, the homogenous unit principle proposes that people "like to become Christians without crossing racial, linguistic, or class barriers."[10] However, targeting the homogenous unit principle is problematic and misguided. Instead of naming White normativity and hegemony, the language of the homogenous unit principle creates an abstract and universal reasoning that is palatable to White fragility. This abstract critique treats all "homogenous" churches the same, whether they be all White, all Black, all Hispanic, all Asian, and so on. Based on that logic Black Churches and White churches under Jim Crow would have the exact same problem of homogeneity. This is the problem of an abstract argument devoid of historical and structural realities. This argument is analogical to saying that anyone talking about race and racism is racist.

---

[8]López, *White by Law*.

[9]DeYoung et al., *United by Faith*, 164.

[10]Donald A. McGavran, *Understanding Church Growth*, 3rd ed., rev. and ed. by C. Peter Wagner (Grand Rapids, MI: Eerdmans, 1990), x. See also Donald A. McGavran, *Ethnic Realities and the Church: Lessons from India* (South Pasadena, CA: William Carey Library, 1979), and C. Peter Wagner, *Our Kind of People: The Ethical Dimensions of Church Growth in America* (Atlanta: John Knox Press, 1979).

In her work, Korie L. Edwards reveals that interracial churches reproduce White hegemony because they

> work to the extent that they are, first, comfortable places for whites to attend. This is because whites are accustomed to their cultural practices and ideologies being the norm and to being structurally dominant in nearly every social institution.[11]

Edwards points out that this White hegemony remains regardless of the race of the lead pastor because proficiency in and support of White religious culture is vital to attract White people.[12] Because White Christians have more choices in their worshiping communities, attracting and retaining them is crucial to the heavenly vision. Simply put, within these interracial churches these White Christians end up being worth more, as the Asian American pastor at the beginning of this chapter came not only to realize but also to repent of.

Disturbingly the optics of interracial churches with its interracial friendships blind people to the underlining demon of racism:

> Blacks in multiracial congregations may be influenced by such congregations to embrace a dominant White racial frame in which the importance of structure is diminished, and such congregations could also be attractive to Blacks who already embrace those perspectives on inequality.[13]

Multiracial churches can actually aggravate racial justice by making their congregants less aware of structural racial realities.

Finally, multiethnic churches can end up with a generic one-size-fits-all approach to discipleship. The issue is focusing on the universality at the expense of particularity, forgetting that the universal questions and concerns are always experienced *as* particular people in particular bodies and histories. When a community becomes more diverse culturally and racially, the work required to learn about everyone's background, to actually see each person in their particular lives and their correspondingly particular discipleship, grows almost exponentially.

---

[11]Korie L. Edwards, *The Elusive Dream: The Power of Race in Interracial Churches* (New York: Oxford University Press, 2008), 139.

[12]Edwards, *Elusive Dream*, 126.

[13]Ryon J. Cobb, Samuel L. Perry, and Kevin D. Dougherty, "United by Faith? Race/Ethnicity, Congregational Diversity, and Explanations of Racial Inequality," *Sociology of Religion* 76, no. 2 (2015): 177-98.

The more diverse the community, the more complicated the discipleship becomes because even though we follow the same Christ, following looks different for everyone. That difference was evident throughout biblical history as well as across different persons of the same time period, like the different callings of the apostles. While different people within a community can learn from each other, the leadership of the church often sets the framework and culture of the community. Too often the preacher ends up saying something along the lines of "despite our differences, we are all one in Christ," which is true. But said with the force of colorblind White dominance, this universalizing message reinforces White hegemony as Korie Edwards notes in her research. Given the ambivalence and fraught nature of multiracial churches, the idea of them being a picture of heaven is functionally whitewashed propaganda. Some call multiethnic churches a mestizo culture; however, this is naive.[14] This approach misunderstands the sheer scope of the problem of White normativity in society, permeating the American church and theological education.

My point in all this is to see multiracial churches as one among many ecclesial expressions; they are like every other one. While there is a place for interracial churches within the broader ecclesial landscape, any Pollyannaish delusions of them being a picture of heaven must be tempered by their limitations and dangers. When they are blind to these problems, multiracial churches can be toxic, doing more harm than good, not a place of heaven, but whitewashed tombs in more ways than one.

ASIAN AMERICANS IN MULTIRACIAL CHURCHES

For Asian American Christians, the experience of a multiethnic church with White hegemony presses toward three directions.

First, multiethnicity with its hidden White hegemony presses Asian Americans toward embracing Whiteness as normative for their spiritual life. In the last chapter, we saw how racial (de)formation leads to a fragmentation or splitting of their identity, where Asian Americans learn to present their more acceptable "White" social self in public. One of the questions that we must ask ourselves is which self goes to church? Which self receives the

---

[14]DeYoung et al., *United by Faith*, 169.

message? Which self participates in the communal life? Which self is dis-
cipled in their church? The multiracial churches with its White hegemony,
through its "White peer approval," encourages and affirms Asian Americans
as they present their model minority selves.[15]

I attended a seminar organized by Asian American pastors serving a
White megachurch. The seminar was designed to share resources and insights for other Asian American pastors. What disturbed me was the level
of condescension of these megachurch pastors toward other Asian
American pastors, especially those serving in ethnic churches. I observed
more than just condescension of megachurch pastors toward smaller
church pastors. I saw an element of racial condescension. Unlike these
"ghetto" ethnic or immigrant pastors, these megachurch pastors were mentored by and served alongside respectable White pastors. These pastors
had no awareness of racial structures that pressed against minorities and
immigrant communities, no awareness of White hegemony that pervades
our society and our theological education. Also, the creativity and innovations that they lauded were for a different ministry context with a different
set of concerns and issues. It did not occur to them that these concepts
could have limited application in other church contexts. That is the arrogance of White normativity, the assumption of universality, that these
Asian American pastors have internalized while serving in predominately
White ministries.

For Asian American pastors leading a multiracial church with this White
normativity mindset, they can pathologize their Asian American identity or
make it the butt of their jokes as a way to break the ice, to say "yes, I understand that I am different, I am in on the joke." Their modus operandi focuses
on the universalizing gospel message, while valorizing their "White" selves
and hiding their Asian American selves.

If the ministry context is a predominately Asian American church desperately trying to be the "biblical" ideal of multiethnicity, White normativity
motivates the Asian American pastor to value White congregants more than
just another Asian American visitor. The Asian American pastor I mentioned at the beginning of this chapter, who repented of his racial favoritism,

---

[15]Richard Delgado, *Critical Race Theory: An Introduction*, 3rd ed. (New York: New York University
Press, 2017), 81.

saw two different visitors to his church: he clearly felt that the Korean international student was less valuable to him than the White family, who would have helped the church to become more diverse. He definitely did not need someone who was going to make his church more "fobby," more Asian. The desire for multiethnicity makes these predominately Asian American churches value non-Asian Americans, especially White folks, more than others, because having them validates that they are good enough for our White-normative society, communicating that they have arrived.

Second, too often multiracial churches function out of a Black/White binary paradigm of diversity with its resulting erasure of Asian Americans. Asian American Christians are seen as honorary Whites, not racial minorities. Indeed, *United by Faith* uncritically says that it is easier for Asian Americans to be a part of multiracial churches because of their "acculturation and structural assimilation."[16] This idea of easy assimilation fails to acknowledge the fragmentation in Asian American identity and its implications for ministry. Just because Asian Americans attend a multiethnic church does not mean that they are actually ministered to well. Their attendance could very well be attributed to racial formation and assimilation pressures as well as other spiritual factors.

The faulty assumptions and limitations of multiethnic ecclesiology presses on Asian American Christians, churches, and pastors with the force of ideological propaganda. Ashamed of their supposed monoculturalness, Asian American churches may try to erase their Asian American identity, which is seen as a stumbling block to God's call for diversity. Trained by White theology, these Asian Americans live as good model minorities, following the White playbook as though they are White. They aspire toward being a multiracial church by erasing their Asian Americanness without realizing that the stumbling blocks on their path toward diversity come from structural Whiteness and racial formation in our society that make them undesirable.[17]

Through the latest expression of protests for Black lives provoked by George Floyd's death, many multiethnic churches were awakened to address structural racism, organize panel discussions and special events and programs

---

[16]DeYoung et al., *United by Faith*, 127.
[17]Russell Jeung, *Faithful Generations: Race and New Asian American Churches* (New Brunswick, NJ: Rutgers University Press, 2004), 158-61.

regarding racism. When anti-Asian racism began to rise with coronavirus misinformation, propagating age-old Yellow peril fears, many Asian American members were disappointed to see no response by the same church leadership. Racial justice was simply about anti-Blackness only. The racial experience of Asian Americans was invisible. I have already stressed the importance of the exceptional nature of the Black experience of White supremacy in chapter seven, that fighting for Asian American visibility should not come at the expense of the Black community and that ultimately the struggle is against Whiteness that marginalizes all people of color. Given all that, the invisibility of Asian Americans within multiethnic churches is toxic and harmful for their spiritual welfare.

If not erased, Asian Americans within multiracial churches easily become Orientalized or homogenized. According to the rubric of liberal multiculturalism—the basis for the way many people think about multiracial churches—each racial group contributes their gifts to the whole. By featuring the distinct gifts of various groups, liberal multiculturalism "museumizes" and "exoticizes" the racial or ethnic characteristics or spirituality in an essentialist way.[18] The particular gifts of each racial group sound good in principle but it does not work for Asian Americans. There is no one worship style, one language, or spiritual practice that can adequately do justice here. So, you sing some Hillsong songs, followed by the gospel choir, then a song in Spanish. The Asian American contribution is up next. Do you sing a song in Korean? Or pray *tong-song-gi-do*? This arrangement Orientalizes Asian Americans as foreigners because Asian languages do not function for Asian Americans in the same way that Spanish does for the Hispanic community. This difference has to do with the US's proximity to Spanish-speaking Mexico as well as the historical fact that most of the Southwest was literally formal Mexico. Korean does not function in the same way for later generations of Korean Americans. As the most diverse and complex of the racial category, Asian Americans end up bearing the heavy burden of trying to find their gift for this multiethnic context, without realizing that the

---

[18]For the problems and limitations of liberal multiculturalism, see Stephen May and Lincoln Dam, "Essentialism," in *Encyclopedia of Critical Whiteness Studies in Education*, ed. Zachary A. Casey (Leiden: Brill, 2021), 179-87. See also Brian Barry, *Culture and Equality: An Egalitarian Critique of Multiculturalism* (Cambridge, UK: Policy, 2001).

problem lies neither in their context nor in their ability but in the very idea of simple multiracial contributions. To clarify, the problem is not the idea of cultural gifts, but the racial prompting that believes racial identity functions the same way among different minorities. This is a trap that Asian Americans can fall into, again giving another reason to pathologize and blame the Asian American for their inadequacy, instead of correctly finding fault in the system.

The other more significant problem here is that of ethnic monopolizing or usually Korean dominance, given the overrepresentation of Korean Americans in Protestant spaces. As we have noted in chapter three, this kind of ethnic monopolizing is damaging and distortive of the whole Asian American community, especially to Asian Americans of South and Southeast Asian heritages. Taking one ethnic heritage to represent the panethnic Asian American community amounts to racial reduction.

Superficial diversity can do more harm than good. For Asian Americans, the ways that we are rendered invisible in racial justice discourses make multiracial spaces perpetuate our erasure from honorary Whiteness to honorary Blackness. In other words, Asian Americans become "White" allies to Black and other people of color. This resultant honorary Blackness is evident when Asian Americans speak of racism and racial realities as only anti-Blackness as though they are not themselves people of color.

CRITICAL MIXED ECONOMY EMBODIED ECCLESIOLOGY

Instead of thinking about multiethnic churches as an ideal and pinnacle of ecclesial expressions, we need to understand how these churches function within a larger mixed economy of different kinds of churches, gathering and ministering in different contexts. The term *mixed economy church*, coined by Archbishop of Canterbury Rowan Williams some two decades ago, pointed to the desperate need to diversify the Church of England to reach the growing ethnic demographics as well as the pressing need to reach to the unchurched or the post-churched.[19] Along those lines, we need

---

[19]See Archbishop's Council on Mission and Public Affairs, *Mission-Shaped Church: Church Planting and Fresh Expressions in a Changing Context* (New York: Seabury, 2010) and Michael Moynagh with Philip Harrold, *Church for Every Context: An Introduction to Theology and Practice* (London: SCM, 2012).

to see the place and role of various kinds of local churches in the body of Christ, that one local expression of the church does not do justice to the diversity of people in their life journeys. This diversity includes race and ethnicity as well.

The idea of contextualizing ecclesiology and focusing on a particular demographic leads us to the homogenous unit principle, much maligned for theologically funding White suburban megachurches. We have already noted how White hegemony still functions within multiracial churches, albeit now much more hidden. Peter Wagner's *Our Kind of People* argued that we need various kinds of churches along ethnic lines, given ethnic diversity, White normativity, and problematic colorblind one-size-fits-all ministry models.[20] Attacking the homogenous unit principle is misguided because such a blunt approach ignores the historic and material differences in various ethnic and racial communities. This critique, in a sense, uses a sledgehammer instead of scalpel. The homogeneous unit principle and the reality of endogamy disturbs us because of our history of segregation and anti-miscegenation laws, but the problem is not some abstract idea of segregation or anti-miscegenation per se, but rather White power and White supremacy, and later a more implicit but even more toxic White normativity. Focusing on the homogeneous unit principle abstracts and universalizes the problem of White exclusive communities in more White-palatable ways because it does not name or draw attention to its Whiteness.

If we are to talk about a mixed economy church with a diversity of ecclesial communities, even for specific ethnic or racial communities, we must attend to the historic and structural forces in our society. The *critical* part in my idea of a critical mixed economy church addresses this specific concern around the homogeneous unit principle. Our mixed economy ecclesiology must incorporate historic and structural dimensions of power and exclusion, as well as material and political inequities within our society as a whole, not just a neighborhood. Framing diversity exclusively in terms of the neighborhood or even the city is problematic. The local context keeps us grounded but we must also deal with the whole of society as well as the ecosystem of American Christianity, including theological institutions, the publishing industry, and

---

[20]C. Peter Wagner, *Our Kind of People: The Ethical Dimensions of Church Growth in America* (Atlanta: John Knox, 1979).

worship song producers. When the dominant normative group, such as a White suburban megachurch, uses the homogeneous unit principle as the most effective strategy for numerical growth, explicitly or implicitly excluding others, the problem is the White normativity that must be taken to task, not the fact that there are minority/ethnic churches around as well. For under-resourced and marginalized communities, having churches that specifically target them makes good sense theologically and missiologically.

Saying that a White member is excluded or marginalized in an Asian American church, and therefore more White pastors need to be hired and more White leaders need to represented on the stage, actually makes logical sense if our problem is simply with the homogeneous unit principle, without a critical awareness of history and structures of our society. This way of arguing is problematic given the pervasive White normativity and the marginalization of Asian Americans in general. Again, it is akin to arguing that talking about the problem of racism is racist.

What about the balkanization of the church with these "segregated" churches?[21] On the one hand, we have the problem of balkanization, and on the other, the White hegemony in multiethnic churches, both toxic and harmful. Having diverse churches of any kind, whether they be ethnic/racial or theological or denominational suffers from their inability to witness to the unity of the body of Christ. A church with diverse membership that is under White hegemony, or any other hidden oppressive normativities, dehumanizes its members and obscures social injustices. Given dangers and challenges on all sides, we need ample humility in our communal journeys. Different kinds of churches will have their particular gifts and challenges. The key is for all churches to be a true and faithful church and not just a social club.

Lastly, the *embodied* aspect of my ecclesiological proposal points to the divine and human realities of the church. An embodied ecclesiology means that we theologically acknowledge the church as comprising of full humanity. The christological Chalcedonian formula of fully God and fully human has been used in theology to account for the divine/human reality, for example, in understanding the nature of Scripture or the relationship

---

[21]See earlier in this chapter for my issues with using the term *segregation* for the diversity of churches.

between human freedom and divine sovereignty.[22] This Chalcedonian idea of affirming human and divine aspects "without confusion, without change, without division, without separation" also can be applied to the dual nature of the church.[23] The Chalcedonian logic of fully human and fully divine rejects a docetic ecclesiology that affirms only the spiritual dimension of the church called and gathered by God, as though it is not of real human beings who bring their own particularities. Of course, an Ebionite ecclesiology that thinks of the church as though it were just a social organization with common interests is inadequate as well.[24] In chapter two, I noted that when thinking about the Chalcedonian formula, the idea of humanity can be misunderstood as an abstract idea, a transcendent ontological category beyond the particular enculturated, embodied realities. So, when we affirm the Chalcedonian dual nature of the church, our affirmation of humanity must avoid this error. Indeed, the wider historic and sociopolitical dimension must be included here as well, because as human beings we cannot be thought of in abstraction from this societal context.

Within the Chalcedonian pattern resides the affirmation of both divine and human realities without confusing the distinction between these two realities. There also resides the crucial asymmetry of divine precedence over the human. George Hunsinger summarizes these various features as "asymmetry, intimacy, and integrity."[25] James Loder relates the two realities to ministry and identifies human socialization and divine transformation at work within the church.[26]

Socialization means assimilating people into a community with its practices, values, and beliefs. This aspect of the church reflects the natural function of any social organization. The task of socialization is an inherent and natural function of the church as a human community and institution. However, the fact that the church's practices, values, and beliefs are Christian in nature does

---

[22]See George Hunsinger, *How to Read Karl Barth: The Shape of His Theology* (New York: Oxford University Press, 1991), 185-218.

[23]See Kimlyn J. Bender, *Karl Barth's Christological Ecclesiology* (Engine, OR: Cascade, 2013).

[24]For more on how the Chalcedonian formula shapes an embodied ecclesiology, see chapter four of my book, Daniel D. Lee, *Double Particularity: Karl Barth, Contextuality, and Asian American Theology* (Minneapolis: Fortress, 2017).

[25]George Hunsinger, *How to Read Karl Barth*, 186.

[26]See James E. Loder Jr., *Educational Ministry in the Logic of the Spirit*, ed. Dana R. Wright (Eugene, OR: Cascade, 2018).

not mean that they are of God. Christianity as a religious expression can become distinct and abstracted from the life of the triune God.[27] Karl Barth argues that Christianity as a "religious" expression is under the judgment of God. His point is not that we should be "religionless" as Christians, but that Christians and the church live between the judgment and grace of God, *simul iustus et peccator* (simultaneously justified and sinner).

Without a continuing conversion, separation and abstraction are a certainty accounting for our waywardness. In his discussion of our need for a continuing conversion, Darrell Guder's language identifies the reduction of the gospel in the translation of a gospel-culture process.[28] Theological compromise does not only reduce, but also accrues, distorting through unfaithful additions to the gospel. Without a contextual apprehension of the gospel, this danger of distortion is ever present to all, given human fallibility. We should note that collective morality tends to be the lowest common denominator of the individual members, as Reinhold Niebuhr avers in *Moral Man and Immoral Society*.[29] Those churches with docetic ecclesiology and acontextual "gospel" culture and "biblical" discipline, supposedly free of cultural distortions, will be especially blindsided by its situatedness and hidden societal normativities.

Transformation by the Holy Spirit points to this continuing conversion, a perpetual reformation, being under the gracious judgment of God, seeking the kind of threefold reconciliation of community that I discussed in chapter four on cultural engagement, involved justification, sanctification, and vocation of the faith community. Along with always being reformed, the transformation by God's Spirit means the church's open anticipation of the mysterious presence and free surprising action of God. The church's practices, values, and beliefs must witness beyond themselves to the true God, never being idealized or idolized in place of the holy God, always on the move toward the active God. This openness to the living God could be expressed through the breakthrough of divine encounter in fervent prayer, provocative

---

[27]Karl Barth, *Church Dogmatics*, vol. 1, part 2, *The Doctrine of the Word of God* (Edinburgh: T&T Clark, 1956), 300.

[28]Darrell L. Guder, *The Continuing Conversion of the Church* (Grand Rapids, MI: Eerdmans, 2000), 97-103.

[29]Reinhold Niebuhr, *Moral Man and Immoral Society: A Study in Ethics and Politics* (New York: Charles Scribner's Sons, 1932).

study, intimate worship, sacrificial service, or authentic community. None of these practices in and of themselves are immune to becoming a mere socialization process. Transformation in the church means that we are at God's mercy, under God's gracious judgment.

Within this generous ecclesiology, all local churches exist and have their place. Given that, churches of every kind share a general common calling along with specific visions and vocations for their congregations. All churches are called to move along their eschatological redemptive trajectory toward great inclusive unity. However, what that inclusivity means and what divisions they address will vary. Dividing walls can, of course, be race, but also ethnicity, class, educational status, sexuality, morality, immigration status, ability, and so on. Regardless of the diversity of its own community, all churches must disciple its members about structural injustices and their part in it. All churches should work toward a growing relationship and partnership with other churches in the neighborhood, city, and beyond, crossing racial, denominational, theological, and other differences. Focusing on race alone more likely functions out of the Black/White binary paradigm of diversity. All churches must attend to the public and political witness of the gospel. For example, it does no good to talk about unity in Christ as a church if its members keep on voting for politicians who want to ignore the poor and the marginalized and support racist and classist policies.

ASIAN AMERICAN CHURCHES

Now that we have an ecclesiological outline for all kinds of churches and have placed multiethnic churches as one expression among many, we are ready to reflect on Asian American churches. When talking about Asian American churches, we are addressing a complex and diverse category, just like the *Asian American* label, as noted in chapter three. There are various kinds of Asian American churches, such as immigrant churches, independent English ministries, and pan-Asian/multiethnic churches.[30]

---

[30]These categories could be sorted and classified even further, especially focusing on the kinds of English ministries that can exist within or alongside the Asian language ministry. See Hoover Wong, *Coming Together or Coming Apart?* (Pasadena, CA: TRACC, 1998) and DJ Chuang, *Multiasian.church: A Future for Asian Americans in a Multiethnic World* (self-pub., 2016).

Immigrant churches are usually made up of a single or a dominant ethnic group and primarily minister to the immigrant generation. Some of them have connections to an ecclesial or denominational affiliation back in Asia, while others are an ethnic-specific segment within a predominantly White denomination in the US. As the children of the immigrant generation grow and mature, a corresponding youth and later English ministry or church develops within or alongside the Asian language congregation.

Independent English ministries form when the children of immigrant churches leave their immigrant church as a group or as individuals. There are a number of forces at work that help create these ministries, which can develop as an exodus out of the ethnic-specific space. Immigrant churches function to protect, affirm, and support immigrant families, along with the idea of the whole family worshiping together. When the English ministry within the immigrant church cannot escape the label of kids church that must follow the cultural norms of the immigrant generation, they leave to seek freedom from the generational and cultural strictures. Formed by White evangelical norms, the second generation seeks to be a pure church beyond culture and ethnicity, "just a church for everyone" as a local pastor acquaintance would say.[31]

The panethnic/multiethnic church follows the church beyond culture and ethnic models toward greater diversity and racial awareness. The move toward diversity beyond one ethnicity could occur progressively as Asian Americans of other ethnicities grow in attendance. Alternatively, the move could be more ideologically driven by the "picture of heaven," critiqued above. Diversity is not just about your neighborhood but society as a whole. Asian American churches seeking to be multiethnic can follow a White narrative failing to attend to raciosociopolitical realities.

Asian American campus ministries should also be included here. Asian American chapters of InterVarsity Christian Fellowship, Epic Movement or Design Movement of Cru, or Asian American ministries within the Navigators all exist within a broader multiethnic context, which makes them generally more aware of their Asian Americanness and open to

---

[31]Kale K. Yu, "Christian Model Minority: Racial and Ethnic Formation in Asian American Evangelicalism," *Journal of Race, Ethnicity, and Religion* 7, no. 4 (2016): 1-24; Prema A. Kurien, *Ethnic Church Meets Megachurch: Indian American Christianity in Motion* (New York: NYU Press, 2017).

ministry innovations given their less hierarchical structure and specific and ever transient community.

Whatever the ministry model, these are all communities of Jesus Christ amid the Asian American Quadrilateral, embodying and witnessing to the gospel as "*contextual community* for Asian heritage, *transitional community* for migration experience, *missional community* for American culture, and *liberational community* for racialization."[32] A dialectical tension exists for these four aspects of Asian American ecclesiology where critical awareness, active theological reflection, and spiritual vigilance could lead to the kind of embodied ecclesiology that reflects the gospel of the incarnate God. In fully owning the context of ecclesial being and ministerial existence, Asian American churches can not only live out God's shalom for our own community, but also bear gifts for the broader world and the global Christian community.

The lack of these critical, theological, and spiritual faculties and disciplines could spell cultural encroachment and captivity, devolving into a mere social club with nominal religious overtones. We might point out the "Babylonian captivity" by the White church in the form of individualism, consumerism, and racism, as Soong-Chan Rah critiques.[33] What Rah rightly points out is the *dominance* and *influence* of White captivity in the American church at large. But of course, along with their particular gifts, Asian American churches, along with churches of every kind, are in danger of their own cultural captivity. No church is immune to these dangers. Vigilance with self-critique and reform never ends until the eschaton.

In this discussion we are acknowledging the *being* of the Asian American church, how God gathers and establishes this faith community, as well as its *becoming,* how in response to divine action, the community grows into who they are, taking up their divine calling as a task set before them. Also, for each of these themes, there exists a dialectical tension between owning Asian Americanness unto God versus making Asian Americanness into an idol apart from God, between a calling or an opportunity versus a temptation or a peril.

---

[32]Lee, *Double Particularity*, 180.

[33]Soong-Chan Rah, *The Next Evangelicalism: Freeing the Church from Western Cultural Captivity* (Downers Grove, IL: InterVarsity, 2009), 18.

On the one hand, Asian American churches are called and tasked to embody the gospel that affirms the humanity of Asian Americans against Orientalist representations, social struggles, political marginalization, and racist attacks. Because the gospel of the resurrection, the good news of the kingdom, encompasses our spiritual, cultural, racial, physical, sociopolitical, economic realities, the church is rightly a place where this holistic gospel comes alive. In that sense, Asian American churches can be a cultural and community hub, a social services center, and base for activism.[34] As Sang Hyun Lee describes, Asian American churches serve as refuge, a place of aid and comfort, and a place of healing.[35] Against racist forces that dehumanize those with Asian heritage, they must recover and affirm these cultural elements as part of their full humanity. Both the humanity of Asian Americans and their Asian heritage, in whatever form and expression this might take, must be affirmed, otherwise, it leads to personal fragmentation and affirmation of only the honorary White selves. The gospel community, in this sense, makes Asian heritage normative and, thus, invisible as simply one part of their identity. The subtle and implicit ways in which Asian Americans can bring their whole selves into God's presence and within the fellowship of other believers at Asian American churches must not be relegated as a social phenomenon, but rather affirmed as a witness to the all-encompassing gospel for humanity in their particularities. A docetic "generic" church that preaches a disembodied gospel is a compromised church with hidden normativity ideologies, a wolf in a sheep's clothing, a pernicious space.

On the other hand, just like every other expression of the church, the particular calling and task of the Asian American church meets with a corresponding temptation or peril. For example, Asian heritage and identity may become a second god alongside God, a false gospel. This happens when Asian heritage is defined or protected in an essentialistic manner, as though it were an eternal constant and not a human construct. God gathers and calls not for the sake of a pristine and pure Asian culture, but for whatever

---

[34]For example, Rah describes these characteristics of wholistic ministry in the Korean American immigrant church in *The Next Evangelicalism*, 164-79.

[35]Sang Hyun Lee, *From a Liminal Place: An Asian American Theology* (Minneapolis: Fortress, 2010), 127-28.

concrete and dynamic cultural existence a particular community may express. Without spiritual vigilance Asian American churches risk devolving into a cultural center with a narrow view of a pure or authentic Asian ethnic identity, so that being a "good Asian" and a "good Christian" problematically become synonymous. The cultural offerings, such as Asian language courses or the celebration of Asian holidays or a general education of ethnic heritage or history, could all be included and affirmed in the life of the faith community as holistic ministry. Asian American churches also risk becoming primarily an extended family or community center with God as merely a sideshow. Here the members might identify themselves more with their local congregation, even over their commitment to Christ, so that they actually lose their "faith" if they no longer attend this particular community. Communal life among Christians does not automatically mean that these are Christian communities and Christian relationships, where Christ mediates the relationships, where we are a community *through* and *in* Christ.[36] A church's ministry in social services and political activism, as well, must be spiritually and theological rooted in the lordship of Jesus Christ, who gives us love and hope to do these kingdom works.

These offerings need to take place with accompanying and substantial theological work and spiritual engagement. Too many Asian American churches and ministries are only culturally or socially Asian American, and not theologically so as well. Theologically, a critical and constructive engagement with Asian American contexts must be taken up, which leads to holistic discipleship as well as communal gifts for the life of the broader neighborhood and church. As discussed above, the Chalcedonian dialect of socialization and transformation applies here, where a true encounter with the living God must be sought and anticipated, not settling for things of God.

Here I have outlined the framework for how to think about ecclesiology in general, providing key distinctions with expressions, models, and aspects of the Asian American church. The particular theological reflection needed for specific Asian American churches across the country must be done by a whole community of minister-theologians.

---

[36]Dietrich Bonhoeffer, *Dietrich Bonhoeffer Works*, vol. 5, *Life Together* and *Prayerbook of the Bible*, ed. Geffrey B. Kelly, trans. Daniel W. Bloesch and James H. Burtness (Minneapolis: Fortress, 1996), 31-33.

INVITATION

In lieu of a conclusion, I offer this invitation to the task of theology for my Asian American readers. I believe others will benefit from this book, but that is not my primary agenda. This book is for my family, my community, my people, Asian Americans in their heterogeneity and diversity.

All Christians do the work of theology, thinking about God and the gospel as related to all of life, although they differ in their critical and conceptual apparatuses and faculties. While formal training does not necessarily result in a deeper relationship with God, the historical and intellectual background grants knowledge of the universal and global church beyond local church experiences and insights. Correspondingly, all Asian American Christians are doing Asian American theology in a similar sense, although there is a wide spectrum of awareness and development. Yes, there are Asian American Christians whose Asian American awareness is so nascent that their theology is a little more than colorblind White theology with some pathologizing of Asian heritage. Of course, many attentive Asian American Christians, even when lacking critical language and limited in their explicit theology, still intuitively discern the kind of subtleties relevant and important for effectively serving their community. The vision of this book is to make those implicit contextual ministry intuitions explicit and theologically rigorous.

The approach of this book has been to focus on the meta themes and concepts that cut across the various ethnic communities within the Asian American label. Methodologically, this panethnic approach is greatly beneficial and even needed, especially regarding the public racial themes. When resources are scarce, attending to the great diversity of the Asian American community proves challenging because this diversity almost becomes an afterthought. However, those who are marginalized and erased, typically through an East Asian American dominance, viscerally feel the problematic limitations of a panethnic approach. Even without the problem of panethnicity, multiple versions of Asian American theology for various ethnic communities are required in order to avoid single story theologies that so easily fall into old or new stereotypes.

The Asian American Christian community needs a plenitude of theological reflection on our ethnic, generational, regional, gender, sexual, confessional, spiritual and every other kind of diversity. This work will not occur automatically, simply with the passage of time. The call must be taken up by each person and each community one at a time with significant investment of time, energy, and resources.

Asian American theology must serve the Asian American Christian community, and in so doing will serve the universal church. While this service to the Asian American Christian community might sound like a truism, temptations and distractions abound, whether they be careerism, racial posturing, or ideological truncation.

If the audience of Asian American theology is the White academy, in a sense oriented toward White-oriented concerns, then White affirmation and acclaim are easier to obtain. Being White-oriented is more politically advantageous for one's career. The academy is predominately White, which rewards and affirms works that address them. However, the Asian American theologian must avoid this temptation if they are to honor their calling.

Viet Nguyen points out the temptation of commodifying Asian American identity, "an enterprise of panethnic entrepreneurship with the academia, reaping the particular and peculiar rewards of academia by symbolic capital of race and resistance."[1] It is possible to use the Asian American community, even Asian American suffering and pain, for one's own promotion and platform. This temptation must be clearly acknowledged if one is to actually serve the Asian American community and not simply use it for one's gain.

In the name of decolonization, resistance to White Eurocentric hegemony can become a fixation. The scope of Asian American theology then narrows down to White hegemony, racism, and colonialism, as though there are no

---

[1]Viet Thanh Nguyen, *Race and Resistance: Literature and Politics Within Asian America* (New York: Oxford University Press, 2002), 5.

problems within the Asian American community itself. While resistance is necessary, such a move makes Asian American theology parasitic, inadvertently and ironically feeding the continuation of White centrality.[2] In a sense, Asian American theology becomes about Asian Americans and not centrally about God. This selective presentation is understandable given that airing dirty laundry of the Asian American community could fuel Orientalism and the internal biases of the White audience. However, this kind of truncation performs a disservice to the Asian American church. We must acknowledge structural inequalities and powers dynamics, but also affirm the common humanity and inhumanity of all, Asian American and non-Asian American.[3]

As I said at the beginning of this book, *Asian American theology is about God revealed in Jesus Christ*, witnessed to by Asian Americans. Because our God is a covenantal God, *Asian American theology is about God revealed in Jesus Christ in covenantal relationship with Asian Americans qua Asian Americans*. Asian American theology means wrestling with this gracious God for the sake of gospel embodiment in the Asian American community. I pray that many will take up this call to Asian American theology.

---

[2]Kuan-Hsing Chen, *Asia as Method: Toward Deimperialization* (Durham, NC: Duke University Press, 2010), 1-2.
[3]Viet Thanh Nguyen, *Nothing Ever Dies: Vietnam and the Memory of War* (Cambridge, MA: Harvard University Press, 2016), 283.

NAME INDEX

SUBJECT INDEX

SCRIPTURE INDEX

Printed in the USA
CPSIA information can be obtained
at www.ICGtesting.com
LVHW091921041124
795688LV00034B/1050